Table of Contents

Italian Greyhound 101: The Ultimate Lovers 1

The History of Italian Greyhounds 2

Physical Characteristics and Traits 12

Personality and Temperament 20

Health and Wellness 30

Grooming and Maintenance 40

Training Your Italian Greyhound 50

Socialization and Interaction 60

Italian Greyhounds and Families 71

Working and Service Italian Greyhounds 81

Sporting and Outdoor Activities 92

Traveling with Your Italian Greyhound 100

Italian Greyhound Clubs and Associations 111

Preparing for a New Italian Greyhound Puppy 122

Puppy Development and Milestones 133

Senior Italian Greyhounds 145

Seasonal Care and Safety 156

Common Behavioral Issues 167

Fun and Games with Your Italian Greyhound 178

Italian Greyhound Legends and Stories 189

Italian Greyhound Art, Photography, and Collectibles 200

Italian Greyhound Rescue and Adoption 211

Italian Greyhounds in the Show Ring 223

Responsible Breeding Practices 234

Creating a Safe and Comfortable Environment 246

Common Italian Greyhound Health Myths and Misconceptions 255

Italian Greyhounds and Special Needs 266

The Future of the Italian Greyhound Breed 278

Training Resources and Techniques 289

Emergency Preparedness and Your Italian Greyhound 301

Celebrating Your Italian Greyhound 311

Have Questions / Comments? 322

Get Another Book Free 324

Italian Greyhound 101

The Ultimate Guide for Italian Greyhound Lovers

Samantha D. Thompson

Created by Xspurts.com[1]

All rights reserved.

Copyright © 2005 onwards .

By reading this book, you agree to the below Terms and Conditions.

Xspurts.com[2] retains all rights to these products.

No part of this book may be reproduced in any form, by photostat, microfilm, xerography, or any other means, or incorporated into any information retrieval system, electronic or mechanical, without the written permission of Xspurts.com[3]; exceptions are made for brief excerpts used in published reviews.

This publication is designed to provide accurate and authoritative information with regard to the subject matter covered, however is for entertainment purposes only. It is sold with the understanding that the publisher is not engaged in rendering legal, accounting, health, relationship or other professional / personal advice. If legal advice or other expert assistance is required, the services of a competent professional should be sought.

First Printed 2023.

ISBN:

DIGITAL VERSION: 978-1-77684-765-5

PHYSICAL VERSION: 978-1-77684-764-8

- A New Zealand Designed Product

Get A Free Book At: go.xspurts.com/free-book-offer[4]

XSPURTS

---

1. https://Xspurts.com
2. https://Xspurts.com
3. https://Xspurts.com
4. https://go.xspurts.com/free-book-offer
5. https://xspurts.com/

The History of Italian Greyhounds

Italian Greyhounds, with their sleek and elegant appearance, have captivated hearts for centuries. Known for their grace and agility, these diminutive canines have a rich history that traces back to ancient civilizations. From their origins in ancient Egypt to their popularity among European aristocracy, Italian Greyhounds have left an indelible mark on the world of dogs.

The story of Italian Greyhounds begins thousands of years ago in the land of the Pharaohs. Depictions of small greyhound-like dogs can be found on ancient Egyptian tomb paintings, suggesting that these sighthounds existed as far back as 4,000 years ago. These early dogs were likely the ancestors of the Italian Greyhounds we know today, and they were highly regarded as companions of the elite.

Fast forward to the Roman Empire, and Italian Greyhounds found themselves in the spotlight once again. The Romans were enamored with these small, graceful canines and often depicted them in their artwork. Italian Greyhounds were highly valued and were even buried alongside their owners, a testament to their status and importance.

During the Middle Ages, Italian Greyhounds faced a period of decline in popularity. However, it was during this time that they found favor among European nobility. Italian Greyhounds were prized for their beauty and companionship, and they became a fixture in royal courts across the continent. They were often seen nestled in the laps of queens and princesses, providing warmth and affection.

In Renaissance Italy, Italian Greyhounds were beloved by the Medici family, who ruled over Florence. The Medici were known for their patronage of the arts and their refined tastes, and they saw the Italian Greyhound as a symbol of elegance and refinement. The breed became synonymous with the Medici court and was depicted in countless paintings and sculptures of the era.

As the centuries progressed, Italian Greyhounds continued to capture the hearts of dog lovers around the world. In the 19th century, they became popular in England, where breeders focused on refining their appearance and temperament. The breed was recognized by the Kennel Club in 1874, solidifying its place in the world of purebred dogs.

Italian Greyhounds made their way to the United States in the late 19th century, where they quickly gained a following. Their graceful movements and gentle nature made them popular both as show dogs and as beloved companions. The Italian Greyhound Club of America was formed in 1903, and the breed gained official recognition by the American Kennel Club in 194

Throughout their history, Italian Greyhounds have maintained their distinctive traits and characteristics. They are known for their slender build, their deep chests, and their long, slender legs. Their coats can come in a variety of colors, including shades of fawn, blue, black, and red. Their sleek appearance is complemented by their expressive eyes and alert expressions.

Italian Greyhounds are sighthounds, which means they have a strong prey drive and an innate instinct to chase after small animals. Despite their small size, they are agile and fast, capable of reaching impressive speeds. However, they are also gentle and affectionate dogs, known for their loyalty and devotion to their human companions.

In modern times, Italian Greyhounds continue to enchant dog lovers with their elegance and charm. They are popular pets in many countries and are often seen strutting their stuff at dog shows around the world. While their numbers may be small compared to some other breeds, their impact on the world of dogs is undeniable.

Origins and Ancestry

The Italian Greyhound, with its delicate frame and graceful demeanor, has a fascinating ancestry that stretches back thousands of years. To understand the origins of this beloved breed, we must delve into the annals of history and explore the influences that have shaped it into the elegant canine companion we know today.

The Italian Greyhound's story begins in ancient Egypt, where depictions of small, sighthound-like dogs can be found on tomb paintings dating back over 4,000 years. These early dogs, believed to be the ancestors of Italian Greyhounds, were cherished companions of the Egyptian elite. Revered for their speed and beauty, they were often depicted hunting alongside their owners or gracing the laps of pharaohs.

From Egypt, the Italian Greyhound's lineage can be traced to the ancient Greeks and Romans. Both cultures held a deep appreciation for the beauty and agility of sighthounds, and it is during this time that the breed began to take on its distinct characteristics. The Greeks referred to these dogs as "Melitanis," and they were prized for their ability to hunt small game.

It was the Romans, however, who played a significant role in shaping the Italian Greyhound as we know it today. The Romans were captivated by the small, elegant sighthounds and often depicted them in their artwork, highlighting their slender build and graceful movements. The breed's popularity soared during the Roman Empire, where it was known as the "Canis Africanus" or "Canis Gallicus." Italian Greyhounds were held in high esteem, and some were even given the prestigious honor of burial alongside their human counterparts.

During the Middle Ages, the popularity of Italian Greyhounds experienced a decline, but their allure would not fade away. It was in Renaissance Italy, specifically under the patronage of the powerful Medici family, that the breed once again gained favor. The Medici, known for their refined tastes, saw the Italian Greyhound as a symbol of elegance and sophistication. These dogs became cherished companions in the Medici court, with many noble families emulating their love for these graceful canines.

As the breed's popularity spread throughout Europe, efforts were made to refine the Italian Greyhound's appearance and temperament. Breeders in England played a pivotal role in this process during the 19th century. They focused on developing a more uniform size and structure, ensuring that the breed retained its elegant form. These efforts led to the establishment of breed standards and the recognition of the Italian Greyhound by the Kennel Club in 187

In the late 19th century, Italian Greyhounds made their way to the United States, where they quickly garnered attention and affection. Their small size, combined with their graceful movements and affectionate nature, made them popular as both show dogs and cherished companions. In 1903, the Italian Greyhound Club of America was formed to promote the breed's welfare and advancement. The American Kennel Club officially recognized the Italian Greyhound in 1948, cementing its place in the realm of purebred dogs.

The Italian Greyhound's lineage can be traced through centuries of refinement and appreciation for its unique qualities. Its slim, streamlined body, deep chest, and long, slender legs showcase its sighthound heritage. The breed's coat can come in a variety of colors, including shades of fawn, blue, black, and red. Its expressive eyes and alert expression add to its overall charm and elegance.

Beyond its physical attributes, the Italian Greyhound possesses an inherent nature that endears it to its human companions. Despite its sighthound lineage, it is a gentle and affectionate breed known for its loyalty and devotion. Italian Greyhounds form strong bonds with their owners and thrive on companionship.

Breed Development and Recognition

The Italian Greyhound, with its sleek and elegant appearance, has a fascinating history of development and recognition as a distinct breed. From its ancient origins to its establishment as a recognized breed, the Italian Greyhound has undergone a journey shaped by dedicated breeders and enthusiasts. Below we will explore the breed's development, recognition, and the standards that define this beloved canine companion.

The Italian Greyhound's lineage can be traced back to ancient civilizations, particularly to ancient Egypt. Depictions of small sighthound-like dogs on Egyptian tomb paintings dating back thousands of years suggest that these early dogs served as the ancestors of the Italian Greyhound we know today. In Egypt, they were highly regarded as companions of the elite and were cherished for their speed, beauty, and loyalty.

As time progressed, the Italian Greyhound's influence spread to ancient Greece and Rome. Both cultures had a profound appreciation for sighthounds and their hunting abilities. In Greece, these dogs were known as "Melitanis," valued for their skill in pursuing and capturing small game. The Romans, too, were enamored by the breed's grace and agility. They depicted Italian Greyhounds in their artwork, showcasing their slender bodies and elegant movements.

During the Middle Ages, the popularity of Italian Greyhounds faced a decline. However, it was during the Renaissance period in Italy that the breed experienced a resurgence. The powerful Medici family, known for their refined tastes, took a keen interest in the breed. Italian Greyhounds became treasured companions in the Medici court, symbolizing elegance and sophistication. Their popularity soared, and noble families across Europe sought to emulate the Medici's love for these graceful canines.

In the 19th century, breeders in England played a significant role in refining the Italian Greyhound's appearance and temperament. Their efforts were focused on establishing a more uniform size and structure for the breed, emphasizing its elegance and beauty. Breed standards were developed, laying the foundation for the Italian Greyhound's recognition as a distinct breed.

In 1874, the Italian Greyhound gained official recognition from the Kennel Club in England, solidifying its status as a breed. The establishment of breed standards ensured consistency in appearance and helped preserve the breed's unique characteristics. These standards defined the Italian Greyhound's size, proportion, coat colors, and overall structure.

The breed's journey continued across the Atlantic, as Italian Greyhounds found their way to the United States. Their small size, gentle nature, and graceful movements made them popular as both show dogs and cherished companions. In 1903, the Italian Greyhound Club of America was founded to promote and protect the breed's welfare. This organization played a crucial role in furthering the breed's development and recognition in the United States.

In 1948, the American Kennel Club officially recognized the Italian Greyhound as a distinct breed. This recognition was a testament to the breed's enduring appeal and its status among purebred dogs. It provided a platform for Italian Greyhound enthusiasts to showcase their dogs in conformation shows and compete for titles and accolades.

Today, the Italian Greyhound continues to captivate dog lovers around the world. Its distinct features, including its slim and streamlined body, deep chest, and long, slender legs, are a testament to its sighthound heritage. The breed's coat can come in various colors, such as fawn, blue, black, and red. Its expressive eyes and alert expression add to its overall charm and grace.

Italian Greyhounds Around the World

Italian Greyhounds, with their elegant appearance and gentle nature, have gained popularity and captivated the hearts of dog lovers around the world. From their ancient origins in Egypt to their presence in modern households, Italian Greyhounds have established themselves as beloved companions in various countries. Below we will explore the global appeal of Italian Greyhounds and their unique roles in different cultures.

Italy, the breed's namesake, holds a special place in the hearts of Italian Greyhound enthusiasts. The breed has a long history in the country, where it was highly valued as a companion of the aristocracy. Italian Greyhounds were cherished by noble families, including the powerful Medici dynasty during the Renaissance period. Even today, Italy continues to celebrate the breed, and Italian Greyhounds can often be seen in Italian artwork, representing elegance and sophistication.

The United Kingdom has also embraced Italian Greyhounds with enthusiasm. It was in England that the breed's modern standards were developed and refined. British breeders played a pivotal role in establishing the breed's characteristics, including its size, structure, and coat colors. Italian Greyhounds gained recognition from the Kennel Club in 1874, and they have since become a beloved breed in the country, both as show dogs and as cherished companions.

Across the Atlantic, the United States has embraced Italian Greyhounds with equal fervor. The breed made its way to the U.S. in the late 19th century and quickly gained popularity. Known for their small size and graceful movements, Italian Greyhounds found favor as lap dogs and loyal companions. The Italian Greyhound Club of America, founded in 1903, has been instrumental in promoting and protecting the breed's welfare in the country. Today, Italian Greyhounds can be found in households across America, cherished for their beauty and affectionate nature.

In Australia, Italian Greyhounds have also made a mark. The breed has gained a following among dog lovers in the country who appreciate its elegance and adaptability to different living environments. Australian breeders and enthusiasts have worked diligently to promote responsible breeding practices and maintain the breed's integrity. Italian Greyhounds can be seen participating in various dog sports and competitions, showcasing their agility and athleticism.

Beyond Europe and the English-speaking world, Italian Greyhounds have gained popularity in countries like Japan. The breed's delicate appearance and gentle nature have resonated with Japanese dog lovers. Italian Greyhounds are often featured in Japanese media and advertisements, further fueling their popularity. In Japan, they are considered a symbol of refined taste and elegance.

In South America, particularly in countries like Brazil and Argentina, Italian Greyhounds have carved out a place for themselves. The breed's elegance and compact size have made them appealing companions in urban environments. Italian Greyhound enthusiasts in these countries actively participate in dog shows, where they can showcase the breed's beauty and grace.

In recent years, Italian Greyhounds have also gained a following in other parts of the world, such as China and South Korea. As these countries experience an increasing interest in purebred dogs, Italian Greyhounds have become sought-after pets. Their compact size and gentle temperament make them well-suited for apartment living in densely populated areas.

Regardless of the geographical location, Italian Greyhounds universally capture the hearts of their owners. Their slender build, deep chest, and long, slender legs give them a distinctive appearance that commands attention. Their coat, which can come in various colors and patterns, adds to their overall charm. Italian Greyhounds are often described as loving, loyal, and affectionate, forming strong bonds with their human companions.

Physical Characteristics and Traits

Italian Greyhounds are renowned for their distinctive physical characteristics and unique traits that make them stand out among other dog breeds. From their slender build to their gentle nature, Italian Greyhounds possess a combination of traits that contribute to their allure and charm. Below we will explore the physical characteristics and traits that define the Italian Greyhound breed.

One of the most striking features of Italian Greyhounds is their slim and streamlined body. They have a graceful appearance, characterized by a deep chest, long and slender legs, and an overall elegant build. Their physique allows them to move with agility and speed, reflecting their sighthound heritage.

The Italian Greyhound's coat is another notable feature. It is short, fine, and smooth to the touch, adding to the breed's sleek appearance. Italian Greyhounds can come in various colors, including shades of fawn, blue, black, and red. Some may exhibit white markings or patterns on their coat, which further enhances their aesthetic appeal.

The breed's head is proportionate to its body, with a long and narrow muzzle. Italian Greyhounds have expressive, dark eyes that exude intelligence and warmth. Their eyes, combined with their alert and inquisitive expressions, contribute to their engaging and captivating presence.

Italian Greyhounds possess a unique trait known as "roaching." This term refers to their tendency to arch their backs when they are excited or feeling playful. This distinctive trait sets them apart from other dog breeds and adds to their endearing charm.

In terms of size, Italian Greyhounds are classified as small dogs. According to breed standards, males typically stand between 13 to 15 inches (33 to 38 centimeters) at the shoulder, while females stand between 12 to 14 inches (30 to 36 centimeters). Their weight usually ranges between 6 to 10 pounds (7 to 5 kilograms), making them a compact and lightweight breed.

Aside from their physical appearance, Italian Greyhounds are known for their gentle and affectionate nature. They form strong bonds with their human companions and thrive on close interaction and companionship. Italian Greyhounds are often described as being loving, loyal, and eager to please.

Despite their small size, Italian Greyhounds possess a resilient and confident demeanor. They carry themselves with poise and grace, displaying a natural elegance in their every movement. They are known for their agile and swift running abilities, reaching impressive speeds despite their compact build.

Being sighthounds, Italian Greyhounds have a strong prey drive. They possess a keen sense of sight and are instinctively attracted to small animals that may resemble prey. It is important for owners to provide a safe and controlled environment for their Italian Greyhounds, ensuring they have proper training and supervision when outside.

Italian Greyhounds are generally well-suited for indoor living, making them adaptable to different living situations, including apartments and houses. However, they do require regular exercise to maintain their physical and mental well-being. Daily walks, playtime, and interactive activities are essential to keep them happy and healthy.

Size and Proportions

Italian Greyhounds, with their delicate and slender appearance, possess distinct size and proportions that contribute to their elegant and graceful demeanor. As a small breed, Italian Greyhounds exhibit unique physical characteristics that set them apart. Below we will explore the size and proportions of Italian Greyhounds, shedding light on their compact yet captivating stature.

Italian Greyhounds are classified as a small breed, characterized by their diminutive size. According to breed standards, males typically stand between 13 to 15 inches (33 to 38 centimeters) at the shoulder, while females stand between 12 to 14 inches (30 to 36 centimeters). These measurements contribute to the breed's compact and lightweight nature.

Proportions play a significant role in defining the Italian Greyhound's overall appearance. The breed possesses a harmonious balance between its various body parts, creating a well-proportioned silhouette. The length of an Italian Greyhound's body is slightly longer than its height at the withers, giving it an elongated yet balanced profile.

One of the distinguishing features of Italian Greyhounds is their deep chest. The chest is well-developed and provides ample space for the heart and lungs. This feature allows the breed to have excellent lung capacity, contributing to its remarkable speed and endurance.

Italian Greyhounds have a slender build, which is further accentuated by their long and slender legs. The legs are proportionate to the size of the body, creating a sleek and streamlined appearance. This proportionality enhances their agility and contributes to their ability to move swiftly.

The breed's head is proportional to its body, displaying a refined and elegant structure. Italian Greyhounds have a long and narrow muzzle, which complements their overall slender build. The muzzle is in balance with the skull, neither appearing too elongated nor too broad.

Italian Greyhounds possess a unique trait known as "rose ears." The ears are small, fine, and carried back, folding over and forming a rose-like shape. This distinctive feature adds to their charm and is a defining characteristic of the breed.

While Italian Greyhounds have a slender frame, they are not fragile. They exhibit a sturdy and well-muscled body, which provides them with the strength and agility necessary for their sighthound heritage. The breed's lightweight physique enables it to achieve remarkable speed and grace in its movements.

The size and proportions of Italian Greyhounds make them well-suited for indoor living. Their compact size allows them to adapt to various living environments, including apartments and houses with limited space. Their small stature makes them portable and easy to handle, which is particularly advantageous for owners who enjoy taking their dogs on outings or trips.

Italian Greyhounds require regular exercise to maintain their physical and mental well-being. Despite their small size, they benefit from daily walks, playtime, and interactive activities. Engaging in exercise not only keeps them fit but also satisfies their natural instincts and helps prevent behavioral issues that may arise from pent-up energy.

Coat Colors and Patterns

Italian Greyhounds, with their sleek and elegant appearance, possess a variety of coat colors and patterns that add to their allure and individuality. From solid hues to intricate markings, the coat of an Italian Greyhound is as unique as the dog itself. Below we will explore the fascinating world of coat colors and patterns in Italian Greyhounds, shedding light on the diverse range found within this beloved breed.

Italian Greyhounds can display a wide array of coat colors, each with its own distinct charm. One of the most common colors is fawn, which ranges from pale cream to deep tan. Fawn Italian Greyhounds often have a warm and inviting appearance, complementing their gentle and affectionate nature. The coat can have variations in shade, with some individuals displaying darker points on the ears, muzzle, and tail.

Another popular color among Italian Greyhounds is blue. This unique hue ranges from a light gray to a deep slate color. Blue Italian Greyhounds possess a striking and ethereal beauty that sets them apart from other color variations. Their coats often have a shimmering quality, adding to their overall elegance.

Black is also seen in the coat color spectrum of Italian Greyhounds. Black Italian Greyhounds exhibit a rich and glossy black coat that exudes sophistication and charm. The intensity of the black can vary, with some individuals having a solid, jet-black coat, while others may have slight variations in shade.

In addition to fawn, blue, and black, Italian Greyhounds can come in other coat colors, such as red and cream. Red Italian Greyhounds showcase a warm and vibrant hue, ranging from a deep mahogany to a lighter copper tone. Cream Italian Greyhounds, on the other hand, have a pale, creamy color that exudes a soft and delicate beauty.

While solid coat colors are common in Italian Greyhounds, there are also individuals with striking patterns and markings. One such pattern is brindle. Brindle Italian Greyhounds have a base color overlaid with dark stripes, creating a unique and eye-catching pattern. The stripes can vary in intensity, creating a range of brindle patterns from subtle to bold.

Italian Greyhounds can also display white markings on their coats, adding contrast and visual interest. White markings may appear on the chest, feet, tip of the tail, or as a blaze on the face. These markings can vary in size and shape, further enhancing the individuality of each dog.

While Italian Greyhounds exhibit a diverse range of coat colors and patterns, it is important to note that all variations are equally desirable within the breed. The Italian Greyhound breed standards recognize and celebrate this diversity, embracing the uniqueness of each dog's coat.

Maintaining the coat of an Italian Greyhound is relatively easy due to its short and fine texture. Regular brushing helps keep the coat clean and free of loose hair. Bathing is only necessary when the dog becomes dirty or starts to develop an odor. Due to their thin skin, Italian Greyhounds are sensitive to extreme temperatures, so it is important to protect them from cold weather by providing suitable clothing.

Unique Features and Attributes

Italian Greyhounds possess a range of unique features and attributes that set them apart from other dog breeds. From their charming personality to their physical characteristics, Italian Greyhounds have captivated the hearts of dog lovers around the world. Below we will explore the distinctive traits and attributes that make Italian Greyhounds truly one-of-a-kind.

One of the most remarkable features of Italian Greyhounds is their elegant and slender build. They have a streamlined body with a deep chest, long and slender legs, and a graceful posture. This distinctive physique allows them to move with agility and grace, showcasing their sighthound heritage. Italian Greyhounds are known for their remarkable speed and agility, despite their small size.

The Italian Greyhound's coat is another standout feature. It is short, fine, and smooth to the touch, contributing to the breed's sleek and polished appearance. Italian Greyhounds come in a variety of coat colors, including fawn, blue, black, and red. These coat colors can range in shades and intensities, adding to the breed's visual diversity.

One unique attribute of Italian Greyhounds is their sensitivity to temperature. Due to their thin skin and lack of body fat, Italian Greyhounds are more susceptible to cold weather. It is important to protect them from extreme temperatures by providing appropriate clothing or keeping them indoors during inclement weather. Their sensitivity to temperature also means they may prefer warm and cozy spots to relax.

Italian Greyhounds are known for their affectionate and gentle nature. They form strong bonds with their human companions and thrive on close interaction and companionship. They enjoy being in the presence of their loved ones and are often described as being "velcro dogs" due to their tendency to stick close to their owners. Their loyal and devoted nature makes them excellent companions for individuals or families seeking a loving and attentive pet.

Despite their small size, Italian Greyhounds possess a resilient and confident demeanor. They are known for their self-assured and independent nature, often displaying a sense of regal poise. Italian Greyhounds are not easily intimidated and have a unique sense of self-awareness. This confidence adds to their overall charm and makes them a joy to be around.

Italian Greyhounds are intelligent and eager to please. They are quick learners and respond well to positive reinforcement-based training methods. They excel in activities that challenge their minds, such as obedience training and agility courses. Their intelligence, combined with their willingness to please, makes them a versatile breed capable of learning a wide range of commands and tricks.

Another distinctive attribute of Italian Greyhounds is their unique trait known as "roaching." When excited or playful, Italian Greyhounds arch their backs, giving the appearance of a slight curve along their spine. This endearing behavior adds to their charm and individuality, setting them apart from other breeds.

Italian Greyhounds possess a strong prey drive due to their sighthound heritage. They have an instinctive desire to chase small animals. It is important for owners to provide a safe and controlled environment for their Italian Greyhounds, particularly when outside. Proper training and socialization can help manage their prey drive and ensure their safety.

Personality and Temperament

Italian Greyhounds are known for their unique personality and gentle temperament, making them beloved companions and cherished members of many households. From their affectionate nature to their intelligence and adaptability, Italian Greyhounds possess a range of traits that contribute to their overall charm. Below we will explore the personality and temperament of Italian Greyhounds, shedding light on the qualities that make them such endearing and delightful dogs.

One of the most notable traits of Italian Greyhounds is their affectionate nature. They form strong bonds with their human companions and thrive on close interaction and companionship. Italian Greyhounds are often described as "velcro dogs" due to their tendency to stick close to their owners, enjoying their presence and seeking comfort in their company. Their loving and attentive nature makes them wonderful companions for individuals or families seeking a devoted and loyal pet.

Italian Greyhounds are known for their gentle and sensitive temperament. They have a deep capacity for empathy and can be attuned to the emotions of their human family members. They often provide comfort and emotional support, making them excellent therapy dogs or companions for individuals in need of emotional assistance. Their sensitivity to their owner's moods and needs adds to their overall charm and endears them to their human companions.

Despite their small size, Italian Greyhounds possess a confident and self-assured demeanor. They have a unique sense of self-awareness and carry themselves with a regal poise. This confidence contributes to their overall presence and distinguishes them from other small dog breeds. Italian Greyhounds are not easily intimidated and exhibit a certain grace and elegance in their every movement.

Italian Greyhounds are intelligent and eager to please. They possess a sharp mind and respond well to positive reinforcement-based training methods. They are quick learners and excel in activities that challenge their mental capabilities. Italian Greyhounds are known to participate in various dog sports and competitions, showcasing their agility, obedience, and ability to learn and execute complex commands.

Italian Greyhounds are adaptable and can thrive in various living environments. While they enjoy being indoors and close to their owners, they are also content with outdoor activities and exploration. Their small size allows them to adapt to apartments and houses with limited space. However, it is important to note that they still require regular exercise to keep them physically and mentally stimulated.

Despite their independent nature, Italian Greyhounds are social dogs that enjoy the company of both humans and other animals. They typically get along well with children, although supervision is necessary to ensure the safety of both the dog and the child. Early socialization is essential to promote positive interactions with other dogs and pets, as well as to help them develop good manners and appropriate behavior.

Italian Greyhounds have a moderate energy level. While they enjoy a good play session or a brisk walk, they are generally not hyperactive or excessively demanding. They are content with a balanced amount of physical exercise and mental stimulation. However, it is important to note that each individual dog may have unique energy requirements, and their exercise needs should be tailored accordingly.

Italian Greyhounds possess a strong prey drive due to their sighthound heritage. They have an instinctive desire to chase small animals. This inclination should be taken into consideration when allowing them off-leash in open spaces. Proper training and supervision are essential to manage their prey drive and ensure their safety.

General Disposition

Italian Greyhounds possess a general disposition that is as endearing as their physical appearance. Known for their affectionate nature, intelligence, and adaptability, Italian Greyhounds make delightful companions and cherished members of many households. Below we will explore the general disposition of Italian Greyhounds, shedding light on their unique qualities and characteristics.

One of the most prominent aspects of the Italian Greyhound's general disposition is their affectionate nature. They form strong bonds with their human companions and thrive on close interaction and companionship. Italian Greyhounds are often described as being "velcro dogs" due to their tendency to stick close to their owners, seeking comfort and providing emotional support. Their affectionate and attentive nature makes them excellent companions for individuals or families seeking a loving and devoted pet.

Italian Greyhounds are known for their gentle temperament and sensitivity. They possess a deep capacity for empathy and are attuned to the emotions of their human family members. They have an innate ability to provide comfort and emotional support, making them ideal therapy dogs or companions for individuals in need. Their sensitivity to their owner's moods and needs adds to their overall charm and endears them to their human companions.

Despite their small size, Italian Greyhounds exhibit a confident and self-assured demeanor. They have a unique sense of self-awareness and carry themselves with a regal poise. This confidence contributes to their overall presence and distinguishes them from other small dog breeds. Italian Greyhounds are not easily intimidated and exhibit a certain grace and elegance in their every movement.

Italian Greyhounds are intelligent and eager to please. They possess a sharp mind and respond well to positive reinforcement-based training methods. They are quick learners and excel in activities that challenge their mental capabilities. Italian Greyhounds are known to participate in various dog sports and competitions, showcasing their agility, obedience, and ability to learn and execute complex commands.

Adaptability is another key aspect of the Italian Greyhound's general disposition. They can thrive in various living environments and adjust well to different lifestyles. While they enjoy being indoors and close to their owners, they are also content with outdoor activities and exploration. Their small size allows them to adapt to apartments and houses with limited space. However, it is important to note that they still require regular exercise and mental stimulation to keep them physically and mentally balanced.

Italian Greyhounds have a moderate energy level. While they enjoy a good play session or a brisk walk, they are generally not hyperactive or excessively demanding. They are content with a balanced amount of physical exercise and mental stimulation. However, it is important to note that each individual dog may have unique energy requirements, and their exercise needs should be tailored accordingly.

Italian Greyhounds are social dogs that generally get along well with both humans and other animals. They tend to be friendly and sociable, enjoying the company of their family members and other pets. However, early socialization is essential to promote positive interactions and ensure good manners and appropriate behavior.

While Italian Greyhounds possess a general disposition that is loving and gentle, it is important to remember that each dog is an individual with its own unique personality. Some Italian Greyhounds may be more reserved or shy, while others may be outgoing and sociable. It is crucial to provide them with a nurturing and supportive environment that meets their individual needs.

Intelligence and Trainability

Italian Greyhounds are not only known for their elegance and beauty but also for their intelligence and trainability. With their sharp minds and eagerness to please, Italian Greyhounds are highly trainable dogs that excel in various activities and commands. Below we will explore the intelligence and trainability of Italian Greyhounds, highlighting their exceptional learning abilities and their readiness to engage in training.

Italian Greyhounds are intelligent dogs that possess a keen intellect. They have the capacity to understand and learn a wide range of commands and tricks. Their intelligence allows them to quickly grasp new concepts and adapt to different training methods. Italian Greyhounds possess a natural curiosity and a desire to explore their environment, which contributes to their learning capabilities.

When it comes to training, Italian Greyhounds are eager to please their owners. They have a strong desire to be rewarded and receive positive reinforcement. This eagerness, combined with their intelligence, makes them responsive to training techniques that focus on positive reinforcement. They thrive in an environment where they receive praise, treats, and other rewards for their achievements. This positive approach encourages their continued engagement and motivation during training sessions.

The intelligence and trainability of Italian Greyhounds make them suitable for a variety of activities and sports. They excel in obedience training, where their ability to learn and follow commands is put to the test. Italian Greyhounds can quickly master basic commands such as sit, stay, come, and heel, as well as more complex commands with consistent training and positive reinforcement.

Italian Greyhounds are also known for their agility and athleticism. They have the physical capabilities to participate in agility courses, where they navigate through various obstacles and perform jumps and weave poles. Their intelligence allows them to understand and execute the sequence of actions required, making them competitive and successful in agility competitions.

In addition to obedience and agility, Italian Greyhounds can also participate in other dog sports, such as rally obedience and scent work. Rally obedience combines obedience training with a series of exercises that are performed together as a team. Italian Greyhounds can showcase their intelligence and trainability by following a designated course and completing each exercise with precision.

Scent work is another activity that Italian Greyhounds can excel in. They have a keen sense of smell, which can be harnessed through scent detection training. Italian Greyhounds can learn to identify specific scents and locate hidden objects or substances. This type of training not only stimulates their mental abilities but also taps into their natural instincts.

While Italian Greyhounds possess remarkable intelligence and trainability, it is important to consider their individual personalities and energy levels. Some Italian Greyhounds may have a more independent streak and require patience and consistent training methods. It is essential to tailor the training approach to meet the needs of each individual dog and provide appropriate mental stimulation to prevent boredom.

Early socialization is crucial for Italian Greyhounds to develop good manners and appropriate behavior. Introducing them to various people, animals, and environments at a young age helps them become well-rounded and confident adults. Socialization also allows them to adapt to new situations and reduces the likelihood of fear or aggression.

The intelligence and trainability of Italian Greyhounds, combined with their gentle and affectionate nature, make them excellent candidates for therapy work. Their ability to learn and respond to commands, as well as their empathetic nature, enables them to provide comfort and emotional support to individuals in need. Italian Greyhounds can bring joy and healing to people in hospitals, nursing homes, and other therapeutic settings.

Socialization and Friendliness

Italian Greyhounds are known for their affectionate nature and friendly disposition, making them excellent companions and beloved family pets. With their gentle demeanor and sociable attitude, Italian Greyhounds have a natural inclination towards socialization and enjoy interacting with humans and other animals. Below we will explore the importance of socialization for Italian Greyhounds and highlight their inherent friendliness that endears them to people and animals alike.

Socialization plays a crucial role in shaping the behavior and temperament of Italian Greyhounds. Early socialization, which involves exposing them to various people, animals, and environments during their developmental stage, helps them become well-rounded and confident adults. It allows them to learn appropriate social behaviors, reduces the likelihood of fear or aggression, and promotes positive interactions with others.

Italian Greyhounds have a friendly and sociable nature. They possess a genuine desire to interact and form connections with humans and other animals. They are known for their gentle and non-aggressive demeanor, which contributes to their ability to get along well with people of all ages, including children. Italian Greyhounds generally exhibit patience and tolerance, making them suitable companions for families and individuals seeking a friendly and affectionate pet.

Italian Greyhounds thrive on companionship and enjoy being in the presence of their human family members. They often form strong bonds with their owners and seek constant contact and attention. Italian Greyhounds are often described as "velcro dogs" due to their tendency to stick close to their owners, providing them with a sense of comfort and security. This inherent need for social interaction and closeness further emphasizes their friendly and sociable nature.

In addition to their affinity for humans, Italian Greyhounds generally exhibit a friendly demeanor towards other animals. With proper socialization and positive experiences, they can develop harmonious relationships with dogs and other pets. However, as with any dog, it is important to introduce them to other animals in a controlled and supervised manner, ensuring that interactions are positive and safe for all involved.

The friendly nature of Italian Greyhounds also extends to strangers. While they may initially be reserved or cautious with unfamiliar individuals, they typically warm up quickly and approach them with curiosity and friendliness. Italian Greyhounds are not typically known for displaying aggressive behaviors towards strangers, making them suitable for individuals or families seeking a sociable and welcoming pet.

Socialization is an ongoing process throughout the life of an Italian Greyhound. Continued exposure to different people, animals, and environments helps maintain their social skills and reinforces positive behavior. Regular walks in the neighborhood, visits to parks, and interactions with other dogs and humans contribute to their continued socialization and help them navigate new situations with ease.

Italian Greyhounds can benefit from training classes and activities that promote socialization, such as obedience training or group playdates with other dogs. These experiences allow them to practice appropriate social behaviors, improve their communication skills, and enhance their overall friendliness.

It is important to note that individual Italian Greyhounds may vary in their level of sociability. Some may exhibit a more reserved or shy disposition, requiring patience and gentle encouragement to feel comfortable in social situations. Respect for their individual personalities and providing them with positive experiences can help them develop confidence and further enhance their friendliness.

Italian Greyhounds' natural friendliness and sociable nature also make them suitable candidates for therapy work. Their ability to form connections and provide comfort to individuals in need is highly valued in therapeutic settings such as hospitals, nursing homes, and schools. Italian Greyhounds can bring joy and emotional support to people, contributing to their overall well-being.

Health and Wellness

Italian Greyhounds are generally healthy and robust dogs with few breed-specific health issues. Their slender build and moderate size contribute to their overall well-being, but it is important to be aware of certain health considerations to ensure the health and wellness of Italian Greyhounds. Below we will explore the health and wellness of Italian Greyhounds, focusing on their general health, potential health concerns, and the measures that can be taken to promote their well-being.

Italian Greyhounds are generally long-lived dogs with a life expectancy of around 12 to 15 years. With proper care and attention, they can lead healthy and active lives. Regular veterinary check-ups are essential to monitor their overall health, detect any potential health issues, and ensure that they receive necessary vaccinations and preventive treatments.

One of the notable health advantages of Italian Greyhounds is their relatively low prevalence of hereditary conditions compared to some other dog breeds. However, like all breeds, Italian Greyhounds may still be susceptible to certain health issues. It is important for potential owners to be aware of these conditions and take appropriate measures to prevent or manage them.

One health concern that can affect Italian Greyhounds is dental disease. Small breeds like Italian Greyhounds are more prone to dental problems, including dental decay, tartar buildup, and gum disease. Regular dental care, including teeth brushing and professional cleanings as recommended by a veterinarian, is crucial to maintain oral health and prevent dental issues.

Italian Greyhounds are also susceptible to orthopedic conditions such as patellar luxation and Legg-Calvé-Perthes disease. Patellar luxation occurs when the kneecap slips out of place, causing discomfort and difficulty in movement. Legg-Calvé-Perthes disease is a condition in which the hip joint deteriorates, leading to pain and lameness. Responsible breeding practices and regular exercise that avoids excessive strain on their joints can help reduce the risk of these conditions.

Like many small breeds, Italian Greyhounds can be prone to obesity if not properly managed. Maintaining a healthy weight is essential to prevent various health issues associated with obesity, such as joint problems, heart disease, and diabetes. Feeding a balanced diet and providing regular exercise in accordance with their energy levels can help prevent obesity and promote overall wellness.

Italian Greyhounds have thin skin and a short coat, which may make them more susceptible to environmental factors such as extreme temperatures and sun exposure. During cold weather, it is important to provide appropriate clothing to keep them warm. In hot weather, it is necessary to provide shade, access to fresh water, and avoid prolonged exposure to direct sunlight to prevent overheating and sunburn.

Italian Greyhounds may also have a higher sensitivity to anesthesia compared to other breeds. It is crucial to inform veterinarians about their breed-specific sensitivity to ensure appropriate anesthetic protocols are followed during surgical procedures or medical treatments.

Maintaining regular exercise is essential for the overall health and well-being of Italian Greyhounds. Although they are not high-energy dogs, they still require daily exercise to prevent weight gain and keep their muscles toned. Regular walks, playtime, and mental stimulation through interactive toys and games are beneficial for their physical and mental health.

When it comes to feeding Italian Greyhounds, it is important to provide them with a balanced and nutritious diet. High-quality dog food that meets their specific nutritional needs is recommended. Feeding schedules and portion control should be tailored to their age, weight, and activity level to prevent overfeeding or undernourishment.

In addition to physical health, the mental well-being of Italian Greyhounds should also be considered. They thrive on human companionship and interaction. Leaving them alone for extended periods can lead to separation anxiety and other behavioral issues.

Common Health Issues in Italian Greyhounds

Italian Greyhounds, despite being generally healthy dogs, are susceptible to certain health issues that are common within the breed. It is important for potential owners and current caretakers to be aware of these conditions to ensure the well-being and proper care of Italian Greyhounds. Below we will explore some of the common health issues that can affect Italian Greyhounds, providing important information on prevention, management, and veterinary care.

Dental disease is a prevalent health concern in Italian Greyhounds. The breed's small size and delicate build make them more susceptible to dental problems, including dental decay, periodontal disease, and tartar buildup. Neglecting dental hygiene can lead to pain, infection, and even tooth loss. Regular dental care, including daily teeth brushing with canine toothpaste, professional dental cleanings, and providing appropriate dental chews, can help maintain good oral health and prevent dental issues.

Patellar luxation is a common orthopedic condition in Italian Greyhounds. It occurs when the kneecap (patella) dislocates or moves out of its normal position, resulting in lameness, pain, and difficulty in walking. The severity of patellar luxation can range from mild to severe, and it can affect one or both hind limbs. In some cases, surgical intervention may be necessary to correct the condition and alleviate discomfort. Proper exercise, avoiding excessive strain on joints, and maintaining a healthy weight can help reduce the risk of patellar luxation.

Italian Greyhounds are also prone to developing Legg-Calvé-Perthes disease, which affects the hip joint. This condition occurs when there is a disruption in the blood supply to the femoral head, leading to the deterioration of the hip joint and subsequent pain and lameness. Legg-Calvé-Perthes disease is most commonly observed in young Italian Greyhounds, and surgical intervention is often required to remove the affected bone and promote healing. Early detection and appropriate treatment can significantly improve the dog's quality of life.

Progressive retinal atrophy (PRA) is an inherited eye disorder that can affect Italian Greyhounds. PRA causes the progressive degeneration of the retina, leading to eventual blindness. It is crucial for breeders to perform appropriate eye examinations on their breeding stock to minimize the occurrence of PRA. Regular eye examinations by a veterinary ophthalmologist can aid in early detection and management of PRA in Italian Greyhounds.

Hypothyroidism is a hormonal disorder that can occur in Italian Greyhounds. It is caused by the underproduction of thyroid hormones by the thyroid gland, leading to a range of symptoms such as weight gain, lethargy, hair loss, and skin problems. Hypothyroidism can usually be managed with lifelong medication in the form of synthetic thyroid hormone supplementation. Regular blood tests and monitoring by a veterinarian are necessary to ensure the proper dosage and management of the condition.

Another health issue that can affect Italian Greyhounds is allergies. They may develop allergies to certain foods, environmental allergens, or substances they come into contact with. Allergies can manifest as skin irritations, itching, redness, and gastrointestinal issues. Identifying and eliminating the allergen from the dog's environment, dietary changes, and appropriate medication prescribed by a veterinarian can help manage and alleviate allergic symptoms.

Italian Greyhounds may also experience sensitivity to certain medications, particularly anesthesia. Due to their small size and unique physiology, Italian Greyhounds may require adjustments in anesthesia protocols during surgical procedures or medical treatments. It is crucial to inform veterinarians about their breed-specific sensitivity to ensure appropriate and safe anesthesia administration.

Exercise and Activity Needs

Italian Greyhounds, despite their small size, have moderate exercise and activity needs that are essential for their overall health and well-being. While they are not high-energy dogs, regular exercise and mental stimulation are important to keep them physically fit, mentally stimulated, and prevent behavioral issues. Below we will explore the exercise and activity needs of Italian Greyhounds, providing valuable insights into the type and amount of exercise they require for a happy and healthy lifestyle.

Italian Greyhounds are sighthounds with a long history of being bred for their speed and agility. Although they are not as physically demanding as some other sighthound breeds, they still require regular exercise to maintain their muscle tone and overall fitness. Engaging in physical activities not only keeps them physically healthy but also provides mental stimulation and helps prevent boredom.

While the exercise needs of Italian Greyhounds can vary based on their age, health, and individual energy levels, a general guideline is to provide them with a daily walk or two, lasting around 20 to 30 minutes each. These walks should be brisk and purposeful, allowing them to explore their surroundings and get some exercise. It is important to note that Italian Greyhounds should be walked on a leash or in a securely fenced area, as their strong prey drive may cause them to chase small animals.

In addition to walks, Italian Greyhounds can benefit from off-leash playtime in a safe and secure environment, such as a fenced backyard or a designated dog park. This allows them to stretch their legs, run, and play freely. It is important to ensure that the area is securely enclosed, as Italian Greyhounds are agile and may attempt to squeeze through small openings.

Italian Greyhounds have an inherent love for running and sprinting. They enjoy short bursts of high-speed activity, which can be satisfied through regular play sessions or short runs in a secure area. Care should be taken not to overexert them, especially in hot weather, as they are more susceptible to heat exhaustion and heat stroke due to their thin coat and low body fat.

In addition to physical exercise, mental stimulation is crucial for the overall well-being of Italian Greyhounds. Engaging their minds helps prevent boredom and destructive behaviors that may result from under-stimulation. Mental stimulation can be achieved through interactive toys, food puzzles, obedience training, or engaging in canine sports and activities that challenge their problem-solving skills.

Despite their exercise needs, it is important to be mindful of the limitations of Italian Greyhounds. They have a delicate build and are prone to injuries, particularly in their joints and bones. Excessive exercise or high-impact activities should be avoided to prevent strain or stress on their fragile structures. Instead, focus on providing low-impact exercises and activities that are gentle on their bodies, such as controlled walks, swimming, or gentle play.

Socialization and interaction with other dogs are important aspects of an Italian Greyhound's exercise routine. They are generally sociable and enjoy the company of other dogs, which can be beneficial for their mental and social development. Regular playdates with well-behaved and properly vaccinated dogs can provide them with opportunities for social interaction, exercise, and mental stimulation.

It is important to consider the age and health of an Italian Greyhound when determining their exercise needs. Puppies require shorter and more frequent exercise sessions to prevent overtiring, while older dogs may have reduced stamina and mobility. In cases of health conditions or injuries, it is essential to consult with a veterinarian to determine appropriate exercise restrictions or modifications.

Diet and Nutrition

A well-balanced diet and proper nutrition are essential for the overall health and well-being of Italian Greyhounds. As a small and active breed, Italian Greyhounds have specific dietary needs that should be met to maintain their optimal health, support their energy levels, and prevent common health issues. Below we will explore the importance of diet and nutrition for Italian Greyhounds, providing valuable insights into their specific dietary requirements and guidelines for maintaining a healthy and balanced diet.

Italian Greyhounds have a relatively high metabolism and require a diet that provides them with the necessary nutrients, calories, and energy to support their active lifestyle. It is important to choose a high-quality dog food that is specifically formulated for small breeds or all life stages. These foods are designed to meet the nutritional needs of small dogs and provide the appropriate balance of proteins, fats, and carbohydrates.

Protein is a crucial component of an Italian Greyhound's diet as it supports their muscle development, repair, and overall growth. Look for dog foods that list high-quality animal proteins, such as chicken, turkey, or fish, as the main ingredients. These proteins should be easily digestible and provide the necessary amino acids for optimal health.

Fat is another important component of an Italian Greyhound's diet, providing them with a concentrated source of energy. Healthy fats, such as those found in fish oil or flaxseed, help maintain a healthy coat and skin, support brain function, and provide essential fatty acids. However, it is important to feed fats in moderation to prevent excessive weight gain.

Carbohydrates, such as whole grains or vegetables, can also be included in an Italian Greyhound's diet in moderate amounts. These carbohydrates provide a source of energy and fiber. However, it is important to choose complex carbohydrates that are easily digestible and avoid excessive amounts of grains that may contribute to weight gain or digestive issues.

Italian Greyhounds have a relatively small stomach capacity, and feeding them smaller, more frequent meals throughout the day can help prevent digestive discomfort and maintain stable blood sugar levels. Dividing their daily food portion into two to three meals is recommended. However, it is important to monitor their calorie intake and adjust portion sizes based on their activity level and body condition to prevent obesity.

While commercial dog food provides a convenient and balanced option, some Italian Greyhound owners choose to feed their dogs a homemade or raw diet. If opting for homemade or raw feeding, it is crucial to consult with a veterinarian or a veterinary nutritionist to ensure the diet is nutritionally complete and balanced. Homemade diets require careful attention to the proper balance of proteins, carbohydrates, fats, and essential nutrients.

In addition to a well-balanced diet, it is important to provide fresh and clean water at all times to keep Italian Greyhounds hydrated. Proper hydration is crucial for their overall health and helps regulate their body temperature, aid digestion, and support organ function.

Italian Greyhounds have a tendency to become overweight if their caloric intake exceeds their energy expenditure. Obesity can lead to various health problems, including joint issues, diabetes, and heart disease. Monitoring their body condition and adjusting their diet and portion sizes accordingly can help prevent obesity. Regular exercise, such as daily walks and play sessions, also contributes to weight management and overall fitness.

It is important to avoid feeding Italian Greyhounds table scraps or excessive treats, as these can contribute to weight gain and disrupt the balance of their diet. Treats should be limited and used as rewards during training or as occasional indulgences. Look for high-quality, small-sized treats that are specifically formulated for small dogs.

Grooming and Maintenance

Italian Greyhounds are elegant and sleek dogs with a short, fine coat that requires minimal grooming. However, proper grooming and maintenance are still essential to keep them looking their best, promote good hygiene, and monitor their overall health. Below we will explore the grooming and maintenance needs of Italian Greyhounds, providing valuable insights into their coat care, dental hygiene, nail care, and other important aspects of their grooming routine.

Italian Greyhounds have a short, smooth coat that is relatively easy to maintain. Their coat does not require regular trimming or professional grooming, but it does benefit from regular brushing to remove loose hair and distribute natural oils, keeping their coat healthy and shiny. A soft bristle brush or grooming mitt is suitable for this purpose. However, it is important to note that Italian Greyhounds have sensitive skin, so it is crucial to use gentle brushing techniques to avoid irritating their skin.

While Italian Greyhounds are not heavy shedders, they still experience seasonal shedding and may require more frequent brushing during these times to remove loose hair. Regular brushing also helps prevent matting and tangles, particularly in areas with longer hair, such as the ears and tail. Pay special attention to these areas to prevent discomfort or skin issues.

Bathing an Italian Greyhound should be done on an as-needed basis. They have a naturally clean and odorless coat, and excessive bathing can strip their skin of natural oils, leading to dryness and irritation. When bathing, use a mild dog shampoo specifically formulated for sensitive skin. It is important to rinse thoroughly to remove all shampoo residue, as leftover residue can cause skin irritation. After bathing, gently towel dry or use a low heat setting on a blow dryer to prevent chilling.

Italian Greyhounds are prone to dental issues, so proper dental care is crucial for their overall health. Brushing their teeth regularly, ideally daily or at least several times a week, helps prevent plaque buildup, tartar formation, and dental disease. Use a soft-bristled toothbrush and a dog-friendly toothpaste. Introduce tooth brushing gradually and make it a positive experience for your Italian Greyhound. Additionally, providing dental chews or toys designed to promote dental health can aid in maintaining their oral hygiene.

Nail care is an important aspect of grooming for Italian Greyhounds. Regular nail trimming is necessary to prevent overgrowth, discomfort, and potential injuries. It is recommended to use a quality nail clipper designed for dogs and to trim the nails carefully, avoiding the quick (the sensitive inner part of the nail that contains blood vessels and nerves). If you are unsure about trimming your Italian Greyhound's nails or if they have dark-colored nails, consider seeking assistance from a professional groomer or veterinarian to ensure safe and proper nail trimming.

Italian Greyhounds have thin and delicate skin, which makes them more prone to sunburn and skin injuries. Protecting them from prolonged exposure to direct sunlight is essential, especially during the summer months. Apply a pet-safe sunscreen or provide them with shade to prevent sunburn. Additionally, during cold weather, consider using doggy sweaters or jackets to provide extra warmth and protection from the elements.

Regular ear cleaning is important to maintain the cleanliness and health of Italian Greyhounds' ears. Check their ears weekly for signs of redness, irritation, or excessive wax buildup. Use a gentle, dog-friendly ear cleaning solution and a cotton ball or pad to clean the visible part of the ear. Avoid inserting anything deep into the ear canal, as this can cause injury or discomfort. If you notice any signs of infection or persistent ear issues, consult a veterinarian for proper diagnosis and treatment.

Coat Care and Shedding

Italian Greyhounds are known for their sleek and short coats, which require minimal grooming compared to other dog breeds. However, proper coat care is still important to keep them looking their best, maintain their skin health, and manage shedding. Below we will explore the coat care and shedding patterns of Italian Greyhounds, providing valuable insights into their grooming routine, shedding characteristics, and tips to keep their coats in optimal condition.

Italian Greyhounds have a single-layered coat that is short, fine, and smooth. Their coat is not prone to matting or excessive shedding, making them relatively low maintenance in terms of coat care. However, regular grooming is still necessary to keep their coats healthy and to monitor their overall skin condition.

Brushing Italian Greyhounds' coats is important to remove loose hair, distribute natural oils, and maintain the shine and health of their coat. A soft bristle brush or grooming mitt is suitable for this breed. Regular brushing, at least once or twice a week, helps to minimize shedding and keeps their coat free from debris and dirt. Brushing also provides an opportunity to inspect their skin for any signs of irritation, dryness, or abnormalities.

While Italian Greyhounds do not have an undercoat, they still experience seasonal shedding. Shedding is a natural process where old and damaged hair is replaced by new growth. During shedding seasons, Italian Greyhounds may experience a slightly increased rate of hair loss. However, their shedding is generally minimal and does not pose a significant issue for most owners.

To manage shedding, regular brushing helps to remove loose hair and reduce the amount of hair that ends up on furniture or clothing. Using a grooming mitt or a brush specifically designed for short coats can be effective in capturing loose hair. Additionally, providing a healthy diet and ensuring proper nutrition can contribute to the overall health of their coat and potentially reduce excessive shedding.

Bathing Italian Greyhounds should be done on an as-needed basis. Their short coats do not require frequent bathing, and over-bathing can strip their skin of natural oils, leading to dryness and potential skin issues. When bathing, it is important to use a mild dog shampoo specifically formulated for sensitive skin. Rinse thoroughly to remove all shampoo residue, as leftover residue can cause skin irritation. After bathing, gently towel dry or use a low heat setting on a blow dryer to prevent chilling.

Maintaining the health of Italian Greyhounds' skin is crucial for a healthy coat. Regular inspection of their skin can help detect any issues such as dryness, redness, or signs of allergies or infections. If any abnormalities are noticed, it is important to consult a veterinarian for proper diagnosis and treatment.

Italian Greyhounds are sensitive to extreme temperatures, both hot and cold. During colder months, they may benefit from wearing doggy sweaters or jackets to provide extra warmth and protection. During hot weather, it is important to ensure they have access to shade and fresh water to prevent overheating. Extreme temperature changes can impact their skin and coat health, so it is important to provide a comfortable environment for them.

Although Italian Greyhounds have a short coat, regular nail trimming is still necessary. Overgrown nails can cause discomfort and potentially affect their gait and overall well-being. Trim their nails carefully, avoiding cutting into the quick (the sensitive inner part of the nail that contains blood vessels and nerves). If you are unsure about trimming their nails or if they have dark-colored nails, seek assistance from a professional groomer or veterinarian.

Nail Trimming and Ear Cleaning

Nail trimming and ear cleaning are important aspects of grooming for Italian Greyhounds. Proper maintenance of their nails and ears not only keeps them comfortable and healthy but also prevents potential issues and discomfort. Below we will explore the importance of nail trimming and ear cleaning for Italian Greyhounds, providing valuable insights into the techniques, tools, and considerations to ensure a safe and effective grooming routine.

Nail trimming is an essential part of Italian Greyhound grooming. Overgrown nails can cause discomfort, affect their gait, and potentially lead to injuries or other health issues. Regular nail trimming helps maintain their paw health and prevents the nails from becoming too long or sharp.

Italian Greyhounds have small and delicate nails, making it important to use proper techniques and suitable tools for their size. Using a high-quality nail clipper specifically designed for dogs is recommended. It is important to avoid using human nail clippers or other inappropriate tools, as they can cause injury or damage to the nails.

When trimming their nails, it is crucial to be cautious and avoid cutting into the quick, which is the sensitive inner part of the nail that contains blood vessels and nerves. Cutting into the quick can cause bleeding and pain. If the nails are light-colored, the quick is usually visible as a pinkish area. However, if the nails are dark-colored, it may be more challenging to identify the quick. In such cases, it is best to trim small amounts at a time, being careful to avoid the quick.

If you are uncertain or uncomfortable with trimming your Italian Greyhound's nails, seeking assistance from a professional groomer or veterinarian is a good option. They have the experience and expertise to handle the process safely and effectively.

In addition to nail trimming, ear cleaning is another important aspect of Italian Greyhound grooming. Regular ear cleaning helps prevent the buildup of wax, debris, and potential ear infections. It is important to keep their ears clean and free from any discomfort or irritation.

To clean their ears, use a gentle and dog-friendly ear cleaning solution recommended by a veterinarian. Avoid using cotton swabs or inserting anything deep into the ear canal, as this can cause injury or discomfort. Instead, soak a cotton ball or pad with the cleaning solution and gently wipe the visible parts of the ear, removing any dirt or excess wax. Pay attention to any signs of redness, inflammation, or discharge, as these may indicate an underlying ear issue. If you notice any abnormalities or persistent ear problems, it is best to consult a veterinarian for proper diagnosis and treatment.

When performing ear cleaning, it is important to make the experience positive and comfortable for your Italian Greyhound. Use treats, praise, and rewards to associate ear cleaning with positive experiences. By establishing a routine and ensuring gentle handling, you can help your Italian Greyhound become more comfortable with the process over time.

It is important to note that Italian Greyhounds have sensitive ears, and excessive cleaning can disrupt the natural balance of their ear canal. Cleaning their ears too frequently or aggressively can lead to dryness, irritation, or even ear infections. Therefore, it is recommended to follow the guidance of a veterinarian regarding the frequency of ear cleaning for your Italian Greyhound.

Along with regular nail trimming and ear cleaning, monitoring and maintaining good hygiene for other parts of your Italian Greyhound's body is also important. Regular brushing to remove loose hair, distribute natural oils, and prevent matting should be incorporated into their grooming routine. Italian Greyhounds have a short and sleek coat, which generally requires minimal brushing. A soft bristle brush or grooming mitt can be used to gently brush their coat, keeping it healthy and shiny.

Dental Health and Oral Care

Maintaining good dental health and providing proper oral care are crucial aspects of overall wellness for Italian Greyhounds. Dental issues can lead to discomfort, pain, and even systemic health problems. Below we will explore the importance of dental health and oral care for Italian Greyhounds, providing valuable insights into common dental problems, preventive measures, and effective oral care practices to ensure their well-being.

Italian Greyhounds, like many other dog breeds, are susceptible to dental problems such as dental decay, gum disease, and tartar buildup. These issues can lead to pain, tooth loss, and bacterial infections that can spread to other organs in the body. Therefore, it is essential to prioritize their dental health and implement preventive measures.

Regular tooth brushing is one of the most effective ways to maintain good oral hygiene for Italian Greyhounds. Daily brushing, if possible, or at least several times a week, is recommended. Use a soft-bristled toothbrush specifically designed for dogs, along with a dog-friendly toothpaste. Human toothpaste should never be used, as it contains ingredients that can be harmful to dogs if ingested.

When introducing tooth brushing, start gradually and make it a positive experience for your Italian Greyhound. Use rewards, praise, and patience to help them become comfortable with the process. Lift their lips and gently brush their teeth in a circular motion, focusing on the outer surfaces. Pay particular attention to the back teeth, as they are more prone to plaque buildup.

If your Italian Greyhound resists tooth brushing, there are alternative options available. Dental wipes or dental sprays can be used to remove plaque and freshen their breath. These products are designed to be gentle on their gums and can be applied with a cloth or sprayed directly into their mouth.

Regular dental check-ups by a veterinarian are essential for maintaining optimal dental health. These visits allow for professional dental cleanings and thorough examinations. Professional cleanings involve the removal of tartar and plaque buildup that cannot be addressed by regular brushing alone. During these cleanings, your Italian Greyhound will be placed under anesthesia to ensure their safety and comfort. The veterinarian will also examine their teeth, gums, and mouth for any signs of dental disease or other oral health issues.

In addition to regular tooth brushing and professional cleanings, there are other measures that can support your Italian Greyhound's dental health. Providing them with appropriate dental chews or toys can help reduce plaque and tartar buildup. These products are designed to promote chewing and provide mechanical cleaning action, which can help remove debris and stimulate the gums.

It is important to note that not all dental chews and toys are created equal. Choose products that are specifically designed for dogs and are the appropriate size for your Italian Greyhound. Avoid items that are too hard or can splinter, as they can cause dental fractures or pose a choking hazard.

Diet can also play a role in maintaining good dental health for Italian Greyhounds. Feeding them a balanced and nutritious diet is essential. Some pet food brands offer dental-specific formulations that have kibble shapes or textures designed to help reduce plaque and tartar buildup. These specialized diets can be beneficial, but it is important to consult with a veterinarian to determine the most suitable option for your Italian Greyhound's specific needs.

Regular monitoring of your Italian Greyhound's oral health is crucial. Examine their mouth for any signs of dental issues, such as bad breath, red or swollen gums, bleeding, excessive drooling, or discolored teeth. These may indicate underlying dental problems that require attention. If you notice any abnormalities, consult with your veterinarian promptly.

Training Your Italian Greyhound

Training your Italian Greyhound is not only crucial for their development and behavior but also strengthens the bond between you and your furry companion. Italian Greyhounds are intelligent and eager to please, making them trainable dogs. With consistency, positive reinforcement, and patience, you can successfully teach them various commands and behaviors. Below we will explore the importance of training for Italian Greyhounds, effective training techniques, and tips to make the training process a positive and rewarding experience.

Training is essential for Italian Greyhounds to develop good manners, obedience, and social skills. It helps them understand their boundaries, promotes mental stimulation, and enhances their overall well-being. Additionally, training is important for their safety, as it enables you to have control over their actions and responses in different situations.

Start training your Italian Greyhound as early as possible. Puppies have a natural curiosity and eagerness to learn, making them more receptive to training. Establishing a foundation of basic commands and behaviors early on sets the stage for more advanced training as they grow older.

Positive reinforcement is a highly effective training method for Italian Greyhounds. Rewarding desired behaviors with treats, praise, or playtime reinforces the behavior and encourages them to repeat it. Italian Greyhounds are sensitive dogs, and harsh training methods or punishment can be counterproductive and potentially damage the trust between you and your dog. Instead, focus on positive reinforcement, patience, and consistency to achieve desired results.

Consistency is key when training Italian Greyhounds. Use clear and consistent cues or commands for different behaviors. For example, use a specific word or gesture for "sit," "stay," or "come." Consistency helps them understand what is expected of them and reduces confusion. Consistently rewarding and reinforcing desired behaviors also reinforces the connection between the behavior and the reward.

Short, frequent training sessions are more effective than long, extended ones. Italian Greyhounds have a relatively short attention span, so keeping training sessions focused and engaging prevents them from becoming bored or overwhelmed. Aim for training sessions of 10 to 15 minutes, a few times a day. Be patient and end the session on a positive note, even if progress is gradual. Remember, training is a gradual process that requires time and repetition.

Socialization is an important aspect of training for Italian Greyhounds. Exposing them to various people, animals, and environments from a young age helps them develop confidence and adaptability. Socialization reduces the likelihood of fear or aggression towards unfamiliar situations or individuals. Take your Italian Greyhound to different places, introduce them to other dogs, and provide positive experiences in various environments. Properly socialized Italian Greyhounds are more well-rounded, confident, and adaptable dogs.

Basic obedience commands are a good starting point for training Italian Greyhounds. Teaching them commands such as "sit," "stay," "come," and "heel" provides a foundation for their behavior and allows you to have control in different situations. Break down the commands into simple steps, use positive reinforcement, and gradually increase the difficulty as they progress. Reward them immediately when they respond correctly to a command.

Crate training is beneficial for Italian Greyhounds, providing them with a safe and comfortable space of their own. Crate training helps with housebreaking, prevents destructive behaviors, and serves as a safe haven when they need to rest or be confined temporarily. Introduce the crate gradually, make it a positive space with comfortable bedding and toys, and use positive reinforcement to encourage them to enter willingly.

Basic Obedience and Manners

Teaching your Italian Greyhound basic obedience and manners is essential for their well-being, safety, and the harmonious coexistence with you and others. Italian Greyhounds are intelligent and trainable dogs, and with consistent training, positive reinforcement, and patience, you can establish a foundation of good behavior and manners. Below we will explore the importance of teaching basic obedience and manners to Italian Greyhounds, effective training techniques, and tips for a successful training experience.

Basic obedience training provides Italian Greyhounds with the necessary skills to understand and respond to commands, enhancing their overall behavior and promoting a positive and respectful relationship between you and your dog. It also establishes a level of control and ensures their safety in different situations.

Positive reinforcement is a highly effective training method for Italian Greyhounds. Rewarding desired behaviors with treats, praise, or playtime reinforces the behavior and encourages them to repeat it. Italian Greyhounds are sensitive dogs, and harsh training methods or punishment can be counterproductive and potentially damage the trust between you and your dog. Instead, focus on positive reinforcement, using treats, praise, and rewards to motivate and reinforce desired behaviors.

Consistency is crucial when training Italian Greyhounds. Use clear and consistent cues or commands for different behaviors. For example, use a specific word or gesture for "sit," "stay," "come," and "heel." Consistency helps them understand what is expected of them and reduces confusion. Consistently rewarding and reinforcing desired behaviors also strengthens the association between the behavior and the reward.

Short, frequent training sessions are more effective than long, extended ones. Italian Greyhounds have a relatively short attention span, so keeping training sessions focused and engaging prevents them from becoming bored or overwhelmed. Aim for training sessions of 10 to 15 minutes, a few times a day. Be patient and end the session on a positive note, even if progress is gradual. Remember, training is a gradual process that requires time and repetition.

Start with the basic commands such as "sit," "stay," "come," and "heel." These commands provide a foundation for their behavior and allow you to have control in different situations. Break down the commands into simple steps, use positive reinforcement, and gradually increase the difficulty as they progress. Reward them immediately when they respond correctly to a command.

Leash training is an important aspect of basic obedience for Italian Greyhounds. Proper leash training ensures their safety during walks and prevents them from pulling or behaving in an uncontrollable manner. Start leash training in a secure and distraction-free area. Use positive reinforcement, treats, and praise to reward them for walking calmly beside you without pulling. Gradually introduce them to different environments and distractions to generalize the behavior.

Teaching your Italian Greyhound to have good manners around people and other animals is essential for their socialization and well-being. This includes teaching them not to jump on people, to greet others politely, and to be calm and well-behaved in various social situations. Consistency, positive reinforcement, and exposure to different people, animals, and environments are key to achieving good manners.

Proper socialization is important for Italian Greyhounds to develop good manners and appropriate behavior. Expose them to various social situations, people, and animals from a young age. Encourage positive interactions and reward them for calm and polite behavior. This helps them become well-rounded and well-behaved dogs in different settings.

Advanced Training Techniques

Italian Greyhounds are intelligent and trainable dogs that excel in advanced training. Once they have mastered basic obedience and manners, you can move on to more advanced training techniques to further stimulate their minds and enhance their skills. Advanced training not only challenges them mentally but also deepens the bond between you and your Italian Greyhound. Below we will explore advanced training techniques specifically tailored for Italian Greyhounds, providing valuable insights into the benefits, methods, and considerations for successful advanced training.

Agility Training: Italian Greyhounds are agile and athletic dogs, making agility training a great option to channel their energy and enhance their physical and mental capabilities. Set up an agility course in your backyard or find a local agility training facility. Teach them to navigate through tunnels, weave poles, and jumps using positive reinforcement and rewards. Agility training improves their coordination, builds confidence, and provides an outlet for their energy.

Trick Training: Italian Greyhounds are eager to please and enjoy learning new things. Trick training not only stimulates their minds but also impresses and entertains others. Teach them fun and impressive tricks like "spin," "roll over," "fetch," or "play dead." Break down each trick into small, achievable steps and use positive reinforcement to encourage their progress. Trick training strengthens the bond between you and your Italian Greyhound while keeping their minds sharp.

Scent Work: Italian Greyhounds have a keen sense of smell, making scent work an engaging and stimulating activity. Introduce them to scent detection training by hiding treats or toys in various locations and encouraging them to find the hidden items using their noses. You can also enroll them in scent work classes or competitions. Scent work provides mental stimulation, builds their confidence, and taps into their natural instincts.

Canine Sports: Italian Greyhounds can participate in various canine sports that cater to their size and abilities. Flyball, lure coursing, and dock diving are popular sports for Italian Greyhounds. These activities allow them to showcase their speed, agility, and athleticism. Participating in canine sports not only keeps them physically active but also fosters their competitive spirit and provides opportunities for socialization with other dogs and owners.

Advanced Obedience: Once your Italian Greyhound has mastered basic obedience commands, you can advance their training by teaching them more complex commands and behaviors. For example, teach them to respond to verbal or hand signals for commands like "leave it," "go to your mat," or "give paw." Advanced obedience training challenges their understanding and responsiveness, reinforcing their good behavior and promoting their mental acuity.

Off-Leash Training: With proper training and trust, Italian Greyhounds can be reliable off-leash. Gradually introduce off-leash training in a safe and controlled environment, such as a fenced-in area or a quiet park. Begin with short distances and gradually increase the distance as their recall improves. Use high-value treats and rewards to reinforce their reliable recall. Off-leash training allows them to enjoy freedom while maintaining their safety and your peace of mind.

Advanced Socialization: Advanced socialization involves exposing your Italian Greyhound to various environments, people, and animals to ensure they remain well-behaved and comfortable in different situations. Take them on outings to crowded areas, introduce them to different types of people and animals, and expose them to new sounds and experiences. Reinforce positive interactions and reward calm and appropriate behavior. Advanced socialization broadens their social skills and strengthens their adaptability.

Troubleshooting Common Behavior Issues

Italian Greyhounds, like any other dog breed, may occasionally exhibit behavior issues that require troubleshooting and corrective measures. Understanding the underlying causes and implementing effective strategies can help address and resolve these issues, leading to a more harmonious relationship between you and your Italian Greyhound. Below we will explore common behavior issues in Italian Greyhounds, their possible causes, and practical solutions to help troubleshoot and correct these behaviors.

Separation Anxiety: Italian Greyhounds are known to form strong bonds with their owners and can develop separation anxiety when left alone. Symptoms may include excessive barking, destructive behavior, or toileting indoors. To address separation anxiety, gradually acclimate your Italian Greyhound to being alone by leaving them for short periods and gradually increasing the duration. Create a safe and comfortable space for them, provide engaging toys, and consider using calming aids like music or pheromone diffusers. Consult a professional if the anxiety persists.

Excessive Barking: Italian Greyhounds are not typically excessive barkers, but they may bark when they feel anxious, bored, or to seek attention. Identify the triggers for their barking and address them accordingly. Ensure they receive sufficient mental and physical stimulation through regular exercise and interactive play. Teach them alternative behaviors such as "quiet" or "speak" commands to redirect their barking. Consistently reward calm behavior and provide them with appropriate outlets for their energy.

Destructive Chewing: Like many dogs, Italian Greyhounds may engage in destructive chewing, especially when they are bored or experiencing anxiety. Provide them with a variety of chew toys and rotate them regularly to keep them engaged. Supervise them when they are out of their crate or confined area to redirect their chewing behavior to appropriate items. Puppy-proof your home by removing or securing valuable or dangerous objects that they may be tempted to chew.

Leash Reactivity: Italian Greyhounds may exhibit leash reactivity, reacting negatively towards other dogs, people, or stimuli while on a leash. This behavior can be managed through proper socialization and positive reinforcement training. Gradually expose them to various stimuli in controlled environments, rewarding calm and positive behavior. Use positive reinforcement training techniques to redirect their attention and focus on you while on the leash. Consider seeking guidance from a professional dog trainer for more specific strategies.

Resource Guarding: Some Italian Greyhounds may exhibit resource guarding behavior, becoming possessive or aggressive when they perceive their food, toys, or space as being threatened. It is important to address resource guarding to prevent potential conflicts. Consult with a professional trainer or behaviorist to develop a training plan that focuses on desensitization and counterconditioning. Gradually teach them to associate positive experiences with people or other animals being near their valued resources.

Jumping on People: Italian Greyhounds, like many dogs, may have a tendency to jump on people when excited or seeking attention. Consistency is key in addressing this behavior. Teach them an alternative behavior, such as sitting or offering a paw, and reward them for calm greetings. Ignore jumping behavior and only give attention when they have all four paws on the ground. Consistently enforce this rule with visitors to reinforce appropriate greeting behavior.

Excessive Energy and Hyperactivity: Italian Greyhounds have bursts of energy but are generally not hyperactive. However, if your Italian Greyhound consistently displays excessive energy or hyperactivity, it may be a result of insufficient mental or physical stimulation. Ensure they receive regular exercise appropriate for their age and health. Engage them in interactive play, mental enrichment activities, and obedience training to channel their energy constructively. Consistency in exercise and mental stimulation can help reduce hyperactivity.

Socialization and Interaction

Socialization and interaction are crucial aspects of raising a well-rounded and well-behaved Italian Greyhound. Proper socialization ensures that your Italian Greyhound develops positive relationships with people, animals, and the environment. It helps them become confident, adaptable, and comfortable in various situations. Below we will explore the importance of socialization and interaction for Italian Greyhounds, effective strategies for socializing them, and the benefits of positive interactions.

Why is Socialization Important?

Socialization is the process of exposing your Italian Greyhound to different people, animals, environments, and stimuli from a young age. It is a critical period in their development, typically occurring between 3 and 14 weeks of age. During this time, they are more receptive to new experiences and less likely to develop fear or anxiety towards unfamiliar situations or individuals.

Socialization provides numerous benefits for Italian Greyhounds:

Confidence Building: Exposing your Italian Greyhound to various situations and stimuli helps build their confidence. Positive experiences during socialization boost their self-assurance, enabling them to navigate the world with ease.

Reduced Fear and Anxiety: Proper socialization helps prevent the development of fear or anxiety towards unfamiliar people, animals, or environments. Italian Greyhounds that are well-socialized are more likely to feel at ease in new situations and be less prone to stress or fear-based behaviors.

Better Adaptability: Dogs that have been properly socialized are more adaptable to different environments and situations. They are better equipped to handle changes and are less likely to become overwhelmed or anxious in new surroundings.

Improved Behavior: Socialization plays a crucial role in shaping your Italian Greyhound's behavior. Through positive interactions, they learn appropriate responses and become more well-behaved in different social settings.

Effective Strategies for Socializing Italian Greyhounds:

Early Exposure: Begin socializing your Italian Greyhound as early as possible. Introduce them to various experiences, people, and animals during their critical socialization period. This includes positive encounters with different individuals of different ages, races, and appearances. It also involves exposing them to different environments, such as parks, cities, and other areas with various sights, sounds, and smells.

Positive Reinforcement: Use positive reinforcement to create positive associations with socialization experiences. Reward your Italian Greyhound with treats, praise, and play for calm and confident behavior in new situations. This reinforces their positive experiences and helps them develop positive associations with unfamiliar people, animals, and environments.

Gradual Exposure: Introduce your Italian Greyhound to new experiences gradually. Start with controlled and familiar environments, and gradually increase the level of exposure to more challenging situations. This gradual approach helps prevent overwhelming your dog and allows them to build confidence at their own pace.

Controlled Interactions: When socializing your Italian Greyhound with other dogs, choose friendly and well-behaved dogs for initial interactions. Supervise these interactions closely, ensuring that they are positive and without any signs of aggression or fear. If necessary, seek the assistance of a professional dog trainer or behaviorist to facilitate controlled socialization experiences.

Ongoing Socialization: Socialization is not a one-time event but an ongoing process throughout your Italian Greyhound's life. Continue to expose them to new experiences, people, and animals regularly. Maintain positive interactions to reinforce their social skills and prevent regression.

Benefits of Positive Interactions:

Positive interactions play a vital role in socialization for Italian Greyhounds:

Building Trust and Bonding: Positive interactions create a strong bond between you and your Italian Greyhound. When they associate positive experiences with your presence, they develop trust and confidence in your guidance.

Introducing Your Italian Greyhound to Other Pets

Introducing a new Italian Greyhound to your household that already has existing pets can be an exciting but delicate process. Proper introductions and gradual acclimation are key to ensuring a harmonious and safe environment for all the pets involved. Italian Greyhounds, known for their gentle and sociable nature, can generally adapt well to living with other pets if introduced correctly. Below we will explore the importance of introducing your Italian Greyhound to other pets, effective strategies for a successful introduction, and tips to promote positive interactions and long-term coexistence.

Why is Proper Introduction Important?

Properly introducing your Italian Greyhound to other pets is crucial for several reasons:

Establishing Positive Relationships: Introductions set the foundation for positive relationships between your Italian Greyhound and existing pets. A successful introduction promotes trust, respect, and companionship among all animals, ensuring a harmonious living environment.

Minimizing Stress and Anxiety: A gradual introduction helps minimize stress and anxiety for both your Italian Greyhound and existing pets. Slow and controlled interactions allow them to adjust to each other's presence, reducing the likelihood of fear, aggression, or territorial behaviors.

Ensuring Safety: A carefully managed introduction process ensures the safety of all pets involved. It allows you to closely monitor their interactions, identify potential issues, and intervene if necessary to prevent any physical harm or emotional distress.

Effective Strategies for Introducing Italian Greyhounds to Other Pets:

Preparation and Patience: Before bringing your Italian Greyhound home, create a designated safe space for them, such as a crate or a separate room. This provides a calm and secure area where they can retreat if needed. Ensure all pets have their own space, beds, and toys to minimize potential resource guarding.

Scent Exchange: Start by introducing the pets' scents to each other before any direct contact. Rub a cloth on your Italian Greyhound and then allow your other pets to sniff it. Similarly, let your Italian Greyhound become familiar with the scents of your existing pets by placing their bedding or toys in their area.

Controlled Visual Introduction: Initially, introduce the pets through a visual barrier, such as a baby gate or a partially opened door. This allows them to observe each other without direct contact. Monitor their reactions and observe their body language for signs of fear, aggression, or curiosity.

Gradual Supervised Interactions: Gradually progress to supervised interactions in controlled environments. Keep your Italian Greyhound on a leash during initial meetings to maintain control and ensure safety. Allow short, positive interactions while closely observing their behavior. Reward calm and friendly interactions with treats and praise.

Neutral Territory: Consider conducting the initial introductions in a neutral territory, such as a park or a neighbor's yard. This helps prevent any territorial behaviors and reduces the chances of conflict. Neutral territories can help alleviate tension and promote neutral and friendly interactions.

Separate Feeding Areas: During the introductory phase, provide separate feeding areas for all pets to minimize potential food-related aggression or competition. Ensure that each pet has their own food and water bowls and that mealtimes are peaceful and uninterrupted.

Gradual Integration: As the pets become more comfortable with each other, gradually increase their interaction time. Allow them to spend more supervised time together while gradually reducing physical barriers. Observe their body language, ensuring that they are relaxed and showing positive signs of acceptance.

1Positive Reinforcement: Reward all pets for calm and friendly behavior during the introduction process. Use treats, praise, and playtime to reinforce positive interactions and establish positive associations with each other's presence.

Meeting New People and Environments

Italian Greyhounds are known for their friendly and sociable nature, making them generally adaptable to new people and environments. However, introducing them to unfamiliar individuals and surroundings requires careful consideration and a gradual approach to ensure their comfort and well-being. Below we will explore the importance of introducing Italian Greyhounds to new people and environments, effective strategies for successful introductions, and tips to promote positive experiences and minimize stress.

Why are Proper Introductions Important?

Properly introducing your Italian Greyhound to new people and environments is important for several reasons:

Building Trust and Confidence: Introductions allow your Italian Greyhound to build trust and confidence in new situations. Positive experiences during introductions contribute to their overall well-being and promote a sense of security and comfort.

Reducing Anxiety and Fear: Gradual introductions help minimize anxiety and fear in Italian Greyhounds. By gradually exposing them to new people and environments, you can help them feel more at ease and reduce the likelihood of stress-related behaviors.

Positive Socialization: Introducing your Italian Greyhound to new people and environments is an opportunity for positive socialization. It helps them develop appropriate social skills, promotes friendly interactions, and builds their confidence in various social settings.

Effective Strategies for Introducing Italian Greyhounds to New People and Environments:

Gradual Exposure: Introduce your Italian Greyhound to new people and environments gradually. Start with low-stress situations and gradually increase the level of exposure. This approach allows them to acclimate at their own pace and build positive associations with each new experience.

Positive Reinforcement: Use positive reinforcement to reward and encourage your Italian Greyhound's calm and confident behavior during introductions. Offer treats, praise, and gentle petting to reinforce their positive experiences and to associate new people and environments with positive outcomes.

Controlled Environments: When introducing your Italian Greyhound to new people or environments, choose controlled settings where you can manage the level of interaction and limit potential stressors. This could be a quiet room in your home or a calm outdoor space.

Familiar Scents: To ease the introduction process, introduce your Italian Greyhound to the scent of new people before physical contact. Have the individuals place an item with their scent, such as a T-shirt, in a designated area for your dog to become familiar with their scent.

Gentle Approach: Encourage new people to approach your Italian Greyhound calmly and gently. Sudden movements or loud voices can startle them. Instruct newcomers to avoid direct eye contact initially, as this can be intimidating for some dogs.

Respect Boundaries: Communicate with new people and educate them about your Italian Greyhound's boundaries. Request that they allow your dog to approach them at their own pace, rather than overwhelming them with immediate physical contact.

1Socialization Classes: Consider enrolling your Italian Greyhound in socialization classes or group training sessions. These controlled environments provide opportunities for them to interact with other dogs and people under the guidance of a professional trainer.

Patience and Observation: Remain patient and observant during introductions. Monitor your Italian Greyhound's body language for signs of stress or discomfort, such as cowering, lip licking, or excessive panting. If you notice any signs of unease, remove them from the situation and give them time to relax.

Tips for Positive Experiences:

Respect Individual Preferences: Understand that not all Italian Greyhounds are naturally outgoing. Some may be more reserved or shy, while others may be more extroverted. Respect your dog's individual preferences and avoid pushing them into interactions that make them uncomfortable.

Safe and Positive Playtime

Playtime is an important aspect of your Italian Greyhound's life, providing them with physical exercise, mental stimulation, and an opportunity to bond with you and other pets. Ensuring safe and positive playtime is crucial to prevent accidents, promote good behavior, and enhance the overall well-being of your Italian Greyhound. Below we will explore the importance of safe and positive playtime, effective strategies for engaging in play, and tips to create a fun and enriching play environment for your Italian Greyhound.

Why is Safe and Positive Playtime Important?

Safe and positive playtime offers numerous benefits for Italian Greyhounds:

Physical Exercise: Playtime allows Italian Greyhounds to burn off excess energy and maintain a healthy weight. Regular exercise through play helps prevent obesity and promotes cardiovascular health and overall physical fitness.

Mental Stimulation: Playtime engages your Italian Greyhound's mind and provides mental stimulation. Interactive games and puzzles challenge their problem-solving skills and help prevent boredom, which can lead to destructive behaviors.

Bonding and Socialization: Playtime strengthens the bond between you and your Italian Greyhound. Interactive play enhances your relationship and builds trust. Playtime with other dogs and people also promotes socialization and positive interactions.

Behavior Management: Engaging in safe and positive play activities helps redirect your Italian Greyhound's energy towards appropriate outlets. It can prevent unwanted behaviors such as excessive barking, chewing, or digging, by providing an alternative and fulfilling activity.

Effective Strategies for Safe and Positive Playtime:

Choose Appropriate Toys: Select toys that are safe, durable, and appropriate for Italian Greyhounds. Avoid toys with small parts that can be swallowed or sharp edges that may cause injury. Opt for toys designed for their size and chewing habits. Interactive puzzle toys and treat-dispensing toys can also provide mental stimulation during play.

Supervise Play Sessions: Always supervise play sessions to ensure the safety of your Italian Greyhound. Pay attention to their behavior and intervene if play becomes too rough or aggressive. Supervision also allows you to redirect their focus if they start exhibiting unwanted behaviors.

Engage in Interactive Play: Participate in interactive play with your Italian Greyhound. This can include games like fetch, tug-of-war, or hide-and-seek. Interactive play strengthens your bond, provides physical exercise, and allows you to monitor their behavior and ensure safe play.

Rotate Toys: Rotate your Italian Greyhound's toys regularly to keep playtime engaging and prevent boredom. This helps maintain their interest in the toys and prevents them from becoming too attached to a single toy, reducing the likelihood of possessive behavior.

Positive Reinforcement: Use positive reinforcement during playtime to reinforce good behavior. Reward your Italian Greyhound with treats, praise, and play for appropriate play behaviors such as gentle mouthing or retrieving toys. This helps them understand the desired play behavior and encourages them to repeat it.

Consider Playdates: Arrange playdates with other well-socialized dogs to provide opportunities for social interaction. Supervise these interactions closely and ensure that all dogs are comfortable and compatible. Playdates can enhance socialization skills, promote healthy play behavior, and provide additional mental and physical stimulation.

1Mental Stimulation Games: Incorporate mental stimulation games into playtime. This can include puzzle toys, scent games, or training sessions with reward-based methods. Mental stimulation games engage their cognitive abilities, provide a challenge, and prevent boredom.

Italian Greyhounds and Families

Italian Greyhounds are not only beloved for their elegant appearance and graceful nature but also for their compatibility with families. These small and affectionate dogs make excellent companions for families of all sizes, bringing joy, love, and a unique charm to the household. Below we will explore the reasons why Italian Greyhounds are a perfect fit for families, their characteristics that make them family-friendly, and the benefits they provide to family members of all ages.

Why are Italian Greyhounds a Perfect Fit for Families?

Italian Greyhounds possess several qualities that make them well-suited for family life:

Affectionate and Loving Nature: Italian Greyhounds have a reputation for being affectionate and loving towards their family members. They thrive on human companionship and enjoy being part of the family unit. Their gentle and cuddly nature makes them wonderful lap dogs and constant sources of comfort and companionship.

Playful and Energetic: Despite their small size, Italian Greyhounds have a playful and energetic side. They love to engage in interactive play with their family members, whether it's a game of fetch, a chase around the yard, or a romp in the park. Their playful nature brings joy and laughter to family activities.

Good with Children: Italian Greyhounds generally get along well with children, making them suitable family pets. They are patient and tolerant, and their small size makes them less intimidating to young children. Proper supervision is essential to ensure gentle interactions between children and Italian Greyhounds, but their friendly nature often makes them an ideal choice for families with kids.

Adaptability: Italian Greyhounds are adaptable and can thrive in various living situations. Whether you live in an apartment or a house with a backyard, Italian Greyhounds can adjust to their environment as long as their exercise and socialization needs are met. This adaptability allows them to seamlessly integrate into different family lifestyles.

Low Maintenance: Italian Greyhounds have short coats that require minimal grooming. They shed minimally and are considered a hypoallergenic breed, making them suitable for families with allergies. Their low maintenance needs free up time for families to focus on spending quality time together rather than extensive grooming routines.

The Benefits of Italian Greyhounds for Family Members:

Companionship: Italian Greyhounds provide unwavering companionship to all family members. They form strong bonds with their human counterparts and are always ready to offer comfort, love, and a listening ear. Their presence can greatly enhance the emotional well-being of family members of all ages.

Teach Responsibility: Caring for an Italian Greyhound can teach children valuable lessons in responsibility and empathy. Assigning age-appropriate tasks, such as feeding, grooming, or walking the dog, instills a sense of responsibility and teaches children the importance of caring for another living being.

Socialization Opportunities: Owning an Italian Greyhound encourages socialization for family members. Walking the dog in the neighborhood or visiting dog parks creates opportunities for interaction with other pet owners and their dogs. This promotes social skills, empathy, and a sense of community.

Emotional Support: Italian Greyhounds have an innate ability to provide emotional support to family members. Their presence can offer comfort during difficult times, reduce stress and anxiety, and provide a source of unconditional love and companionship.

1Encourages Physical Activity: Italian Greyhounds need regular exercise, and involving the whole family in their exercise routine encourages physical activity for everyone. Taking daily walks, playing in the yard, or engaging in interactive games keeps both the Italian Greyhound and family members active and promotes a healthy lifestyle.

Children and Italian Greyhounds

Italian Greyhounds are known for their gentle and affectionate nature, making them excellent companions for children. Their small size, playful demeanor, and adaptability make them well-suited to family life, particularly in households with young ones. Below we will explore the unique bond between children and Italian Greyhounds, the benefits of this relationship, and considerations for creating a safe and harmonious environment for both.

The Bond between Children and Italian Greyhounds:

The bond between children and Italian Greyhounds is truly special. Here's why:

Gentle and Tolerant: Italian Greyhounds have a gentle and tolerant nature that makes them well-suited for children. They are patient and forgiving, even in the face of a child's energetic and sometimes clumsy behavior. This temperament allows for a positive and harmonious relationship between the two.

Companionship and Emotional Support: Italian Greyhounds offer unwavering companionship and emotional support to children. They provide a listening ear, comfort in times of sadness or stress, and a constant presence that can alleviate feelings of loneliness or anxiety.

Playful and Energetic: Italian Greyhounds share a natural inclination for play and fun with children. Their playful demeanor can keep children entertained for hours, whether it's engaging in a game of fetch, chasing each other in the yard, or simply cuddling on the couch. Their energy and enthusiasm make them compatible playmates.

Teach Responsibility and Empathy: Caring for an Italian Greyhound can teach children valuable life lessons in responsibility and empathy. Assigning age-appropriate tasks, such as feeding, grooming, or walking the dog, instills a sense of responsibility and nurtures empathy by emphasizing the needs and well-being of another living being.

Benefits of the Relationship:

The relationship between children and Italian Greyhounds offers numerous benefits:

Emotional Well-being: The presence of an Italian Greyhound can greatly contribute to a child's emotional well-being. They offer unconditional love and support, providing a source of comfort and stability. This can boost a child's self-esteem, reduce stress, and enhance overall emotional resilience.

Physical Activity: Owning an Italian Greyhound encourages physical activity for children. Taking the dog for regular walks, playing in the yard, or engaging in interactive games promotes a healthy and active lifestyle. This regular exercise benefits both the child and the dog, fostering a sense of well-being and physical fitness.

Socialization and Communication Skills: Italian Greyhounds can play a significant role in developing a child's socialization and communication skills. Walking the dog in the neighborhood or visiting dog parks creates opportunities for interaction with other pet owners and their dogs. This promotes social skills, empathy, and a sense of community.

Learning Responsibility: Caring for an Italian Greyhound fosters a sense of responsibility in children. By being involved in the daily care routine, children learn the importance of fulfilling the needs of another living being. This responsibility helps them develop organizational skills, punctuality, and a sense of commitment.

Education and Learning: Owning an Italian Greyhound can present educational opportunities for children. They can learn about the breed's history, characteristics, and proper care. This knowledge fosters a love for animals and may even inspire a future career in veterinary medicine or animal-related fields.

Seniors and Italian Greyhounds

Italian Greyhounds are not only cherished for their elegance and grace but also for their compatibility with seniors. These small and affectionate dogs can bring immense joy, companionship, and a renewed sense of purpose to the lives of older adults. Below we will explore the unique bond between seniors and Italian Greyhounds, the benefits of this companionship, and considerations for creating a safe and fulfilling environment for both.

The Bond between Seniors and Italian Greyhounds:

The bond between seniors and Italian Greyhounds is truly special. Here's why:

Companionship: Italian Greyhounds provide loyal and unwavering companionship to seniors. They thrive on human connection and form deep and meaningful bonds with their owners. Their constant presence offers emotional support, reduces feelings of loneliness, and provides a source of love and comfort.

Affectionate Nature: Italian Greyhounds are known for their affectionate nature, which is particularly beneficial for seniors. Their gentle demeanor and cuddly nature can bring immense joy and a sense of fulfillment to older adults, providing a calming and soothing presence in their lives.

Low Maintenance: Italian Greyhounds have short coats that require minimal grooming. They shed minimally and are considered a hypoallergenic breed, making them suitable for seniors with allergies or those who may have limited mobility or energy for extensive grooming routines. Their low maintenance needs allow seniors to focus on the joys of companionship without excessive care responsibilities.

Calm Demeanor: Italian Greyhounds have a calm and relaxed demeanor, which can have a positive impact on seniors. Their peaceful presence can help reduce stress, lower blood pressure, and create a tranquil environment. This calmness can be particularly beneficial for seniors who may experience anxiety or have a need for a more serene living space.

Benefits of the Relationship:

The relationship between seniors and Italian Greyhounds offers numerous benefits:

Emotional Well-being: The companionship of an Italian Greyhound can significantly improve the emotional well-being of seniors. They provide unconditional love, comfort, and support, helping to alleviate feelings of loneliness, depression, and anxiety. The presence of a devoted pet can bring immense joy and a sense of purpose to a senior's life.

Physical Health: Caring for an Italian Greyhound can have positive effects on a senior's physical health. Regular walks and gentle play sessions with their furry companion provide light exercise and promote cardiovascular health. This increased physical activity can help improve mobility, flexibility, and overall well-being.

Social Interaction: Italian Greyhounds encourage social interaction for seniors. Taking the dog for walks in the neighborhood or visiting dog-friendly parks provides opportunities for conversation and connection with other pet owners and dog lovers. These interactions foster a sense of community, combat isolation, and promote overall social well-being.

Routine and Structure: Italian Greyhounds thrive on routine, providing seniors with a sense of structure and purpose. Caring for a pet establishes a daily routine, including feeding, grooming, and exercise. This regular schedule can add a sense of meaning and responsibility to a senior's day, promoting mental stimulation and a sense of accomplishment.

Increased Happiness and Reduced Stress: The presence of an Italian Greyhound can increase happiness and reduce stress levels in seniors. The love and companionship provided by these gentle dogs have a positive impact on mental and emotional well-being. The act of stroking a dog's soft coat can release endorphins, promoting feelings of happiness and relaxation.

Multi-Dog Households

Multi-Dog Households: Harmonious Living with Italian Greyhounds

Italian Greyhounds are social and friendly dogs, making them an excellent choice for multi-dog households. The addition of an Italian Greyhound to a home with other canine companions can create a lively and harmonious environment. However, successfully managing a multi-dog household requires careful consideration, proper introductions, and ongoing attention to ensure the well-being and happiness of all dogs involved. Below we will explore the dynamics of multi-dog households, effective strategies for introducing Italian Greyhounds to other dogs, and tips for maintaining a peaceful coexistence.

Understanding the Dynamics of Multi-Dog Households:

Multi-dog households offer unique dynamics and social interactions among the dogs involved. Here are some important factors to consider:

Pack Hierarchy: Dogs naturally establish a pack hierarchy within their social group. It's essential to understand that introducing a new Italian Greyhound can potentially impact the existing hierarchy. Observing and managing the social dynamics among the dogs can help prevent conflicts and establish a harmonious balance.

Individual Personalities: Each dog has its own personality and temperament. Some dogs may be more dominant, while others may be more submissive. It's important to consider the individual personalities of each dog when introducing a new Italian Greyhound to the mix. Understanding their unique traits can help anticipate potential challenges and address them effectively.

Resources and Territory: Dogs have a natural instinct to protect resources and territory. This can include food, toys, sleeping areas, and even attention from their owners. Ensuring that each dog has access to their own resources and territory helps minimize competition and potential conflicts.

Effective Strategies for Introducing Italian Greyhounds to Other Dogs:

Introducing a new Italian Greyhound to an existing pack requires careful planning and a gradual approach. Here are some strategies to facilitate a successful introduction:

Neutral Territory: Conduct the initial introduction in a neutral territory that is unfamiliar to all the dogs. This helps minimize territorial behaviors and reduces the likelihood of conflicts. Neutral spaces, such as a park or a friend's backyard, create a neutral ground for the dogs to meet and interact.

Controlled Visual and Scent Introduction: Before any physical contact, allow the dogs to observe and scent each other. Use a visual barrier, such as a baby gate, to allow the dogs to see and smell each other without direct contact. This allows them to become familiar with each other's presence in a controlled and safe manner.

Gradual On-Leash Introduction: Begin with on-leash introductions, keeping the dogs at a comfortable distance from each other. Allow them to sniff and interact in a controlled manner while maintaining control over their movements. Watch for signs of stress or aggression and intervene if necessary.

Positive Reinforcement: Reward calm and friendly behavior during the introduction process. Use treats, praise, and play to reinforce positive interactions and create positive associations between the dogs. This helps establish a positive and harmonious relationship from the beginning.

Supervised Interaction: Gradually increase the duration and intensity of the interactions while closely supervising the dogs. Allow them to interact off-leash in a controlled environment, such as a fenced backyard or a secure dog park. Continue to observe their behavior and intervene if any signs of tension or aggression arise.

Working and Service Italian Greyhounds

The Versatility of Italian Greyhounds: Working and Service Companions

Italian Greyhounds are often recognized for their elegance and grace, but they also possess an impressive range of abilities that make them well-suited for various working and service roles. Despite their small size, these intelligent and adaptable dogs can excel in tasks such as therapy work, assistance work, and even certain dog sports. Below we will explore the unique capabilities of Italian Greyhounds in working and service roles, their training requirements, and the benefits they provide in these important roles.

The Abilities of Italian Greyhounds in Working and Service Roles:

Italian Greyhounds possess several qualities that make them valuable assets in working and service roles:

Sensitivity and Empathy: Italian Greyhounds are highly sensitive and attuned to human emotions. They have an innate ability to provide comfort and emotional support, making them well-suited for therapy work. Their gentle nature and intuition allow them to connect with people and provide solace in various environments, including hospitals, nursing homes, and schools.

Agility and Speed: Despite their small size, Italian Greyhounds are agile and have impressive speed. These qualities make them suitable for various dog sports, such as agility and lure coursing. Their athleticism and ability to navigate obstacles with ease make them successful competitors in these disciplines.

Intelligence and Trainability: Italian Greyhounds are intelligent and eager to please, which enhances their trainability. They can quickly learn and respond to commands, making them capable of performing a wide range of tasks in service roles. Their willingness to learn and work alongside their handlers is a testament to their intelligence and adaptability.

Alertness and Awareness: Italian Greyhounds possess a keen sense of alertness and are highly aware of their surroundings. This attribute is particularly valuable in assistance work, where they can be trained to provide alerts or assistance to individuals with specific needs, such as those with hearing impairments or medical conditions.

Training Requirements for Working and Service Roles:

Training is a crucial aspect of preparing Italian Greyhounds for working and service roles. Here are some important considerations:

Socialization: Early and thorough socialization is essential to expose Italian Greyhounds to a wide range of people, animals, and environments. This helps them develop the confidence and adaptability necessary for working in different settings. Proper socialization also ensures they can remain calm and focused in potentially distracting situations.

Obedience Training: Italian Greyhounds require a solid foundation in obedience training to ensure they can follow commands reliably. Basic obedience training, including commands such as sit, stay, come, and heel, establishes the groundwork for more advanced tasks and facilitates effective communication between the dog and their handler.

Task-Specific Training: Depending on the specific working or service role, Italian Greyhounds may require specialized training. For example, therapy dogs may undergo training to be calm and gentle in various environments, while assistance dogs may be trained in specific tasks such as retrieving items, alerting to sounds, or providing mobility assistance. Tailoring the training to the specific role is crucial for success.

Positive Reinforcement: Italian Greyhounds respond well to positive reinforcement training methods, which involve rewarding desired behaviors with treats, praise, or play. This positive approach not only enhances their motivation and engagement but also strengthens the bond between the dog and their handler.

Benefits of Italian Greyhounds in Working and Service Roles:

Italian Greyhounds provide several benefits when fulfilling working and service roles:

Emotional Support: Italian Greyhounds excel at providing emotional support in therapy work. Their gentle and empathetic nature can uplift the spirits of individuals in need, offering comfort, and companionship in challenging circumstances.

Guide Dogs and Assistance Roles

Guide dogs and assistance dogs play a crucial role in assisting individuals with visual impairments or disabilities. While certain dog breeds are commonly associated with these roles, Italian Greyhounds may not be the first breed that comes to mind. However, with their intelligence, adaptability, and gentle nature,

Italian Greyhounds have proven to be effective and dedicated guide dogs and assistance companions. Below we will explore the unique capabilities of Italian Greyhounds in guide and assistance roles, their training requirements, and the impact they have on the lives of individuals with disabilities.

The Abilities of Italian Greyhounds as Guide Dogs and Assistance Companions:

Italian Greyhounds possess several qualities that make them well-suited for guide and assistance roles:

Intelligence and Trainability: Italian Greyhounds are intelligent and eager to please, which enhances their trainability. They can quickly learn and respond to commands, making them capable of performing various tasks to assist individuals with disabilities. Their ability to understand and execute complex instructions is essential for the success of their role.

Sensitivity and Empathy: Italian Greyhounds are highly sensitive and attuned to their environment and the needs of their handlers. They have a natural ability to provide emotional support and comfort, which is invaluable for individuals with visual impairments or disabilities. Their empathy allows them to anticipate their handler's needs and provide assistance accordingly.

Size and Mobility: Italian Greyhounds' small size makes them agile and maneuverable, making them effective guides in various environments. They can navigate through crowded spaces, tight corners, and other challenging situations with ease. Their compact stature also allows them to fit comfortably in different modes of transportation, providing greater accessibility for their handlers.

Alertness and Awareness: Italian Greyhounds possess a keen sense of alertness and are highly aware of their surroundings. This quality is particularly important for guide dogs, as they need to be vigilant in identifying potential obstacles or hazards in their path. Their alertness and quick responses contribute to the safety and well-being of their handlers.

Training Requirements for Guide and Assistance Roles:

Training is a crucial aspect of preparing Italian Greyhounds for guide and assistance roles. Here are some important considerations:

Specialized Training Programs: Italian Greyhounds destined for guide or assistance roles typically undergo specialized training programs conducted by reputable organizations. These programs focus on obedience training, socialization, task-specific training, and exposure to various environments and situations. The training curriculum is designed to develop the necessary skills and behaviors required for successful guide and assistance work.

Obedience and Task Training: Italian Greyhounds receive extensive obedience training to ensure they respond reliably to their handler's commands. They learn essential commands such as forward, stop, left, right, and curb recognition. In addition to obedience training, they are trained in specific tasks tailored to the needs of their handlers. These tasks may include navigating obstacles, finding objects, or providing stability and support during mobility.

Socialization: Proper socialization is vital for Italian Greyhounds in guide and assistance roles. They are exposed to various environments, people, animals, and sensory stimuli to ensure they remain calm, focused, and adaptable in different situations. Socialization also helps them develop positive interactions with the public and other animals they may encounter during their work.

Partnership Development: Guide and assistance dogs undergo a process called "matching" or "partnering" to ensure compatibility between the dog and their handler. This process considers factors such as the handler's lifestyle, physical needs, and personal preferences. The goal is to establish a strong bond and mutual trust between the dog and their handler, leading to a successful partnership.

Search and Rescue Italian Greyhounds

When it comes to search and rescue operations, certain dog breeds often come to mind, such as German Shepherds or Labrador Retrievers. However, the remarkable abilities of Italian Greyhounds should not be overlooked. These small and agile dogs possess an exceptional sense of smell, intelligence, and determination that make them valuable assets in search and rescue missions. Below we will explore the unique capabilities of Italian Greyhounds in search and rescue work, their training requirements, and the impact they have on locating missing individuals in various scenarios.

The Abilities of Italian Greyhounds in Search and Rescue:

Italian Greyhounds possess several qualities that make them well-suited for search and rescue work:

Keen Sense of Smell: Despite their small size, Italian Greyhounds have a remarkable sense of smell. Their olfactory capabilities allow them to detect and follow scent trails, even in challenging environments. This keen sense of smell is invaluable in search and rescue operations, where locating missing individuals quickly can be a matter of life and death.

Agility and Speed: Italian Greyhounds are agile and possess impressive speed, allowing them to navigate through various terrains with ease. Their ability to maneuver quickly and efficiently makes them valuable in search operations conducted in rugged or hard-to-reach areas. Their small size also enables them to access spaces that larger dogs may struggle to reach.

Intelligence and Trainability: Italian Greyhounds are intelligent and highly trainable. They possess a strong desire to please their handlers and excel in learning complex tasks. This intelligence allows them to adapt to different search and rescue scenarios, making them versatile assets in various environments, such as wilderness, urban, or disaster situations.

Determination and Focus: Italian Greyhounds have a natural determination and focus, which are vital traits in search and rescue work. They possess an unwavering commitment to the task at hand and are capable of working tirelessly for extended periods. Their determination and focus contribute to their success in locating missing individuals, even in challenging conditions.

Training Requirements for Search and Rescue Work:

Training plays a crucial role in preparing Italian Greyhounds for search and rescue operations. Here are some important considerations:

Scent Discrimination: Italian Greyhounds undergo intensive scent training to develop their ability to discriminate between different scents and track specific individuals. They are trained to follow human scent trails and indicate the presence of a person by barking, sitting, or using other trained behaviors.

Search Techniques: Italian Greyhounds learn various search techniques, depending on the type of search and rescue operation they will be involved in. This training includes area searches, trailing, and even air scent work. They are trained to search systematically and cover large areas efficiently.

Obedience and Communication: Italian Greyhounds receive thorough obedience training to ensure they respond reliably to their handler's commands. Clear communication between the dog and handler is essential during search and rescue missions, as the handler needs to guide the dog effectively and interpret their behavioral cues accurately.

Environmental Exposure: Search and rescue training involves exposing Italian Greyhounds to different environments and scenarios they may encounter during operations. This includes exposure to various surfaces, weather conditions, noises, and distractions to ensure they remain focused and undeterred by challenging surroundings.

The Impact of Italian Greyhounds in Search and Rescue Operations:

The presence of Italian Greyhounds in search and rescue operations has a significant impact:

Improved Efficiency: Italian Greyhounds contribute to the efficiency of search and rescue operations by covering ground quickly and effectively. Their speed and agility enable them to navigate difficult terrains, allowing for thorough searches in areas that may be inaccessible to larger dogs or human search teams.

Therapy and Emotional Support Dogs

Therapy and emotional support dogs play a vital role in providing comfort, companionship, and assistance to individuals in need. While certain dog breeds are commonly associated with these roles, Italian Greyhounds should not be overlooked. With their gentle nature, affectionate demeanor, and intuitive understanding, Italian Greyhounds have proven to be exceptional therapy and emotional support dogs. Below we will explore the unique capabilities of Italian Greyhounds in therapy work, their training requirements, and the positive impact they have on the well-being of individuals.

The Capabilities of Italian Greyhounds as Therapy and Emotional Support Dogs:

Italian Greyhounds possess several qualities that make them well-suited for therapy and emotional support roles:

Gentle and Calming Presence: Italian Greyhounds have a gentle and calming presence that can provide immense comfort to individuals in need. Their affectionate nature and innate ability to sense and respond to human emotions make them ideal companions in therapeutic settings.

Intuitive Understanding: Italian Greyhounds are highly intuitive and empathetic. They can sense the emotions and needs of individuals, offering solace and support in times of distress. Their ability to provide a listening ear, offer unconditional love, and provide physical contact through cuddling can be deeply therapeutic for those experiencing emotional or psychological challenges.

Adaptability and Size: Italian Greyhounds' small size makes them highly adaptable to various environments, including hospitals, nursing homes, and schools. Their size allows them to comfortably sit on beds, laps, or be held by individuals who may have limited mobility. This adaptability allows them to reach individuals who may benefit from their presence but may be unable to interact with larger dogs.

Sensitivity to Touch: Italian Greyhounds have a natural affinity for human touch. Their soft, velvety coats are inviting to touch, providing a soothing and tactile experience for individuals in need of emotional support. This sensitivity to touch can help reduce stress, lower blood pressure, and promote relaxation and emotional well-being.

Training Requirements for Therapy and Emotional Support Roles:

Training is a crucial aspect of preparing Italian Greyhounds for therapy and emotional support roles. Here are some important considerations:

Temperament Assessment: Italian Greyhounds selected for therapy and emotional support roles undergo temperament assessments to ensure they possess the appropriate qualities. These assessments evaluate their social skills, adaptability, tolerance for handling, and ability to remain calm and focused in different environments.

Obedience Training: Therapy and emotional support dogs, including Italian Greyhounds, undergo comprehensive obedience training. This training ensures they can follow basic commands reliably and exhibit good manners in public settings. Obedience training helps create a well-behaved and manageable companion during therapy sessions or when providing emotional support.

Socialization: Proper socialization is essential for Italian Greyhounds in therapy and emotional support roles. They are exposed to a wide range of people, environments, and situations to develop confidence, adaptability, and appropriate behavior. Socialization also helps them become comfortable with various stimuli they may encounter during their work, such as medical equipment or crowded spaces.

Handler Partnership: Italian Greyhounds work closely with their handlers, who are responsible for their training, guidance, and well-being. Developing a strong bond and partnership between the dog and handler is crucial for effective therapy and emotional support work. Handlers must understand the needs and cues of their Italian Greyhound to ensure a harmonious and successful interaction with individuals in need.

Sporting and Outdoor Activities

The Adventure Partners: Italian Greyhounds in Sporting and Outdoor Activities

Italian Greyhounds, known for their elegance and grace, might not be the first breed that comes to mind when thinking about sporting and outdoor activities. However, these small and agile dogs possess a surprising amount of athleticism, energy, and enthusiasm that make them excellent companions for various sporting and outdoor pursuits. Below we will explore the unique capabilities of Italian Greyhounds in sporting and outdoor activities, their suitability for different pursuits, and the benefits they bring to their owners in these adventurous endeavors.

The Athletic Abilities of Italian Greyhounds:

Italian Greyhounds possess several qualities that make them well-suited for sporting and outdoor activities:

Agility and Speed: Despite their small size, Italian Greyhounds are remarkably agile and fast. They can navigate obstacles and maneuver through challenging terrains with ease. Their graceful and light-footed nature enables them to excel in activities that require quick bursts of speed, such as agility courses and flyball.

Stamina and Endurance: Italian Greyhounds may be small, but they have surprising stamina and endurance. They can maintain a steady pace over long distances, making them suitable for activities such as hiking, jogging, and even participating in dog marathons. Their ability to keep up with their owners during extended outdoor adventures is impressive.

Versatility: Italian Greyhounds are versatile athletes and can participate in various sporting activities. From lure coursing to dock diving and obedience trials to rally obedience, Italian Greyhounds can showcase their skills and compete alongside other breeds in a wide range of competitions and events.

Intuitive Nature: Italian Greyhounds have an intuitive nature that allows them to understand their owners' cues and respond accordingly. This makes them highly trainable and adaptable to different sporting activities. Their ability to follow directions and work closely with their handlers contributes to their success in various sports.

Suitability for Different Sporting and Outdoor Activities:

Italian Greyhounds can excel in a range of sporting and outdoor activities:

Lure Coursing: Lure coursing is a sport that simulates the chase of prey. Italian Greyhounds, with their exceptional speed and agility, are well-suited for this activity. They eagerly pursue the artificial lure, showcasing their natural instinct and drive.

Agility: Italian Greyhounds can excel in agility courses, which involve navigating obstacles, tunnels, and jumps in a timed event. Their nimbleness, combined with their intelligence and willingness to please, allows them to perform intricate maneuvers and complete courses with precision.

Flyball: Flyball is a high-energy team sport that involves relay racing and jumping over hurdles. Italian Greyhounds' speed and athleticism make them valuable team members in flyball competitions. They demonstrate their agility and quick reflexes while racing against other dogs in a thrilling and fast-paced environment.

Hiking and Jogging: Italian Greyhounds make excellent companions for hiking and jogging enthusiasts. Their endurance and willingness to explore outdoor environments make them ideal partners for outdoor adventures. With their compact size, they can navigate narrow trails and challenging terrain with ease.

Obedience Trials: Italian Greyhounds can participate in obedience trials, demonstrating their obedience skills and ability to follow commands. Their intelligence, combined with their eagerness to please, allows them to excel in obedience exercises, such as heeling, retrieving, and staying in place.

The Benefits of Sporting and Outdoor Activities for Italian Greyhounds and Owners:

Engaging in sporting and outdoor activities offers numerous benefits for both Italian Greyhounds and their owners:

1Physical Exercise: Sporting and outdoor activities provide essential physical exercise for Italian Greyhounds. These activities help maintain their overall health, promote cardiovascular fitness, and prevent obesity.

Italian Greyhounds and Hiking

Exploring Nature's Trails: Italian Greyhounds and Hiking Adventures

Hiking is a popular outdoor activity that allows individuals to connect with nature, exercise, and enjoy breathtaking scenery. While Italian Greyhounds may not be the first breed that comes to mind when thinking of hiking companions, these elegant and athletic dogs are more than capable of joining their owners on outdoor adventures. With their agility, endurance, and adventurous spirit, Italian Greyhounds can make excellent hiking partners. Below we will explore the unique capabilities of Italian Greyhounds in hiking, considerations for their safety and well-being on the trails, and the benefits of experiencing nature together.

The Adventurous Spirit of Italian Greyhounds:

Italian Greyhounds possess several qualities that make them well-suited for hiking:

Agility and Nimbleness: Italian Greyhounds are agile and nimble, enabling them to traverse various terrains with ease. Their light-footedness and grace make them adept at maneuvering over rocks, roots, and uneven surfaces commonly encountered on hiking trails.

Endurance and Stamina: Despite their small size, Italian Greyhounds have surprising endurance and stamina. They can keep up with their owners on long hikes, maintaining a steady pace over extended distances. Their energy levels and enthusiasm for outdoor activities make them suitable companions for more adventurous hiking trails.

Size and Portability: Italian Greyhounds' compact size is an advantage on the hiking trails. They can navigate narrow paths and squeeze through tight spaces, making them versatile hikers. Additionally, their smaller stature allows for easy transport in backpacks or carriers if needed during particularly challenging sections of the hike.

Curiosity and Adaptability: Italian Greyhounds are curious by nature and thrive on exploring new environments. They eagerly embrace the sights, scents, and sounds of the outdoors, enhancing the hiking experience for both dog and owner. Their adaptability allows them to adjust to different trail conditions and weather changes encountered during hikes.

Safety Considerations for Hiking with Italian Greyhounds:

While Italian Greyhounds can make excellent hiking companions, it's essential to consider their safety and well-being on the trails:

Trail Difficulty and Length: Consider the difficulty level and length of the trail when hiking with Italian Greyhounds. Start with shorter, less challenging trails to gauge their endurance and capabilities. Gradually progress to longer and more demanding hikes as their fitness levels increase. Be mindful of their limitations and avoid trails with steep climbs, rugged terrain, or extreme weather conditions.

Protective Gear: Provide your Italian Greyhound with appropriate protective gear for hiking. A well-fitted harness can help distribute the force evenly if you need to assist or lift your dog over obstacles. Consider using booties to protect their paws from sharp rocks, thorns, or hot surfaces. Additionally, a reflective collar or vest enhances visibility, especially during low-light conditions.

Hydration and Nutrition: Carry enough water for both you and your Italian Greyhound, as staying hydrated is crucial during hikes. Collapsible water bowls are lightweight and convenient for providing water breaks along the trail. Pack nutritious snacks or treats to replenish their energy levels during extended hikes.

Leash and Recall Training: Ensure your Italian Greyhound is comfortable walking on a leash and responds well to recall commands. Even if the trail allows off-leash hiking, it's important to have control over your dog in potentially dangerous or sensitive areas. Respect trail regulations and be considerate of other hikers and wildlife.

Agility and Obedience Competitions

Unleashing the Agility and Obedience Stars: Italian Greyhounds in Competition

Agility and obedience competitions are exciting events that showcase the skills, athleticism, and intelligence of dogs and their handlers. While Italian Greyhounds may not be the most commonly associated breed with these competitions, their exceptional agility, speed, and trainability make them formidable competitors. With their graceful presence and unwavering focus, Italian Greyhounds have the potential to shine in both agility and obedience arenas. Below we will explore the unique capabilities of Italian Greyhounds in agility and obedience competitions, the training required to excel in these disciplines, and the rewards and benefits for both dogs and their dedicated handlers.

The Agile Abilities of Italian Greyhounds:

Italian Greyhounds possess several qualities that make them well-suited for agility and obedience competitions:

Speed and Agility: Despite their small size, Italian Greyhounds are renowned for their incredible speed and agility. They can navigate obstacles, weave through poles, and leap over jumps with grace and precision. Their lightning-fast reflexes and nimble movements contribute to their success in agility courses.

Intelligence and Trainability: Italian Greyhounds are intelligent and highly trainable dogs. They quickly grasp new concepts and eagerly respond to commands. Their ability to learn complex routines and execute them flawlessly showcases their intelligence and adaptability in obedience competitions.

Focus and Drive: Italian Greyhounds possess a remarkable level of focus and drive, which is essential for excelling in agility and obedience events. They maintain their attention on their handlers, eagerly awaiting cues and directions. This intense focus allows them to execute precise movements and complete challenging tasks.

Athleticism and Stamina: Italian Greyhounds have surprising athleticism and stamina. They can perform with intensity and endurance, making them valuable competitors in agility courses that require speed, endurance, and quick turns. Their ability to maintain energy and focus throughout a competition contributes to their success.

Training for Agility and Obedience Competitions:

Training plays a crucial role in preparing Italian Greyhounds for agility and obedience competitions. Here are some important considerations:

Foundation Training: Italian Greyhounds undergo foundation training to establish basic skills, such as recall, sit, stay, and heel. This training builds the groundwork for more advanced exercises and helps create a strong bond between the dog and handler.

Agility Training: Agility training focuses on teaching Italian Greyhounds to navigate obstacles, including jumps, tunnels, weave poles, and A-frames. They learn to follow their handler's cues and complete a set course within a specified time, emphasizing accuracy and speed.

Obedience Training: Obedience training focuses on teaching Italian Greyhounds to respond reliably to commands such as sit, stay, come, and heel. They learn to perform these commands with precision and focus, showcasing their obedience and responsiveness.

Socialization and Distraction Training: Italian Greyhounds undergo socialization and distraction training to become comfortable in various environments and situations. They learn to perform under distractions, such as loud noises, crowds, and other dogs, while maintaining their focus on their handler's commands.

Rewards and Benefits of Agility and Obedience Competitions:

Participating in agility and obedience competitions offers numerous rewards and benefits for both Italian Greyhounds and their handlers:

Mental Stimulation: Agility and obedience competitions provide mental stimulation for Italian Greyhounds. The challenge of learning complex routines, following cues, and navigating obstacles engages their intellect, keeping them mentally sharp and fulfilled.

1Physical Exercise: Agility competitions require Italian Greyhounds to demonstrate their athletic prowess, promoting physical fitness and conditioning. The intense running, jumping, and weaving involved in agility courses provide an excellent workout that helps maintain their overall health and well-being.

Traveling with Your Italian Greyhound

Embarking on Adventures: Traveling with Your Italian Greyhound

Traveling is an exciting and enriching experience that allows individuals to explore new places, create lasting memories, and bond with loved ones. For Italian Greyhound owners, the thought of leaving their beloved companion behind during travel can be disheartening. However, with proper preparation and considerations, Italian Greyhounds can make wonderful travel companions. Their adaptable nature, small size, and affectionate temperament make them well-suited for various travel adventures. Below we will explore the unique aspects of traveling with Italian Greyhounds, including transportation options, accommodation considerations, and safety measures to ensure a memorable and enjoyable journey for both dog and owner.

Transportation Options for Italian Greyhounds:

When it comes to traveling with Italian Greyhounds, it's important to consider transportation methods that prioritize their comfort and safety:

Car Travel: Traveling by car is a popular choice for Italian Greyhound owners. Ensure your Italian Greyhound is secured in a well-ventilated crate or a specially designed car harness to prevent injury or distraction while driving. Make frequent stops for bathroom breaks, exercise, and hydration, and never leave your dog unattended in a parked car.

Air Travel: If air travel is necessary, check with airlines regarding their pet policies and requirements. Some airlines allow small dogs, like Italian Greyhounds, to travel in the cabin with their owners as carry-on baggage. However, it's important to familiarize yourself with specific airline regulations, crate requirements, and necessary documentation well in advance.

Train and Bus Travel: Some train and bus companies allow small dogs to travel alongside their owners. Check with the respective company regarding their pet policies, crate requirements, and any additional fees. Ensure your Italian Greyhound remains calm and well-behaved throughout the journey to ensure a positive travel experience for all passengers.

Accommodation Considerations:

Finding suitable accommodation is essential when traveling with Italian Greyhounds. Consider the following factors to ensure a comfortable and pet-friendly stay:

Pet-Friendly Accommodation: Look for hotels, vacation rentals, or campgrounds that explicitly allow pets. Many establishments offer pet-friendly amenities, such as designated areas for exercise and pet-friendly policies. It's always recommended to inform the accommodation in advance about your Italian Greyhound's presence to ensure a seamless check-in process.

Room Comfort: Choose accommodations that provide adequate space for your Italian Greyhound to move around comfortably. Ensure there are no hazards or escape routes in the room, such as loose wires or open windows. Bringing familiar bedding and toys can create a sense of familiarity and security for your dog in a new environment.

Outdoor Spaces: Prioritize accommodations that provide easy access to outdoor spaces where your Italian Greyhound can stretch their legs, relieve themselves, and get some exercise. Research nearby parks, walking trails, or off-leash areas where you can safely enjoy outdoor activities together.

Safety Measures during Travel:

Maintaining the safety and well-being of your Italian Greyhound during travel is of utmost importance. Consider the following measures to ensure a safe journey:

Identification and Microchipping: Ensure your Italian Greyhound wears a secure collar with an identification tag containing your contact information. Additionally, consider microchipping your dog as an added precaution. Keep a recent photograph of your dog on hand in case of an emergency or if they go missing.

Health and Vaccinations: Before traveling, visit your veterinarian to ensure your Italian Greyhound is up to date on vaccinations and preventive medications. Carry a copy of their medical records, including vaccination certificates and any necessary health certificates required for travel.

Road Trips and Car Safety

Adventures on Wheels: Road Trips and Car Safety for Italian Greyhounds

Road trips offer a fantastic opportunity for adventure, exploration, and quality time with loved ones. As Italian Greyhound owners, the thought of embarking on a road trip can be incredibly exciting, but it also comes with the responsibility of ensuring the safety and well-being of our beloved companions. Italian Greyhounds, with their small size and gentle nature, can make excellent travel partners. Below we will explore the unique considerations for road trips with Italian Greyhounds, including car safety measures, comfort during the journey, and essential supplies to ensure a safe and enjoyable travel experience for both dog and owner.

Car Safety Measures for Italian Greyhounds:

When it comes to road trips, prioritizing the safety of Italian Greyhounds is of utmost importance. Here are some car safety measures to consider:

Secure Restraint: Italian Greyhounds should always be properly restrained while traveling in a car. The most secure option is to use a well-ventilated crate or a specially designed car harness. These restraints prevent your Italian Greyhound from moving around the vehicle, reducing the risk of injury in case of sudden stops or accidents.

Backseat Placement: It is safest to place your Italian Greyhound in the backseat of the car. This reduces the risk of injury from airbag deployment, which can be dangerous for small dogs. Additionally, placing them in the backseat provides a more stable and comfortable environment during the journey.

Avoid Free Roaming: Never allow your Italian Greyhound to roam freely in the car during travel. Unrestrained movement can be distracting for the driver and increase the risk of injury to your dog in the event of sudden maneuvers or collisions. Keep them securely confined to their designated space.

Window Safety: While it may be tempting to let your Italian Greyhound enjoy the breeze through an open window, it is crucial to ensure their safety. Do not allow your dog to stick their head out of the window, as it exposes them to the risk of injury from debris or objects flying by. Keep windows partially open or consider using window shades to provide fresh air without compromising safety.

Comfort and Well-being during the Journey:

Ensuring the comfort and well-being of your Italian Greyhound during the road trip enhances their travel experience. Consider the following tips:

Familiarize with the Car: Help your Italian Greyhound become familiar with the car before the journey. Gradually introduce them to the vehicle, allowing them to explore and associate positive experiences such as treats or playtime inside the car. This familiarity can help reduce anxiety and make them more comfortable during the trip.

Comfortable Seating: Create a comfortable space for your Italian Greyhound in the car. Place a soft and cozy bedding material in their designated area to provide a comfortable surface for lounging and resting. Consider using a non-slip mat or a cushioned pet seat cover to ensure stability and prevent slipping during the journey.

Climate Control: Maintain a comfortable climate within the car to ensure your Italian Greyhound's well-being. Avoid exposing them to extreme temperatures, both hot and cold. If the weather is warm, ensure sufficient ventilation and use sunshades to protect them from direct sunlight. In colder temperatures, provide a warm blanket or jacket to keep them cozy.

Regular Breaks: Plan for regular breaks during the road trip to allow your Italian Greyhound to stretch their legs, relieve themselves, and have a drink of water. These breaks provide opportunities for exercise, mental stimulation, and bathroom breaks. Find pet-friendly rest areas or parks along the route to give them a chance to explore and release pent-up energy.

Air Travel and Regulations

Soaring High: Air Travel and Regulations for Italian Greyhounds

Air travel offers a convenient and efficient way to transport ourselves and our furry friends across great distances. For Italian Greyhound owners, the thought of taking to the skies with their beloved companions may raise questions about the rules, regulations, and considerations specific to air travel. With their small size and gentle demeanor, Italian Greyhounds can make excellent travel companions on airplanes. Below we will explore the unique aspects of air travel for Italian Greyhounds, including airline regulations, preparations for the journey, and tips for ensuring a smooth and stress-free experience for both dog and owner.

Understanding Airline Regulations:

When it comes to air travel with Italian Greyhounds, it's crucial to familiarize yourself with the specific regulations and requirements of the airlines you plan to fly with. Here are some common considerations:

Pet Policies: Different airlines have varying pet policies, including restrictions on the number of pets allowed in the cabin, specific weight limits, and breed restrictions. Research and choose an airline that allows small dogs like Italian Greyhounds to travel in the cabin, as this is generally the preferred option for their comfort and safety.

Cabin vs. Cargo: Some airlines may require pets to travel in the cargo hold, especially for longer flights or larger dogs. However, Italian Greyhounds, being small in size, often have the privilege of traveling in the cabin with their owners. This allows for better monitoring and ensures their well-being throughout the journey.

Crate Requirements: Airlines typically have specific requirements for the size, material, and construction of the crate or carrier used to transport pets in the cabin. Ensure that the crate meets the airline's regulations and is appropriately sized to allow your Italian Greyhound to stand, turn around, and lie down comfortably.

Health and Documentation: Most airlines require a health certificate issued by a veterinarian within a specified timeframe before the flight. Ensure your Italian Greyhound is up to date on vaccinations and preventive medications. Additionally, carry a copy of their medical records, including vaccination certificates and any necessary health certificates required for travel.

Preparations for Air Travel:

Proper preparation is essential to ensure a smooth and stress-free experience when traveling with your Italian Greyhound by air. Consider the following preparations:

Crate Training: Familiarize your Italian Greyhound with the travel crate well in advance of the flight. Gradually introduce them to the crate, associate positive experiences with it, and create a comfortable and secure environment. This will help reduce anxiety and make the crate a familiar and safe space during the journey.

Identification and Contact Information: Ensure your Italian Greyhound wears a secure collar with an identification tag that includes your contact information. It is also recommended to consider microchipping your dog as an additional form of identification. Keep a recent photograph of your dog on hand in case of an emergency or if they go missing.

Comfort and Familiarity: Line the crate with bedding material that smells familiar to your Italian Greyhound. This can include blankets or clothing items with your scent on them. Familiar scents can help alleviate stress and provide a sense of security during the flight.

Exercise and Bathroom Breaks: Prior to the flight, provide your Italian Greyhound with ample exercise and bathroom breaks. This will help them expend energy and reduce the need to relieve themselves during the flight. However, avoid vigorous exercise shortly before the flight to prevent overstimulation and excessive thirst.

Dog-Friendly Accommodations and Destinations

Tail-Wagging Vacations: Dog-Friendly Accommodations and Destinations for Italian Greyhounds

Planning a vacation is an exciting opportunity to escape the ordinary and create lasting memories with your Italian Greyhound. However, leaving your furry friend behind can be a tough decision. Fortunately, there is a growing number of dog-friendly accommodations and destinations that welcome Italian Greyhounds with open arms. From cozy hotels to breathtaking outdoor spaces, these establishments cater to the needs of both you and your four-legged companion. Below we will explore the concept of dog-friendly accommodations, highlight some popular destinations, and provide tips for a memorable and enjoyable trip with your Italian Greyhound.

The Rise of Dog-Friendly Accommodations:

In recent years, the travel industry has recognized the importance of catering to pet owners and their furry companions. This has led to an increase in dog-friendly accommodations that offer comfort, convenience, and a range of amenities to ensure a pleasant stay. Italian Greyhounds, known for their gentle demeanor and compact size, fit perfectly into the world of dog-friendly travel. Here are a few types of accommodations to consider:

Pet-Friendly Hotels: Many hotels now offer designated pet-friendly rooms or floors, allowing you to enjoy your stay with your Italian Greyhound. These rooms often provide additional amenities such as pet beds, food bowls, and even welcome treats. Some hotels may also have pet-friendly policies that extend to common areas, including outdoor spaces or dining areas.

Vacation Rentals: Renting a pet-friendly vacation home or cottage can be an excellent choice for Italian Greyhound owners. These accommodations often offer more space, a backyard or outdoor area, and the flexibility to create a home-away-from-home experience. Vacation rentals also provide the advantage of privacy and a sense of familiarity for both you and your dog.

Campgrounds and RV Parks: For those who enjoy camping or traveling with a recreational vehicle (RV), dog-friendly campgrounds and RV parks are great options. These destinations often have designated pet-friendly areas, trails for walks, and sometimes even dog parks. Camping can be a wonderful bonding experience, allowing you and your Italian Greyhound to reconnect with nature.

Popular Dog-Friendly Destinations:

When it comes to planning a vacation with your Italian Greyhound, choosing the right destination is crucial. Here are a few popular dog-friendly destinations that offer a range of activities and attractions:

Beaches and Coastal Towns: Many beaches and coastal towns are known for their dog-friendly policies. These destinations provide opportunities for your Italian Greyhound to enjoy sandy paws, refreshing swims, and long walks along the shoreline. Check local regulations regarding dog access and leash requirements before visiting.

National Parks and Hiking Trails: National parks and hiking trails offer breathtaking natural beauty and the chance for you and your Italian Greyhound to explore the great outdoors. Before visiting, ensure that the park allows dogs and review any specific regulations regarding leashes and trail access. Respect wildlife and pack essentials such as water, waste bags, and comfortable harnesses for your Italian Greyhound.

City Exploration: Many cities are becoming more dog-friendly, offering parks, cafes, and attractions that welcome well-behaved dogs. Research dog-friendly neighborhoods and establishments before your visit, ensuring that your Italian Greyhound can accompany you on urban adventures. Keep in mind leash regulations, and be considerate of other pedestrians and businesses.

Tips for a Memorable Trip with Your Italian Greyhound:

To ensure a memorable and enjoyable trip with your Italian Greyhound, consider the following tips:

Plan Ahead: Research and make reservations at dog-friendly accommodations well in advance of your trip. Some establishments have limited pet-friendly rooms or specific requirements, so it's best to secure your accommodations early.

Italian Greyhound Clubs and Associations

A Community of Canine Enthusiasts: Italian Greyhound Clubs and Associations

Italian Greyhounds, with their elegant appearance and gentle demeanor, have garnered a devoted following of passionate enthusiasts around the world. These enthusiasts form a tight-knit community through various clubs and associations dedicated to the breed. Italian Greyhound clubs provide a platform for breed enthusiasts to connect, share knowledge, and promote responsible dog ownership. Below we will explore the significance of Italian Greyhound clubs and associations, their role in breed preservation and education, as well as the benefits they offer to both owners and their beloved Italian Greyhounds.

Preserving and Promoting the Breed:

Italian Greyhound clubs and associations play a vital role in preserving and promoting the breed's heritage and characteristics. These organizations actively work towards maintaining the breed standard and ensuring the overall health and well-being of Italian Greyhounds. Here are some key ways in which clubs contribute to breed preservation:

Breed Standards and Guidelines: Italian Greyhound clubs establish and uphold the official breed standards set by kennel clubs and breed organizations. These standards outline the ideal characteristics, structure, and temperament of the breed, serving as a benchmark for breeders, judges, and enthusiasts.

Responsible Breeding Practices: Clubs promote responsible breeding practices by setting guidelines for breeders to follow. They encourage health testing, genetic screening, and responsible selection of breeding stock to minimize hereditary health issues and maintain the overall quality of the breed.

Education and Information: Italian Greyhound clubs provide educational resources and information to breeders, owners, and prospective owners. They conduct seminars, workshops, and educational events that cover various aspects of the breed, including health, grooming, training, and responsible ownership. These resources help ensure that Italian Greyhound owners are well-informed and equipped to provide the best care for their dogs.

Rescue and Rehoming Efforts: Many Italian Greyhound clubs and associations have dedicated rescue programs that aim to find loving homes for Italian Greyhounds in need. They collaborate with shelters, volunteers, and foster homes to provide temporary care and facilitate the adoption process. These initiatives contribute to the welfare and well-being of Italian Greyhounds beyond the scope of breeding and show activities.

Community and Connection:

Italian Greyhound clubs create a sense of community and connection among breed enthusiasts. They offer opportunities for owners and enthusiasts to come together, share experiences, and develop lasting friendships. Here's how Italian Greyhound clubs foster a sense of community:

Breed-specific Events and Competitions: Italian Greyhound clubs organize and host various events, including specialty shows, agility trials, lure coursing, and obedience competitions. These events provide a platform for Italian Greyhound owners to showcase their dogs, learn from experienced judges, and socialize with fellow enthusiasts.

Meet-ups and Playdates: Clubs often organize meet-ups and playdates where Italian Greyhounds and their owners can come together for socialization and exercise. These informal gatherings allow dogs to interact, develop social skills, and build camaraderie while owners exchange knowledge, tips, and stories.

Online Communities: In addition to physical gatherings, Italian Greyhound clubs maintain online platforms and social media groups where members can connect and engage with one another. These virtual spaces serve as forums for discussions, sharing photos and stories, seeking advice, and staying up-to-date with the latest happenings in the Italian Greyhound community.

Mentorship and Support: Italian Greyhound clubs provide mentorship and support to newcomers and novice owners. Experienced members willingly offer guidance, share their expertise, and answer questions, ensuring that new Italian Greyhound owners feel welcomed and supported in their journey.

Breed Clubs and RegionalGroups

Unifying Passion: Breed Clubs and Regional Groups for Italian Greyhounds

Italian Greyhounds have captured the hearts of dog enthusiasts worldwide with their elegance, grace, and affectionate nature. In order to foster a sense of community and promote the welfare of the breed, Italian Greyhound breed clubs and regional groups have emerged. These organizations serve as a hub for breed enthusiasts to connect, share knowledge, organize events, and support one another. Below we will explore the significance of breed clubs and regional groups for Italian Greyhounds, their role in fostering camaraderie, and the benefits they offer to both owners and their beloved companions.

Building Community and Fostering Camaraderie:

Breed clubs and regional groups play a pivotal role in building a sense of community among Italian Greyhound enthusiasts. They provide a platform for like-minded individuals to come together, exchange experiences, and develop lasting friendships. Here are some key ways in which these organizations foster camaraderie:

Shared Passion and Support: Breed clubs and regional groups unite individuals who share a common love for Italian Greyhounds. By bringing together owners, breeders, and enthusiasts, these organizations create a supportive network where members can seek advice, share triumphs and challenges, and celebrate the joys of Italian Greyhound ownership.

Events and Activities: Breed clubs and regional groups organize a wide range of events and activities tailored to the interests of Italian Greyhound enthusiasts. These may include specialty shows, lure coursing competitions, obedience trials, and educational seminars. These events offer opportunities for members to showcase their dogs, learn from experts, and engage in friendly competition.

Regional Gatherings: Regional groups often organize gatherings in specific geographic areas to bring together Italian Greyhound owners in the vicinity. These gatherings provide a chance for members to meet face-to-face, share experiences, and participate in activities such as group walks, playdates, or picnics. Regional groups foster a sense of belonging and create local support networks for Italian Greyhound owners.

Online Communities: In addition to physical events, breed clubs and regional groups maintain online platforms and social media groups. These virtual spaces enable members to connect, share stories and photos, seek advice, and stay updated on the latest news and events. Online communities create a sense of unity and facilitate communication among Italian Greyhound enthusiasts from different regions.

Benefits for Owners and Italian Greyhounds:

Participating in breed clubs and regional groups offers numerous benefits for Italian Greyhound owners and their beloved companions:

Educational Resources: Breed clubs and regional groups provide access to a wealth of educational resources about Italian Greyhounds. They offer information on breed history, care and grooming, health issues, training tips, and responsible breeding practices. These resources empower owners to make informed decisions and provide the best possible care for their Italian Greyhounds.

Mentorship and Guidance: Experienced members of breed clubs and regional groups often serve as mentors to newcomers. They willingly share their knowledge, offer guidance, and provide support to those who are new to Italian Greyhound ownership. Mentorship programs create a supportive environment where owners can learn from seasoned enthusiasts and navigate the intricacies of owning an Italian Greyhound.

Health and Genetic Screening: Breed clubs and regional groups emphasize the importance of health testing and genetic screening for Italian Greyhounds. They promote responsible breeding practices, encouraging breeders to screen for common hereditary health issues and prioritize the overall health and well-being of the breed. By supporting responsible breeding, these organizations contribute to the long-term health of Italian Greyhounds.

Advocacy and Rescue Efforts: Breed clubs and regional groups often take an active role in advocating for the welfare of Italian Greyhounds. They collaborate with animal welfare organizations and rescue groups to support Italian Greyhounds in need.

Rescue and Adoption Organizations

A Second Chance at Love: Rescue and Adoption Organizations for Italian Greyhounds

Rescue and adoption organizations play a vital role in finding loving homes for animals in need, including the beloved Italian Greyhound. These organizations work tirelessly to rescue, rehabilitate, and rehome Italian Greyhounds that have been abandoned, surrendered, or found as strays. They provide a lifeline for these gentle and affectionate dogs, offering them a second chance at a happy and fulfilling life. Below we will explore the significance of rescue and adoption organizations for Italian Greyhounds, their dedication to the welfare of the breed, and the benefits they offer to both adopters and the dogs themselves.

Rescuing and Rehabilitating Italian Greyhounds:

Rescue and adoption organizations serve as a safety net for Italian Greyhounds in distress. Their primary objective is to rescue dogs from unfortunate situations and provide them with necessary care and rehabilitation. Here are some key aspects of their work:

Rescue Operations: These organizations actively seek out Italian Greyhounds in need, whether they are abandoned, neglected, or at risk of euthanasia in shelters. They work closely with animal control agencies, shelters, and concerned individuals to identify Italian Greyhounds that require assistance.

Veterinary Care: Upon rescue, Italian Greyhounds receive immediate medical attention. This includes comprehensive health evaluations, vaccinations, spaying or neutering, and treatment for any existing health conditions. Rescue organizations ensure that the dogs are in good health before they are made available for adoption.

Rehabilitation and Training: Some Italian Greyhounds rescued by these organizations may require rehabilitation and behavior modification due to previous neglect or trauma. Dedicated volunteers and trainers work patiently with these dogs, helping them overcome their fears, building their confidence, and preparing them for successful adoption into loving homes.

Foster Care: Rescue organizations rely on foster homes to provide temporary care and a nurturing environment for Italian Greyhounds awaiting adoption. Foster families play a crucial role in assessing the dogs' temperament, addressing their specific needs, and preparing them for life in a home setting.

Finding Forever Homes:

The ultimate goal of rescue and adoption organizations is to find permanent, loving homes for Italian Greyhounds. Here's how they facilitate the adoption process:

Adoption Applications and Screening: Prospective adopters go through an application and screening process to ensure they are a suitable match for an Italian Greyhound. Organizations review applications, conduct interviews, and sometimes perform home visits to assess the environment and determine if it is suitable for the dog's specific needs.

Education and Guidance: Rescue organizations educate potential adopters about the breed's characteristics, care requirements, and any specific considerations related to Italian Greyhounds. They provide guidance on proper training, socialization, and integration into the adoptive family, ensuring that the dogs are placed in knowledgeable and committed homes.

Matching Dogs with Adopters: Rescue organizations carefully match Italian Greyhounds with potential adopters based on their lifestyle, preferences, and the dog's individual needs. This process aims to create harmonious and lasting relationships between the dogs and their new families.

Post-Adoption Support: Adoption doesn't end with the placement of an Italian Greyhound into a new home. Rescue organizations provide ongoing support and resources to adopters, answering questions, addressing concerns, and offering guidance as the dog settles into their new environment.

Benefits for Adopters and Italian Greyhounds:

Rescue and adoption organizations offer numerous benefits for both adopters and Italian Greyhounds:

Saving a Life: By adopting from a rescue organization, individuals give an Italian Greyhound a second chance at life. They provide a safe and loving home, offering the dog an opportunity to thrive and experience the love and care they deserve.

Competitions and Events

Unleashing the Spirit: Competitions and Events for Italian Greyhounds

Italian Greyhounds, with their sleek build and graceful movements, are no strangers to the world of competitions and events. These gatherings offer a platform for owners and enthusiasts to showcase the beauty, athleticism, and intelligence of the breed. Whether it's on the agility course, in the show ring, or during lure coursing, Italian Greyhounds shine brightly, capturing the hearts of onlookers. Below we will explore the significance of competitions and events for Italian Greyhounds, the various types of competitions they participate in, and the benefits these experiences offer to both dogs and their owners.

Showcasing Breed Excellence:

Dog competitions and events provide a unique opportunity to celebrate the breed-specific traits and characteristics of Italian Greyhounds. These gatherings allow dogs to demonstrate their beauty, movement, and temperament to judges, fellow enthusiasts, and the general public. Here are some of the key competitions in which Italian Greyhounds often participate:

Conformation Shows: Conformation shows are designed to evaluate breeding stock based on how well they adhere to the breed standard. Judges assess various aspects of the Italian Greyhound, including their structure, movement, coat, and temperament. These shows provide a platform for breeders and owners to present their Italian Greyhounds and receive recognition for their adherence to breed standards.

Agility Trials: Agility trials test a dog's speed, agility, and ability to navigate through a series of obstacles. Italian Greyhounds, with their athleticism and agility, excel in these events. They showcase their ability to maneuver jumps, tunnels, weave poles, and other obstacles, guided by their owners or handlers. Agility trials highlight the bond between the dog and their handler and the intelligence and trainability of Italian Greyhounds.

Lure Coursing: Lure coursing allows Italian Greyhounds to tap into their inherent hunting instincts. In this competition, dogs chase a mechanized lure across a field, simulating the thrill of a live hunt. The course replicates the unpredictability and speed of a fleeing prey, and Italian Greyhounds showcase their incredible speed, agility, and focus as they pursue the lure.

Obedience Trials: Obedience trials assess a dog's ability to follow commands and perform various tasks with precision and accuracy. Italian Greyhounds, known for their intelligence and eagerness to please, demonstrate their obedience skills through exercises such as heeling, retrieving, and staying in place. Obedience trials highlight the strong bond between the dog and their owner and the Italian Greyhound's capacity for learning and responsiveness.

Benefits for Dogs and Owners:

Participating in competitions and events offers numerous benefits for Italian Greyhounds and their owners:

Bonding and Socialization: Competitions and events provide opportunities for Italian Greyhounds and their owners to bond and strengthen their relationship. Training for competitions involves regular practice sessions, communication, and teamwork, fostering trust and understanding between the dog and their owner.

Mental Stimulation: Competitions challenge Italian Greyhounds mentally, stimulating their intellect and problem-solving abilities. Engaging in activities such as agility, obedience, and lure coursing keeps their minds sharp, promotes focus, and prevents boredom.

Physical Fitness and Exercise: Participating in competitions and events ensures that Italian Greyhounds receive regular exercise and physical activity. These activities help maintain their physical fitness, muscle tone, and overall well-being. The structured exercise provided by competitions contributes to the prevention of obesity and the development of a healthy lifestyle.

Social Connections: Competitions and events offer a social setting where Italian Greyhound owners can connect with fellow enthusiasts. These gatherings create a community of like-minded individuals who share a common passion for the breed.

Preparing for a New Italian Greyhound Puppy

Welcoming a Bundle of Joy: Preparing for a New Italian Greyhound Puppy

Bringing a new Italian Greyhound puppy into your home is an exciting and joyous occasion. These elegant and affectionate companions require proper preparation to ensure they have a smooth transition and a healthy start to their lives. From creating a safe environment to gathering essential supplies, being well-prepared is key to providing the best care for your new furry friend. Below we will explore the important steps and considerations involved in preparing for a new Italian Greyhound puppy, setting the stage for a happy and fulfilling journey together.

Creating a Safe and Welcoming Environment:

Preparing your home for the arrival of your Italian Greyhound puppy involves creating a safe and welcoming environment. Here are some key steps to take:

Puppy-Proofing: Italian Greyhound puppies are curious and prone to exploring their surroundings. Ensure that your home is puppy-proofed by removing any potential hazards such as toxic plants, electrical cords, small objects that can be swallowed, and household chemicals. Secure loose wires and cover electrical outlets to prevent accidents.

Designated Puppy Area: Set up a designated area where your Italian Greyhound puppy can rest, eat, and play. This can be a small room or a sectioned-off area with a comfortable bed, food and water bowls, and appropriate chew toys. Use baby gates or barriers to confine the puppy to this area initially, gradually expanding their access to other parts of the house as they grow older and become familiar with their surroundings.

Safe Containment: Italian Greyhounds are agile and can easily slip through small spaces. Ensure that your yard is securely fenced to prevent any escape attempts. Consider installing a fence with small gaps or adding an additional inner fence to create a secure play area. Supervise outdoor activities to ensure the puppy's safety.

Gathering Essential Supplies:

To ensure a smooth transition for your Italian Greyhound puppy, gather the necessary supplies in advance. Here are some essential items to have on hand:

Food and Water Bowls: Choose sturdy, non-tip bowls that are appropriate for your puppy's size. Opt for stainless steel or ceramic bowls that are easy to clean and won't harbor bacteria.

High-Quality Puppy Food: Consult with your breeder or veterinarian to determine the best type of puppy food for your Italian Greyhound. High-quality, nutritionally balanced food specially formulated for puppies will support their growth and development.

Comfortable Bedding: Provide a cozy bed or crate with soft bedding for your Italian Greyhound puppy to rest and sleep. Ensure the bed or crate is appropriately sized to accommodate the puppy's size and provide a sense of security.

Chew Toys and Enrichment: Italian Greyhound puppies have a natural inclination to chew. Provide a variety of chew toys to satisfy their teething needs and redirect their chewing away from inappropriate items. Interactive toys and puzzle feeders can also provide mental stimulation and prevent boredom.

Establishing a Routine:

A consistent routine is crucial for the well-being and development of your Italian Greyhound puppy. Establishing a routine from the beginning helps them feel secure and provides structure. Consider the following aspects when developing a routine:

Feeding Schedule: Italian Greyhound puppies require regular meals throughout the day. Consult with your breeder or veterinarian for guidance on feeding frequency and portion sizes. Stick to a consistent feeding schedule to establish good eating habits.

Potty Training: Establish a potty training routine to teach your Italian Greyhound puppy where and when to eliminate. Take them outside to designated potty areas after meals, playtime, and naps. Praise and reward them for successful elimination to reinforce desired behavior.

Choosing a Breeder or Adoption Source

Navigating the Path: Choosing a Breeder or Adoption Source for your Italian Greyhound

Choosing the right breeder or adoption source is a crucial step when adding an Italian Greyhound to your family. Whether you decide to work with a breeder or opt for adoption, finding a reputable and responsible source ensures that you bring home a healthy and well-cared-for puppy. This chapter explores the factors to consider when selecting a breeder or adoption source for your Italian Greyhound, empowering you to make an informed and responsible choice for your new furry companion.

Reputable Breeders:

Working with a reputable breeder can provide you with a well-bred Italian Greyhound puppy that meets breed standards and possesses good health and temperament. Here are some key factors to consider when choosing a breeder:

Health Screening and Genetic Testing: Responsible breeders prioritize the health of their dogs and perform health screenings and genetic tests to identify and mitigate potential hereditary issues. They should be able to provide you with documentation of the health tests performed on the parents, such as eye exams and DNA tests for specific genetic conditions.

Breed Knowledge and Involvement: Reputable breeders demonstrate a deep understanding and passion for the Italian Greyhound breed. They actively participate in breed clubs, events, and competitions, showing their commitment to preserving and improving the breed. They should be knowledgeable about breed-specific characteristics, health concerns, and proper care and should be able to answer your questions thoroughly.

Socialization and Environment: A responsible breeder provides a nurturing and stimulating environment for their puppies. They ensure that the puppies are well-socialized from an early age, exposed to various sounds, sights, and experiences. Puppies raised in a home environment rather than a commercial breeding facility tend to have better social skills and adaptability.

Transparency and Support: Reputable breeders are transparent and open about their breeding practices. They are willing to provide references from previous puppy buyers and share information about the puppy's lineage, including any notable achievements or titles of the parents. They also offer ongoing support and guidance, willing to answer questions and provide assistance throughout the dog's life.

Adoption Sources:

Adopting an Italian Greyhound through a rescue organization or shelter is another wonderful way to bring home a loving companion. Here are key considerations when choosing an adoption source:

Rescue or Shelter Reputation: Research the reputation and credibility of the rescue organization or shelter you are considering. Look for organizations with a proven track record of responsible rescue and adoption practices. Check for positive reviews, feedback from previous adopters, and their involvement in the Italian Greyhound community.

Transparency and Screening Process: A reputable adoption source will have a thorough screening process in place to ensure that the Italian Greyhounds they place in homes are matched with suitable adopters. This process may involve an application, interviews, and a home visit to assess your readiness and commitment to caring for an Italian Greyhound.

Health and Behavior Assessment: Good rescue organizations conduct thorough health evaluations and behavioral assessments of the Italian Greyhounds in their care. They provide any necessary veterinary care, including vaccinations, spaying or neutering, and addressing any existing health issues before adoption. They should also be transparent about the dog's medical history and any behavioral challenges.

Support and Education: Reputable adoption sources offer support and guidance throughout the adoption process and beyond. They should be available to answer your questions, provide resources on Italian Greyhound care and training, and offer assistance if any challenges arise after the adoption. Look for organizations that prioritize the well-being and long-term success of the dog and adopter relationship.

Puppy-Proofing Your Home

Creating a Safe Haven: Puppy-Proofing Your Home for an Italian Greyhound

Welcoming a new Italian Greyhound puppy into your home is an exciting and joyous time. As you prepare for their arrival, one important aspect to consider is puppy-proofing your living space. Just like human infants, Italian Greyhound puppies are curious and explore their surroundings with boundless energy. Ensuring a safe environment is essential for their well-being. Below we will explore the significance of puppy-proofing your home, key areas to focus on, and essential measures to keep your Italian Greyhound puppy safe.

Understanding the Curious Nature of Italian Greyhound Puppies:

Italian Greyhound puppies are known for their inquisitive and adventurous nature. They are naturally curious about their surroundings and have a tendency to explore everything within their reach. It's essential to anticipate potential hazards and remove them to create a safe and secure environment for your new furry friend.

Identifying Potential Hazards:

To effectively puppy-proof your home, you need to identify potential hazards and take appropriate measures to eliminate or minimize them. Here are some key areas to focus on:

Household Chemicals: Italian Greyhound puppies are small and vulnerable, making them more susceptible to the dangers of household chemicals. Store cleaning products, detergents, pesticides, and other hazardous substances in locked cabinets or high shelves out of their reach.

Toxic Plants: Some common household plants, such as lilies, azaleas, and ivy, can be toxic to Italian Greyhounds if ingested. Research and remove any potentially harmful plants from your home or place them in areas inaccessible to your puppy.

Small Objects: Italian Greyhound puppies have a natural inclination to explore their environment by mouthing and chewing objects. Keep small items such as buttons, coins, jewelry, and children's toys out of their reach to prevent choking hazards or intestinal blockages.

Electrical Cords: Puppies may find electrical cords enticing to chew on, which can lead to electric shocks or injuries. Secure cords against walls using cord concealers or cover them with cord protectors to prevent access.

Taking Essential Safety Measures:

In addition to identifying potential hazards, there are several safety measures you can implement to ensure the well-being of your Italian Greyhound puppy. Here are some important steps to take:

Containment: Create a designated puppy-proof area in your home where your Italian Greyhound puppy can safely explore. Use baby gates or barriers to restrict access to hazardous areas such as the kitchen, laundry room, or basement. Gradually expand their access to other areas as they grow older and become more familiar with their environment.

Secure Trash Bins: Italian Greyhound puppies are naturally curious and may explore trash bins in search of interesting smells or potential food scraps. Use lidded trash bins or place them in areas that are inaccessible to your puppy to prevent them from accessing potentially harmful items.

Secure Doors and Windows: Ensure that all doors and windows are securely closed and fitted with screens or appropriate barriers to prevent your Italian Greyhound puppy from escaping or falling out. Italian Greyhounds are agile and can easily squeeze through small openings or jump over low fences.

Secure Countertops and Shelves: Italian Greyhound puppies are excellent jumpers and climbers. Remove any items from countertops or low shelves that your puppy may be tempted to jump on and potentially knock over, causing injury or damage.

Secure Furniture: Assess the stability of furniture items such as bookcases, cabinets, and shelves. Use furniture straps or anchors to prevent them from tipping over if your Italian Greyhound puppy tries to climb or explore them.

Essential Supplies and Gear

Equipping for Adventure: Essential Supplies and Gear for Your Italian Greyhound

As you prepare to welcome an Italian Greyhound into your home, it's important to gather the necessary supplies and gear to ensure their comfort, safety, and well-being. From everyday essentials to specialized items tailored to the unique needs of Italian Greyhounds, having the right tools at your disposal will help you provide the best care for your new furry friend. Below we will explore the essential supplies and gear required for your Italian Greyhound, ensuring they are ready to embark on a life of adventure by your side.

Comfortable Bedding:

A comfortable bed is essential for your Italian Greyhound's rest and relaxation. Opt for a bed specifically designed for small breeds, with soft and supportive padding. Italian Greyhounds are known for their love of warmth, so consider a bed with built-in heating or provide cozy blankets to keep them snug during colder seasons.

Appropriate Collar and Leash:

Selecting a collar and leash that fit properly is crucial for the safety and control of your Italian Greyhound. Since they have delicate necks, choose a lightweight and adjustable collar that won't put undue pressure on their throat. A sturdy leash with a comfortable grip will enable you to guide your Italian Greyhound during walks and outdoor activities.

Harness:

Many Italian Greyhound owners prefer using a harness instead of a collar for walking and leash attachment. Harnesses distribute pressure more evenly across the body, reducing the risk of neck injury. Look for a well-fitting, secure harness specifically designed for small breeds, ensuring that it doesn't restrict their movement or cause discomfort.

ID Tags and Microchip:

Ensure your Italian Greyhound can be easily identified in case they get lost by having proper identification. Attach an ID tag with your contact information to their collar or harness. Additionally, consider microchipping your Italian Greyhound, which provides a permanent form of identification that can be scanned by veterinarians and shelters.

Food and Water Bowls:

Choose sturdy, non-tip bowls made of stainless steel or ceramic for your Italian Greyhound's food and water. These materials are easy to clean and won't harbor bacteria. Opt for bowls specifically designed for small breeds to accommodate their size and prevent discomfort while eating or drinking.

High-Quality Dog Food:

Italian Greyhounds have specific dietary requirements, and feeding them high-quality dog food is essential for their health and well-being. Consult with your breeder or veterinarian to determine the appropriate type of dog food for your Italian Greyhound based on their age, size, and specific dietary needs.

Treats:

Treats are a valuable tool for training, rewarding good behavior, and strengthening the bond with your Italian Greyhound. Choose small, soft treats specifically designed for small breeds. Consider treats that promote dental health or are tailored to address specific dietary concerns, such as sensitive stomachs or allergies.

Grooming Supplies:

Italian Greyhounds have short coats that require minimal grooming. However, having the necessary grooming supplies on hand is still important to keep them clean and healthy. This includes a soft-bristle brush or grooming mitt to remove loose hair, a dog-specific toothbrush and toothpaste for dental care, and nail clippers or a grinder to maintain their nails at a suitable length.

Safety Gear:

Ensure your Italian Greyhound's safety by investing in essential safety gear. If you have a pool or live near water, a life jacket is recommended, as Italian Greyhounds are not natural swimmers due to their slim build. Reflective gear, such as a harness or collar with reflective strips, is crucial for nighttime walks or outdoor adventures, providing visibility and ensuring the safety of you and your dog.

Puppy Development and Milestones

Unveiling the Journey: Puppy Development and Milestones of Italian Greyhounds

Welcoming a new Italian Greyhound puppy into your life is an exciting and rewarding experience. As they grow from adorable bundles of fur into graceful companions, understanding their developmental milestones is key to providing them with the care and support they need. Below we will explore the fascinating journey of Italian Greyhound puppy development, highlighting key milestones in their physical, cognitive, and social development.

Birth to Two Weeks:

The first two weeks of an Italian Greyhound puppy's life are spent primarily nursing, sleeping, and growing. At birth, they are blind, deaf, and completely reliant on their mother. During this time, their senses gradually develop, and they begin to crawl and interact with their littermates.

Three to Four Weeks:

Around three weeks of age, Italian Greyhound puppies start to open their eyes, revealing their beautiful gaze to the world. Their sense of hearing also begins to develop, allowing them to respond to sounds. They start to take their first wobbly steps, exploring their surroundings and engaging in playful interactions with their littermates.

Five to Seven Weeks:

Italian Greyhound puppies become more mobile and confident during this stage. They begin to develop their primary teeth, and their sense of smell becomes more refined. Socialization with humans and other animals becomes crucial during this period, as they learn important social cues and begin to understand their place in the pack.

Eight to Twelve Weeks:

At eight weeks, Italian Greyhound puppies are ready to leave their litter and join their new families. This period is crucial for bonding and continued socialization. They will continue to refine their motor skills, explore their environment, and learn important life lessons through play and interaction.

Physical Development:

Italian Greyhounds have a unique growth pattern. They tend to reach their full height by around six months of age but continue to fill out and develop muscle tone until they are around one year old. It's important to provide them with a balanced diet that supports their growth and prevents excessive weight gain, which can strain their delicate bones and joints.

Cognitive Development:

Italian Greyhounds are known for their intelligence and quick learning abilities. As they grow, their cognitive skills develop rapidly. They become more attentive and responsive to training cues, learning basic commands and engaging in problem-solving activities. Mental stimulation through puzzle toys, interactive games, and positive reinforcement training is crucial to keep their minds sharp and prevent boredom.

Social Development:

Socialization plays a significant role in shaping the behavior and temperament of Italian Greyhound puppies. Early exposure to different people, animals, environments, and stimuli helps them develop confidence, adaptability, and appropriate social skills. It's essential to expose them to a wide range of positive experiences during their critical socialization period, which typically occurs between three and sixteen weeks of age.

During this time, introduce your Italian Greyhound puppy to various sights, sounds, and experiences. Gradually expose them to new environments, such as parks, busy streets, and different types of surfaces. Encourage positive interactions with other well-behaved dogs and people of different ages and appearances.

Puppy Training:

The early stages of development provide an ideal opportunity to start basic training with your Italian Greyhound puppy. Begin with basic commands such as sit, stay, and come, using positive reinforcement techniques such as treats, praise, and rewards. Consistency, patience, and gentle guidance are key to building a strong foundation for their future obedience and manners.

It's important to remember that Italian Greyhounds are sensitive by nature and respond best to positive, reward-based training methods. Harsh or forceful training techniques can cause anxiety or reluctance to learn. Seek the guidance of a professional dog trainer to ensure you are using effective and humane training methods.

Growth Stages and Changes

The Ever-Unfolding Journey: Growth Stages and Changes in Italian Greyhounds

Watching an Italian Greyhound grow and mature is a fascinating and rewarding experience. From their tiny, delicate frames to their graceful and elegant stature, Italian Greyhounds undergo various growth stages and changes throughout their lives. Understanding these developmental milestones is essential for providing them with appropriate care and support. Below we will explore the growth stages and changes in Italian Greyhounds, from puppyhood to adulthood, shedding light on the remarkable journey of these beloved companions.

Puppyhood: The Foundation of Growth

Italian Greyhound puppies are born fragile and helpless, relying on their mother for nourishment and protection. During the first few weeks, they undergo rapid growth and development, both physically and mentally. Their eyes and ears gradually open, revealing a world of sights and sounds previously unknown to them. They begin to explore their surroundings, develop motor skills, and interact with their littermates.

Nutrition plays a vital role during this critical stage. Italian Greyhound puppies require a diet rich in essential nutrients, including high-quality proteins, fats, vitamins, and minerals, to support their rapid growth and development. Consult with your veterinarian to ensure you are providing a balanced and appropriate diet for your growing puppy.

Adolescence: The Awkward Phase

As Italian Greyhounds enter adolescence, they undergo significant changes in their physical and behavioral development. This stage is often marked by growth spurts, where their limbs may appear lanky and disproportionate. It is important to provide them with proper nutrition and exercise to support their growth and maintain healthy bone and muscle development.

Behaviorally, Italian Greyhound adolescents may exhibit increased independence and stubbornness. They may test boundaries and challenge authority. Consistent and positive reinforcement-based training is essential during this stage to establish good behavior patterns and reinforce appropriate manners.

Adulthood: The Peak of Maturity

Italian Greyhounds reach their adult size and physical maturity around one year of age. Their lanky frames fill out, and their muscles develop, showcasing their elegant and sleek appearance. By this stage, their growth rate slows down significantly, and they settle into their adult body shape.

Maintaining an appropriate weight is crucial for Italian Greyhounds to prevent strain on their delicate bones and joints. Monitor their diet and provide regular exercise to keep them fit and healthy. Be mindful of their tendency to gain weight easily, as excess weight can lead to health issues such as joint problems and obesity.

Coat Changes: From Puppy Fluff to Adult Glamour

The coat of an Italian Greyhound undergoes changes as they transition from puppyhood to adulthood. As puppies, they often have a soft, fluffy coat that may change in texture and density as they mature. The adult coat of an Italian Greyhound is short, smooth, and sleek, providing them with protection and insulation.

Regular grooming is necessary to keep their coat in optimal condition. Brushing them weekly helps remove loose hair and keeps their skin healthy. Italian Greyhounds are considered low-shedding dogs, making them a suitable choice for those with allergies. However, it is important to note that no dog is completely hypoallergenic, and individual reactions may vary.

Dental Development: Nurturing Healthy Smiles

Proper dental care is essential for the overall health and well-being of Italian Greyhounds. Like other dog breeds, they experience teething during their puppyhood. It is important to provide appropriate chew toys and treats designed for teething puppies to alleviate discomfort and promote healthy dental development. Additionally, regular teeth brushing and dental check-ups are crucial to prevent dental issues such as plaque buildup, gum disease, and tooth decay.

Socialization and Training Milestones

The Dance of Connection: Socialization and Training Milestones for Italian Greyhounds

Italian Greyhounds are intelligent and sensitive companions, capable of forming deep bonds with their human families. Socialization and training play crucial roles in shaping their behavior and ensuring their well-being. From the early stages of puppyhood to adulthood, Italian Greyhounds go through various milestones in their social and training journey. Below we will explore the importance of socialization and training milestones for Italian Greyhounds, highlighting key aspects and sharing insights into their unique needs.

Puppy Socialization: The Foundation of Confidence

Early socialization is vital for Italian Greyhound puppies to develop confidence, adaptability, and positive associations with the world around them. The critical period for socialization typically occurs between three and sixteen weeks of age. During this time, puppies are more receptive to new experiences and form lasting impressions.

Introduce your Italian Greyhound puppy to various environments, sounds, surfaces, people, and animals in a controlled and positive manner. Gradually expose them to different stimuli, ensuring they have positive experiences. This includes interactions with other well-behaved dogs, meeting people of different ages and appearances, and exposure to different environments such as parks, busy streets, and public spaces.

Training Milestones: Building a Strong Foundation

Italian Greyhounds are intelligent and eager to please, making them quick learners when provided with positive reinforcement training. Start training your Italian Greyhound puppy as early as possible to establish a strong foundation for obedience, manners, and appropriate behavior.

Basic Commands: Begin with basic commands such as sit, stay, come, and down. Use positive reinforcement techniques, including treats, praise, and rewards, to motivate and encourage your Italian Greyhound puppy. Consistency and patience are key to successful training sessions.

Potty Training: Establish a regular routine for potty breaks, both during the day and at night. Italian Greyhounds are generally clean dogs and prefer to eliminate in designated areas. Be diligent in providing ample opportunities for them to relieve themselves outside, rewarding them when they eliminate in the appropriate spot.

Leash Training: Leash training is essential for Italian Greyhounds to walk safely and comfortably. Introduce them to the leash gradually, allowing them to become familiar with wearing it before venturing outside. Use positive reinforcement to encourage walking politely on the leash and reward them for good leash manners.

Social Skills: Continued socialization throughout their lives is essential for Italian Greyhounds to maintain good social skills. Expose them to a variety of people, animals, and environments, ensuring positive interactions and experiences. Encourage appropriate play behavior and discourage any signs of aggression or fear.

Advanced Training: Beyond the Basics

As your Italian Greyhound progresses in their training, you can move on to more advanced commands and activities. Advanced training provides mental stimulation and helps strengthen the bond between you and your dog. Here are some examples of advanced training for Italian Greyhounds:

Agility: Italian Greyhounds excel in agility due to their agility, speed, and grace. Consider enrolling your Italian Greyhound in agility classes where they can navigate obstacles, tunnels, and jumps, showcasing their natural abilities.

Tricks and Freestyle: Italian Greyhounds are eager to please and enjoy learning new tricks. Teach them entertaining and impressive tricks such as spin, bow, or play dead. You can also explore freestyle training, combining tricks and dance moves to create a choreographed routine.

1 Therapy and Assistance Training: Italian Greyhounds are well-suited for therapy work and can provide comfort and emotional support to those in need. If your Italian Greyhound has a calm and gentle temperament, consider pursuing therapy or assistance dog training to assist individuals with physical or emotional challenges.

Health Checkups and Vaccinations

Guardians of Well-being: Health Checkups and Vaccinations for Italian Greyhounds

Ensuring the health and well-being of your Italian Greyhound is a top priority as a responsible pet owner. Regular health checkups and vaccinations play a crucial role in maintaining their overall wellness and protecting them from preventable diseases. Below we will explore the importance of health checkups and vaccinations for Italian Greyhounds, shedding light on the key aspects and providing valuable insights into their unique healthcare needs.

Importance of Health Checkups:

Regular health checkups are essential for monitoring the overall health and detecting any potential health issues in Italian Greyhounds. These checkups, performed by a veterinarian, involve a comprehensive examination to assess the physical condition, identify early signs of illness or disease, and provide appropriate preventive care. Here are the key reasons why health checkups are vital for Italian Greyhounds:

Early Detection: Regular health checkups allow veterinarians to detect any health issues in their early stages. Early detection can significantly improve the prognosis and increase the chances of successful treatment.

Vaccination Assessment: During checkups, veterinarians assess the vaccination status of Italian Greyhounds and recommend necessary vaccinations to ensure they are protected against common diseases.

Preventive Care: Health checkups also provide an opportunity to discuss preventive care measures such as parasite control, dental hygiene, and proper nutrition. Veterinarians can offer guidance on maintaining your Italian Greyhound's overall well-being.

Vaccinations for Italian Greyhounds:

Vaccinations are crucial for preventing the spread of contagious and potentially life-threatening diseases among Italian Greyhounds. Vaccines work by stimulating the immune system to recognize and fight specific diseases. Here are some essential vaccinations for Italian Greyhounds:

Core Vaccinations:

Rabies: Rabies is a fatal disease that affects the nervous system of animals and humans. Rabies vaccination is mandatory in many countries and is typically administered once a year or as per local regulations.

Distemper: Distemper is a highly contagious viral disease that affects the respiratory, gastrointestinal, and nervous systems. Vaccination against distemper is typically administered in a series of shots during puppyhood and then followed by booster shots.

Non-Core Vaccinations:

Non-core vaccinations are optional and depend on various factors such as geographic location, lifestyle, and exposure risks. Consult with your veterinarian to determine which non-core vaccines are recommended for your Italian Greyhound. Some common non-core vaccines include:

Canine Influenza: Canine influenza is a contagious respiratory disease that can cause coughing, sneezing, and other flu-like symptoms in dogs. Vaccination may be recommended, especially for Italian Greyhounds that interact with other dogs frequently or participate in dog shows or group activities.

Bordetella: Bordetella, also known as kennel cough, is a highly contagious respiratory infection. It is commonly required for dogs that board in kennels, attend daycare, or participate in group training sessions or competitions.

It's important to follow the recommended vaccination schedule and maintain regular booster shots to ensure continued protection. Vaccination needs may vary based on local regulations, regional disease prevalence, and individual risk factors.

Additional Preventive Measures:

In addition to vaccinations, there are other important preventive measures to consider for the health and well-being of your Italian Greyhound:

Parasite Control:

Parasites such as fleas, ticks, and intestinal worms can pose significant health risks to Italian Greyhounds. Regular preventive treatments, including topical or oral medications, are crucial to protect your pet from these parasites. Consult with your veterinarian to determine the appropriate parasite control measures for your Italian Greyhound based on their lifestyle and local risks.

Senior Italian Greyhounds

Embracing the Golden Years: Senior Italian Greyhounds

Italian Greyhounds bring joy, companionship, and boundless energy to our lives. As they gracefully age, it's essential to adapt their care to meet their changing needs. Senior Italian Greyhounds deserve special attention, love, and support to ensure they enjoy a happy and healthy life in their golden years. Below we will explore the unique aspects of caring for senior Italian Greyhounds, shedding light on their specific needs and providing valuable insights into ensuring their well-being.

Understanding the Aging Process:

Like all living beings, Italian Greyhounds undergo natural changes as they age. It's important to recognize and embrace these changes to provide the best possible care for senior Italian Greyhounds. Here are some key aspects of the aging process in Italian Greyhounds:

Slowing Down: Senior Italian Greyhounds may exhibit a decrease in energy levels and a tendency to sleep more. They may not be as active or playful as they were in their younger years. It's important to respect their need for rest and provide them with a comfortable and quiet space.

Joint and Mobility Issues: As Italian Greyhounds age, they may experience joint stiffness, arthritis, or other mobility issues. Providing them with soft bedding, orthopedic support, and low-impact exercise can help alleviate discomfort and maintain mobility.

Changes in Senses: Senior Italian Greyhounds may experience changes in their vision and hearing. Regular veterinary checkups can help monitor their sensory health and provide appropriate support or treatment as needed.

Dental Health: Dental issues, such as gum disease and tooth decay, become more common in senior Italian Greyhounds. Regular dental care, including teeth brushing and professional cleanings, is crucial to prevent dental problems and maintain their overall health.

Tailoring Nutrition for Senior Italian Greyhounds:

Proper nutrition is essential for the well-being of senior Italian Greyhounds. As they age, their dietary needs change, requiring adjustments to accommodate their evolving health. Here are some considerations for senior Italian Greyhound nutrition:

Weight Management: Maintaining a healthy weight is crucial for senior Italian Greyhounds to prevent strain on their joints and organs. Adjust their diet to ensure they are receiving appropriate portions and monitor their weight regularly. Consult with your veterinarian to determine the ideal weight range for your senior Italian Greyhound.

Nutritional Balance: Senior Italian Greyhounds may require a diet that is lower in calories but still rich in essential nutrients. Choose a high-quality, age-appropriate commercial dog food or consider a balanced homemade diet under the guidance of a veterinarian or canine nutritionist. Ensure their diet includes lean proteins, healthy fats, and a variety of fruits and vegetables.

Joint Support: Incorporating supplements such as glucosamine and chondroitin can provide joint support for senior Italian Greyhounds. These supplements help promote joint health and mobility, alleviating discomfort caused by age-related conditions like arthritis.

Hydration: Adequate hydration is vital for senior Italian Greyhounds' overall health. Ensure clean, fresh water is readily available to them at all times. Monitor their water intake to prevent dehydration.

Physical and Mental Stimulation:

Although senior Italian Greyhounds may have decreased energy levels, it's important to provide them with appropriate physical and mental stimulation to keep their bodies and minds active.

Exercise: Engage your senior Italian Greyhound in regular, low-impact exercise tailored to their abilities. Gentle walks, slow-paced play sessions, and swimming can help maintain muscle tone, joint flexibility, and cardiovascular health. Adjust the duration and intensity of exercise to accommodate their energy levels and any physical limitations.

Recognizing the Signs of Aging

Embracing the Journey: Recognizing the Signs of Aging in Italian Greyhounds

Italian Greyhounds are cherished companions known for their grace, beauty, and joyful demeanor. As our beloved Italian Greyhounds age, it is important to be attuned to the signs of aging and adapt their care accordingly. By recognizing and understanding these signs, we can provide the support and attention they need to live their golden years to the fullest. Below we will explore the signs of aging in Italian Greyhounds, shedding light on the physical and behavioral changes that may occur, and offering insights into providing the best possible care.

Physical Changes:

Gray Hair and Coat: Just like humans, Italian Greyhounds may develop gray or white hair as they age. It is common for the muzzle and face to show signs of graying. The coat may also become thinner and less vibrant. Regular grooming and appropriate nutrition can help maintain a healthy coat.

Loss of Muscle Tone: Aging Italian Greyhounds may experience a gradual loss of muscle tone, resulting in a less firm and toned appearance. This is a natural part of the aging process. Regular exercise and a balanced diet can help maintain muscle strength and overall fitness.

Weight Changes: Senior Italian Greyhounds may be more prone to weight gain or loss. Hormonal changes and a decrease in activity levels can contribute to weight gain, while dental issues or health conditions may lead to weight loss. Regular monitoring of their weight and adjustments to their diet and exercise routine can help maintain a healthy weight.

Changes in Mobility: Joint stiffness, arthritis, and other age-related conditions can impact an Italian Greyhound's mobility. They may have difficulty climbing stairs, jumping onto furniture, or walking for extended periods. Providing comfortable bedding, ramps or steps, and low-impact exercise can help support their mobility and alleviate discomfort.

Behavioral Changes:

Decreased Energy and Activity: Aging Italian Greyhounds may exhibit decreased energy levels and a preference for more rest and relaxation. They may not engage in vigorous play as they once did. Allow them to set the pace and provide a quiet and comfortable space for them to rest.

Increased Sleep: Senior Italian Greyhounds tend to sleep more and may have a different sleep pattern compared to when they were younger. They may nap more frequently throughout the day and have a deeper sleep. Creating a cozy and quiet sleep environment is important to support their rest.

Cognitive Changes: Some aging Italian Greyhounds may experience cognitive decline, which can manifest as disorientation, confusion, or changes in behavior. They may forget familiar routines or people. Providing mental stimulation through puzzle toys, interactive games, and training can help keep their minds active.

Sensory Changes: Italian Greyhounds may experience changes in their vision and hearing as they age. They may develop cataracts, experience vision loss, or become more sensitive to loud noises. Regular veterinary check-ups can help identify and address any changes in their sensory abilities.

Caring for Aging Italian Greyhounds:

Regular Veterinary Check-ups: Regular visits to the veterinarian are essential for monitoring the health of aging Italian Greyhounds. These check-ups allow for early detection of any health issues and the implementation of appropriate treatment plans.

1Age-Appropriate Nutrition: Adjusting the diet of aging Italian Greyhounds is crucial to meet their changing nutritional needs. Senior-specific dog food formulas may contain fewer calories, added joint supplements, and easily digestible ingredients. Consult with your veterinarian to determine the best diet for your aging Italian Greyhound.

Joint Support and Comfort: Provide comfortable bedding and consider adding orthopedic support to help alleviate joint stiffness and discomfort. Warm blankets or heated beds can provide added comfort, especially for those with arthritis.

Special Care and Accommodations

Tailored Comfort: Special Care and Accommodations for Italian Greyhounds

Italian Greyhounds are beloved companions known for their elegance, affectionate nature, and unique physical attributes. These delightful dogs require special care and accommodations to ensure their well-being and happiness. By understanding their specific needs and making necessary adjustments, we can provide a safe and comfortable environment for our Italian Greyhound friends. Below we will explore the special care and accommodations required for Italian Greyhounds, shedding light on their unique characteristics and providing valuable insights into creating an optimal living space for them.

Climate Considerations:

Italian Greyhounds have a thin coat and minimal body fat, making them more sensitive to extreme temperatures. It is important to provide them with a climate-controlled environment, especially during hot summers and cold winters. Here are some tips to help maintain their comfort:

In hot weather, provide access to shaded areas, use fans or air conditioning to keep them cool, and avoid taking them out during the hottest parts of the day.

During cold weather, provide them with warm bedding, sweaters or coats for outdoor excursions, and limit their exposure to extreme cold.

Safety Measures:

Italian Greyhounds have a slender build and delicate bone structure, making them prone to injuries. It is essential to create a safe environment to minimize the risk of accidents. Consider the following safety measures:

Secure fencing: Italian Greyhounds have a strong prey drive and may be inclined to chase small animals. Ensure that your yard is securely fenced to prevent them from escaping and getting into potentially dangerous situations.

Stair and furniture safety: Due to their height and lightweight build, Italian Greyhounds can easily injure themselves by jumping from heights or navigating stairs. Use pet gates or barriers to restrict access to areas with stairs and provide pet-friendly stairs or ramps to assist them in reaching elevated surfaces.

Comfortable Resting Areas:

Italian Greyhounds are known for their love of cozy and comfortable spots to rest and sleep. Providing them with appropriate bedding and resting areas is essential for their well-being. Consider the following:

Soft bedding: Italian Greyhounds have thin skin and are prone to developing pressure sores. Provide soft and supportive bedding to cushion their joints and protect their sensitive skin. Orthopedic or memory foam beds can provide added comfort, especially for senior Italian Greyhounds or those with joint issues.

Elevated beds: Italian Greyhounds often prefer elevated beds that allow them to see their surroundings while resting. Consider providing them with raised beds or window perches to fulfill their desire for a vantage point.

Exercise and Mental Stimulation:

Despite their petite size, Italian Greyhounds still require regular exercise and mental stimulation to keep them physically and mentally healthy. Consider the following:

Daily walks: Italian Greyhounds benefit from daily walks to fulfill their exercise needs. However, be mindful of their delicate legs and use a harness rather than a collar to prevent neck injuries.

Playtime: Engage in interactive play sessions with toys that stimulate their natural instincts, such as chasing and retrieving toys or puzzle toys that provide mental stimulation.

Dental Care:

Dental hygiene is crucial for Italian Greyhounds' overall health. They are prone to dental issues such as tooth decay and gum disease. Incorporate regular dental care practices into their routine:

Regular brushing: Brush your Italian Greyhound's teeth regularly using a dog-specific toothbrush and toothpaste. Start the habit early to ensure their comfort with the process.

Dental treats and toys: Provide dental treats or toys designed to promote oral health, such as those that help clean teeth and massage gums.

End-of-Life Considerations

Honoring Their Journey: End-of-Life Considerations for Italian Greyhounds

The bond we share with our Italian Greyhounds is a cherished one, built on years of love, loyalty, and companionship. As our beloved Italian Greyhounds age, it is important to approach their end-of-life stage with compassion, understanding, and a commitment to their comfort and well-being. Below we will explore the end-of-life considerations for Italian Greyhounds, shedding light on the emotional and practical aspects that arise during this challenging time and offering guidance on how to provide the best possible care.

Recognizing the Signs:

Understanding the signs that indicate your Italian Greyhound is approaching the end of their life is essential. While each dog is unique, some common signs include:

Decreased appetite or refusing food

Difficulty breathing or shortness of breath

Increased lethargy and decreased activity

Loss of bladder and bowel control

Chronic pain or discomfort

Significant weight loss

Changes in behavior or personality

If you observe any of these signs, it is crucial to consult with your veterinarian to assess your Italian Greyhound's condition and discuss the best course of action.

Palliative Care and Pain Management:

Palliative care focuses on providing comfort, pain relief, and quality of life for Italian Greyhounds with life-limiting conditions. It aims to minimize pain and discomfort, allowing them to experience as much joy and contentment as possible during their final days. Here are some considerations for palliative care:

Pain management: Work closely with your veterinarian to develop a pain management plan tailored to your Italian Greyhound's needs. This may include medications, therapies such as acupuncture or physical therapy, and modifications to their environment to enhance comfort.

Home environment: Create a calm and soothing environment for your Italian Greyhound. Provide a cozy and quiet space where they can rest undisturbed, away from loud noises and excessive activity. Ensure their living area is free from hazards that could cause accidents or injury.

Emotional Support:

As our Italian Greyhounds approach the end of their lives, they may experience a range of emotions, and we, as their caregivers, have an important role in providing emotional support. Consider the following:

Spend quality time: Engage in activities that bring comfort and joy to your Italian Greyhound, such as gentle grooming, cuddling, or simply being present with them. These moments can help strengthen the bond and provide reassurance.

Maintain routines: Stick to familiar routines and schedules as much as possible. Consistency can provide a sense of security and familiarity during uncertain times.

Seek support: Reach out to supportive friends, family, or online communities who have experienced or are going through similar situations. Sharing your thoughts and feelings can provide comfort and understanding.

Hospice Care and Euthanasia:

In some cases, when a dog's quality of life declines significantly, the humane choice may be to consider euthanasia. This decision is never easy, but it is important to prioritize your Italian Greyhound's well-being and prevent unnecessary suffering. Here are some considerations:

Consultation with a veterinarian: Engage in open and honest discussions with your veterinarian about your Italian Greyhound's condition, prognosis, and options for end-of-life care. They can provide guidance, answer your questions, and support you in making the best decision for your pet.

Hospice care: If you choose not to pursue euthanasia immediately, hospice care can be an option. Hospice focuses on providing comfort and supportive care during the final stages of a pet's life. It involves managing pain, keeping them clean and comfortable, and ensuring their emotional well-being.

Seasonal Care and Safety

Navigating the Seasons: Seasonal Care and Safety for Italian Greyhounds

Italian Greyhounds are delightful companions known for their elegance, sensitivity, and love for their human families. As responsible pet owners, it is essential to understand the seasonal care and safety considerations for our Italian Greyhounds to ensure their well-being throughout the year. Each season brings unique challenges and opportunities, and by taking the necessary precautions, we can create a safe and enjoyable environment for our furry friends. Below we will explore the seasonal care and safety tips for Italian Greyhounds, highlighting the specific considerations for each season.

Springtime Splendor:

Spring brings new life and vibrant colors, but it also presents certain risks for Italian Greyhounds. Here are some tips to ensure their safety during this season:

Allergies: Just like humans, Italian Greyhounds can experience seasonal allergies. Keep an eye out for symptoms such as itching, sneezing, watery eyes, or skin irritations. Consult with your veterinarian if you suspect your dog is suffering from allergies.

Fleas and Ticks: Springtime increases the presence of fleas and ticks. Use flea and tick preventatives recommended by your veterinarian to protect your Italian Greyhound from these parasites. Regularly check their coat for any signs of infestation and promptly remove any ticks.

Gardening Safety: Spring is a time for gardening, but certain plants can be toxic to dogs. Ensure that your garden is free from poisonous plants such as lilies, azaleas, and tulips. Keep your Italian Greyhound away from fertilizers, pesticides, and other potentially harmful substances.

Summertime Safety:

Summer brings sunshine and outdoor adventures, but it also poses risks associated with heat and increased outdoor activities. Consider the following to keep your Italian Greyhound safe and comfortable:

Hydration: Ensure your Italian Greyhound has access to fresh water at all times, especially during hot weather. Carry a portable water bowl and provide water breaks during walks or outdoor activities.

Sun Protection: Italian Greyhounds have thin coats and are prone to sunburn. Apply pet-safe sunscreen to their exposed areas, such as the nose, ears, and belly, when spending extended periods outdoors. Provide shaded areas to protect them from direct sunlight.

Heat Safety: Italian Greyhounds are sensitive to heat and can quickly succumb to heatstroke. Avoid walks or outdoor activities during the hottest parts of the day. Walk them early in the morning or late in the evening when temperatures are cooler. Never leave your Italian Greyhound in a parked car, as the temperature inside can rise rapidly and be life-threatening.

Autumn Precautions:

Autumn brings cooler temperatures and colorful foliage, but it also comes with its own set of considerations. Here are some tips to ensure your Italian Greyhound's safety during this season:

Falling Leaves and Mushrooms: Keep your Italian Greyhound away from piles of leaves, as they may hide hazards such as sharp objects or toxic mushrooms. Mushrooms can be extremely dangerous if ingested, so regularly inspect your yard and walking areas to remove any potential risks.

Daylight Changes: As the days become shorter, it is important to adjust your walking schedule and ensure your Italian Greyhound is visible during evening walks. Use reflective gear or attach a reflective collar or leash to enhance their visibility.

Temperature Changes: Autumn brings fluctuating temperatures. Keep your Italian Greyhound warm by providing them with appropriate sweaters or jackets when the weather turns chilly. Ensure they have a warm and comfortable bed to rest in during colder nights.

Hot Weather Tips and Precautions

Beat the Heat: Hot Weather Tips and Precautions for Italian Greyhounds

Italian Greyhounds are elegant and sensitive companions known for their affectionate nature and unique physical attributes. With their sleek coats and delicate constitution, they require special attention and care during hot weather. As responsible pet owners, it is our duty to ensure their safety and well-being during summer months when temperatures rise. Below we will explore hot weather tips and precautions specifically tailored to Italian Greyhounds, providing essential information to help keep them cool, comfortable, and protected from the heat.

Hydration is Key:

Proper hydration is crucial for Italian Greyhounds to regulate body temperature and prevent dehydration. Here are some tips to ensure they stay adequately hydrated:

Fresh Water Access: Provide fresh, clean water at all times, both indoors and outdoors. Monitor the water level and refill it regularly, especially on hot days, to ensure your Italian Greyhound always has access to water.

Ice Cube Treats: Offer ice cubes as a refreshing treat. Italian Greyhounds may enjoy licking or playing with them, and it can help cool them down while providing some entertainment.

Travel with Water: When going on outings or walks, carry a portable water bottle and a collapsible water bowl to provide your Italian Greyhound with water breaks along the way.

Limit Outdoor Activities:

When the temperature rises, it is important to limit your Italian Greyhound's exposure to the heat. Follow these guidelines to keep them safe and comfortable:

Walks and Exercise: Adjust your walking schedule to early mornings or late evenings when temperatures are cooler. Avoid walks during the hottest parts of the day to prevent overheating and paw pad burns from hot pavement.

Provide Shade: Create shaded areas in your yard using umbrellas, canopies, or trees. Ensure your Italian Greyhound has a cool spot to rest and relax when outdoors.

Indoor Playtime: Engage in indoor activities to keep your Italian Greyhound mentally stimulated and physically active. Puzzle toys or interactive games can provide entertainment without exposing them to excessive heat.

Cooling Techniques:

Implementing cooling techniques can help your Italian Greyhound beat the heat and maintain a comfortable body temperature:

Wet Towel or Cooling Mat: Wet a towel with cool water and place it over your Italian Greyhound's body or create a cooling mat by freezing a damp towel. These techniques can provide instant relief from the heat.

Cooling Vests or Bandanas: Invest in a cooling vest or bandana specifically designed for dogs. These products use evaporative cooling technology to keep your Italian Greyhound cool during outdoor activities.

Swimming Opportunities: If your Italian Greyhound enjoys water, consider providing a shallow pool or a safe water source for them to splash around and cool off. Always supervise them near water to ensure their safety.

Protect from Sunburn:

Italian Greyhounds have thin coats and light skin, making them susceptible to sunburn. Take the following measures to protect them from harmful UV rays:

1Avoid Midday Sun: Limit exposure to the sun during peak hours when the sun's rays are strongest. Opt for shaded areas or keep your Italian Greyhound indoors during this time.

Pet-Safe Sunscreen: Apply pet-safe sunscreen to areas vulnerable to sunburn, such as the nose, ears, and belly. Consult your veterinarian to find a suitable sunscreen product for your Italian Greyhound.

Protective Clothing: Consider using lightweight clothing or a dog-specific sun shirt to provide additional sun protection. Ensure the clothing fits properly and does not cause discomfort or restrict movement.

Cold Weather Care and Protection

Embracing the Chill: Cold Weather Care and Protection for Italian Greyhounds

Italian Greyhounds are graceful and sensitive companions known for their affectionate nature and unique physical attributes. With their sleek coats and lean bodies, they may require extra care and attention during cold weather to keep them safe and comfortable. As responsible pet owners, it is essential to understand the specific needs of Italian Greyhounds in chilly temperatures and take necessary precautions to ensure their well-being. Below we will explore cold weather care and protection tips tailored to Italian Greyhounds, providing valuable information to keep them warm, happy, and healthy during the winter season.

Protecting from the Elements:

Italian Greyhounds are more susceptible to cold weather due to their thin coats and minimal body fat. Here are some measures to shield them from the elements:

Sweaters or Coats: Invest in well-fitted, warm sweaters or coats specifically designed for Italian Greyhounds. These garments can provide an extra layer of insulation and keep them comfortable during outdoor activities.

Paw Protection: Protect your Italian Greyhound's paws from the cold ground, ice, and salt used for de-icing. Consider using paw wax or applying pet-friendly booties to prevent paw pad injuries and exposure to harsh chemicals.

Shelter: Provide a warm and cozy shelter for your Italian Greyhound when they are outside. A well-insulated dog house or a covered area with blankets or bedding can offer protection from the wind and cold.

Indoor Comfort:

While Italian Greyhounds may enjoy spending time outdoors, they are primarily indoor dogs. Ensure their indoor environment is cozy and warm:

Temperature Control: Maintain a comfortable indoor temperature, ideally between 65-75°F (18-24°C). Use space heaters or heating pads in designated areas to provide additional warmth, but ensure they are pet-safe and used under supervision.

Soft Bedding: Offer soft and warm bedding options for your Italian Greyhound. Provide blankets, pet beds, or heated mats to create a comfortable resting place away from drafts.

Avoid Drafts: Protect your Italian Greyhound from drafts by closing windows and doors or using draft stoppers. Avoid placing their bed or favorite resting spot near cold areas, such as drafty windows or doors.

Adjusting Walks and Exercise:

Cold weather does not mean your Italian Greyhound has to forgo outdoor activities entirely. However, it's important to make adjustments to keep them safe and comfortable:

Shorter Walks: Consider shortening your Italian Greyhound's walks during extremely cold weather. Keep an eye on their behavior and signs of discomfort. If they start shivering or lifting their paws, it may be a sign that it's time to head back indoors.

Midday Walks: Plan walks during the warmer parts of the day, such as mid-morning or early afternoon when the sun is out and temperatures are slightly higher. This can help avoid the coldest times of the day, usually early morning and evening.

Indoor Exercise: On particularly frigid days, engage your Italian Greyhound in indoor exercises. Set up obstacle courses, play interactive games, or teach them new tricks to keep them mentally stimulated and physically active.

Nutrition and Hydration:

Proper nutrition and hydration play a vital role in maintaining your Italian Greyhound's overall health during the winter season:

1Adequate Food Intake: Monitor your Italian Greyhound's food intake and adjust their diet if necessary. During colder months, they may require slightly more calories to maintain their body temperature. Consult with your veterinarian to ensure they are receiving a balanced diet.

Holiday Hazards and Safety Measures

Celebrating Safely: Holiday Hazards and Safety Measures for Italian Greyhounds

The holiday season is a time of joy, festivities, and quality time spent with loved ones, including our beloved Italian Greyhounds. However, amidst the merriment, it's important to be aware of potential hazards that can pose a risk to our furry friends. Italian Greyhounds, known for their sensitivity and inquisitive nature, require extra attention and care during this time. Below we will explore holiday hazards and provide essential safety measures to ensure the well-being of Italian Greyhounds throughout the festive season.

Decorations and Ornaments:

The allure of holiday decorations can be irresistible to curious Italian Greyhounds. Here are some precautions to protect them from potential dangers:

Christmas Trees: Ensure your Christmas tree is securely anchored to prevent tipping. Consider using a tree gate or barrier to restrict access. Keep fragile ornaments and tinsel out of reach to prevent ingestion or choking hazards.

Electrical Cords: Secure loose electrical cords and keep them hidden or inaccessible to your Italian Greyhound. Chewing on cords can result in electric shock or injury. Consider using cord covers or protective tubing.

Plants: Many popular holiday plants, such as poinsettias, mistletoe, and holly, are toxic to dogs if ingested. Keep these plants out of reach or opt for pet-safe alternatives.

Holiday Food and Treats:

The holiday season brings an array of delicious food and treats, but not all are safe for Italian Greyhounds. Consider the following:

Chocolate and Sweets: Keep chocolate, candies, and baked goods containing xylitol (a common sugar substitute) out of reach. Chocolate and xylitol can be toxic to dogs and may cause severe health complications.

Table Scraps: Resist the temptation to share table scraps with your Italian Greyhound. Rich and fatty foods, such as turkey skin, gravy, or stuffing, can cause digestive upset or even pancreatitis. Stick to their regular diet and offer dog-friendly treats instead.

Bones and Hazards: Avoid giving your Italian Greyhound cooked bones, as they can splinter and cause choking or digestive blockages. Dispose of leftover bones securely. Keep garbage bins tightly sealed to prevent scavenging.

Noise and Stress:

Italian Greyhounds are sensitive to noise and can become stressed or anxious during loud holiday celebrations. Consider the following tips:

Quiet Retreat: Create a quiet and comfortable space where your Italian Greyhound can retreat to when they need a break from the noise and commotion. Provide a cozy bed, familiar toys, and calming music or white noise to help them relax.

Safe Haven: During fireworks or noisy gatherings, consider using a crate or playpen to provide a safe haven for your Italian Greyhound. Cover the crate with a blanket or use a noise-canceling device to muffle loud sounds.

Calming Techniques: Explore natural calming remedies, such as lavender-infused diffusers, anxiety wraps, or pheromone sprays, to help ease your Italian Greyhound's anxiety. Consult with your veterinarian about potential options.

Guests and Introductions:

Having guests over during the holidays can be exciting but overwhelming for Italian Greyhounds. Ensure a positive and stress-free experience with the following guidelines:

1Controlled Introductions: Introduce your Italian Greyhound to new guests gradually and in a controlled manner. Allow them to approach at their own pace, and provide treats or positive reinforcement to create positive associations.

Quiet Space: Set up a designated area for your Italian Greyhound away from the bustling holiday gatherings. Inform your guests about your dog's boundaries and the importance of respecting their space.

Common Behavioral Issues

Navigating Behavioral Challenges: Addressing Common Behavioral Issues in Italian Greyhounds

Italian Greyhounds are adored for their elegant appearance, affectionate nature, and unique personality traits. However, like any dog breed, they can experience behavioral challenges that may require attention and training. Understanding these common behavioral issues is essential for creating a harmonious and fulfilling relationship with your Italian Greyhound. Below we will explore some typical behavioral issues that Italian Greyhounds may exhibit and discuss effective strategies for addressing them.

Separation Anxiety:

Italian Greyhounds are known for their strong attachment to their owners, which can sometimes lead to separation anxiety. Signs of separation anxiety may include excessive barking, destructive behavior, or inappropriate elimination when left alone. Here are some strategies to help alleviate separation anxiety:

Gradual Departures: Practice gradual departures by starting with short periods of time away and gradually increasing the duration. This helps your Italian Greyhound become accustomed to your absence.

Create a Safe Space: Designate a comfortable and secure area for your Italian Greyhound when you are not at home. Provide them with engaging toys, a cozy bed, and items that carry your scent to help them feel more at ease.

Behavior Modification: Consult with a professional dog trainer or behaviorist to develop a behavior modification plan that addresses your Italian Greyhound's separation anxiety. This may involve desensitization exercises and positive reinforcement techniques.

Excessive Barking:

Italian Greyhounds, like many small breeds, may have a tendency to bark excessively. While occasional barking is normal, persistent or excessive barking can be problematic. Here are some approaches to manage and reduce excessive barking:

Identify Triggers: Observe and identify the triggers that cause your Italian Greyhound to bark excessively. It could be boredom, anxiety, territorial behavior, or attention-seeking. Understanding the underlying cause can help address the issue effectively.

Distraction and Diversion: Redirect your Italian Greyhound's attention to a more appropriate behavior when they start barking excessively. Engage them in a toy or offer a treat to divert their focus.

Positive Reinforcement: Use positive reinforcement training techniques to reward your Italian Greyhound for calm and quiet behavior. Teach them the "quiet" command and provide treats or praise when they stop barking on command.

Housetraining Issues:

Italian Greyhounds, like any dog, may experience housetraining challenges, especially during puppyhood. Consistency, patience, and positive reinforcement are key when addressing housetraining issues:

Establish a Routine: Create a consistent schedule for feeding, potty breaks, and outdoor walks. Take your Italian Greyhound to the designated potty area after meals, waking up, and playtime.

Reward and Reinforce: Use positive reinforcement, such as treats, praise, and petting, to reward your Italian Greyhound for eliminating in the appropriate spot. Avoid punishment or scolding for accidents, as it may create anxiety or confusion.

Supervision and Crate Training: When indoors, closely supervise your Italian Greyhound to prevent accidents. Consider crate training to create a safe and comfortable den-like space where your dog can stay when you are unable to supervise.

Leash Reactivity:

Some Italian Greyhounds may exhibit leash reactivity, which can manifest as lunging, barking, or aggressive behavior when encountering other dogs or stimuli on walks. Here are some techniques to address leash reactivity:

1Positive Reinforcement Training: Use positive reinforcement techniques to reward your Italian Greyhound for calm behavior on walks. Gradually expose them to triggers at a distance where they remain calm and reward them for positive responses.

Separation Anxiety and Boredom

Easing the Strain: Combating Separation Anxiety and Boredom in Italian Greyhounds

Italian Greyhounds are cherished companions known for their affectionate nature and unwavering loyalty. However, like many dogs, they can experience separation anxiety and boredom when left alone for extended periods. Separation anxiety is a distressing condition that arises from a strong attachment to their owners, while boredom can lead to frustration and undesirable behavior. Understanding these issues and implementing effective strategies is crucial to ensure the well-being of Italian Greyhounds. Below we will explore separation anxiety and boredom in Italian Greyhounds and discuss practical solutions to alleviate these challenges.

Separation Anxiety:

Italian Greyhounds are prone to separation anxiety due to their deep bond with their owners. When left alone, they may exhibit various signs of distress, including excessive barking, destructive behavior, and inappropriate elimination. Here are some strategies to help manage separation anxiety:

Gradual Departures: Practice gradual departures by gradually increasing the time you spend away from your Italian Greyhound. Start with short intervals and gradually extend the duration. This helps them become accustomed to your absence and reduces anxiety.

Establish a Routine: Create a consistent daily routine that includes exercise, mental stimulation, and quality time with your Italian Greyhound. Having a predictable schedule can help them feel more secure and less anxious when you are not around.

Desensitization: Teach your Italian Greyhound to associate your departure cues with positive experiences. Perform these cues, such as picking up your keys or putting on your coat, without leaving. Over time, they will learn that these cues do not necessarily mean you are leaving.

Interactive Toys and Puzzles: Provide your Italian Greyhound with interactive toys and puzzles that can keep them mentally stimulated and engaged when you are not home. These toys can help distract them from feelings of anxiety and provide a positive outlet for their energy.

Boredom:

Boredom can be a significant contributor to undesirable behaviors in Italian Greyhounds. Without mental and physical stimulation, they may become restless and engage in destructive behaviors. Here are some ways to combat boredom:

Exercise: Engage your Italian Greyhound in regular exercise sessions to expend their energy and stimulate their minds. Daily walks, playtime, and interactive activities such as agility training can help keep them mentally and physically fit.

Enrichment Toys: Provide your Italian Greyhound with a variety of interactive toys that challenge their problem-solving skills. Treat-dispensing toys or puzzle toys can keep them engaged and mentally stimulated.

Rotating Toys: Rotate your Italian Greyhound's toys regularly to keep their interest and prevent monotony. Introduce new toys periodically to keep their playtime exciting and engaging.

Training and Tricks: Engage in positive reinforcement training sessions with your Italian Greyhound. Teach them new tricks, obedience commands, or participate in canine sports like agility or nose work. Training sessions provide mental stimulation and strengthen the bond between you and your dog.

Additional Strategies:

In addition to the above techniques, consider the following strategies to address separation anxiety and boredom:

Calming Aids: Consider using calming aids such as pheromone diffusers or sprays, calming music, or anti-anxiety wraps. These can help create a soothing environment for your Italian Greyhound and promote relaxation.

1Professional Help: If your Italian Greyhound's separation anxiety or boredom persists despite your efforts, seek assistance from a professional dog trainer or behaviorist. They can provide personalized guidance and develop a behavior modification plan tailored to your dog's needs.

Doggy Daycare or Pet Sitters: Consider enrolling your Italian Greyhound in doggy daycare or hiring a reliable pet sitter when you need to be away for extended periods.

Barking and Howling

Decoding the Melodies: Understanding Barking and Howling in Italian Greyhounds

Italian Greyhounds, with their gentle and affectionate nature, are not typically known for excessive barking or howling. However, like any dog breed, they may engage in vocalizations to communicate their needs, express emotions, or alert their owners. Understanding the reasons behind barking and howling in Italian Greyhounds is essential for effective communication and maintaining a harmonious living environment. Below we will explore the various factors that contribute to barking and howling in Italian Greyhounds and discuss strategies to manage and address these behaviors.

Communication and Expression:

Italian Greyhounds use barking and howling as a means of communication. Here are some common reasons why they engage in vocalizations:

Alerting: Italian Greyhounds have a keen sense of hearing and may bark or howl to alert their owners of potential threats or unusual occurrences. This is their way of notifying you that something has caught their attention or that they feel the need to protect their territory.

Excitement: Barking and howling can also be a sign of excitement. Italian Greyhounds may vocalize when they are thrilled to see their owners, anticipating playtime or engaging in activities that they find enjoyable.

Attention-Seeking: Like many dogs, Italian Greyhounds may bark or howl to gain attention. They may do so when they feel ignored or when they want something, such as food, water, or interaction.

Anxiety and Fear:

Italian Greyhounds are sensitive dogs that can experience anxiety and fear, leading to excessive vocalizations. Here are some factors that may contribute to anxiety-related barking and howling:

Separation Anxiety: Italian Greyhounds are prone to separation anxiety, which can manifest as distress vocalizations when left alone. They may bark or howl as a means to express their distress and attempt to seek comfort.

Fearful Triggers: Italian Greyhounds may bark or howl when confronted with fearful stimuli, such as loud noises, unfamiliar people, or other animals. They use vocalizations as a way to communicate their discomfort and attempt to create distance from perceived threats.

Boredom and Loneliness:

Barking and howling can also result from boredom or loneliness in Italian Greyhounds. These active and intelligent dogs require mental stimulation and companionship. Here are some considerations to address these factors:

Insufficient Exercise: Inadequate physical exercise and mental stimulation can contribute to restlessness and boredom, leading to excessive vocalizations. Ensuring regular exercise and engaging activities can help alleviate these behaviors.

Lack of Social Interaction: Italian Greyhounds thrive on companionship and may vocalize when they feel lonely or isolated. Providing sufficient social interaction, playtime, and quality time together can reduce their need to vocalize for attention.

Environmental Triggers:

Italian Greyhounds may also respond vocally to environmental stimuli. Here are some common triggers that may lead to barking or howling:

Other Dogs: Italian Greyhounds are known to be social creatures and may vocalize in response to other dogs in their surroundings. They may bark or howl to communicate or establish their presence.

Noises and Disturbances: Loud noises, such as sirens, fireworks, or construction sounds, can startle Italian Greyhounds and prompt vocal responses. They may bark or howl as a natural reaction to perceived threats or to express discomfort.

1Lack of Stimulation: If Italian Greyhounds are understimulated or confined to a monotonous environment for extended periods, they may resort to barking or howling as a means to express their frustration or seek attention.

Resource Guarding and Aggression

Navigating the Territories: Understanding Resource Guarding and Aggression in Italian Greyhounds

Italian Greyhounds are known for their gentle and affectionate nature, making them beloved companions. However, like any dog breed, they may exhibit resource guarding behaviors and aggression under certain circumstances. Resource guarding refers to the protective behavior displayed by dogs when they feel the need to defend their valued possessions. Understanding the reasons behind resource guarding and aggression in Italian Greyhounds is crucial for maintaining a safe and harmonious living environment. Below we will explore the factors contributing to resource guarding and aggression in Italian Greyhounds and discuss strategies to manage and address these behaviors effectively.

Resource Guarding:

Resource guarding can occur when Italian Greyhounds perceive a particular item or space as valuable and feel the need to protect it. This behavior is rooted in the dog's instinctual drive to secure resources for survival. Here are some common triggers for resource guarding:

Food: Italian Greyhounds may exhibit resource guarding behaviors when it comes to their food, especially if they have experienced food scarcity or competition in the past. They may growl, snap, or show aggression to prevent others from approaching their food bowl or treats.

Toys and Objects: Italian Greyhounds may guard toys, bones, or other objects they consider valuable. They may display possessive behaviors such as growling, stiffening, or even biting when others approach or attempt to take the item.

Territory: Italian Greyhounds can display resource guarding behaviors when it comes to their designated spaces or resting areas. They may exhibit territorial aggression by growling, barking, or even biting to defend their perceived territory.

Aggression:

Aggression in Italian Greyhounds can arise from various factors, including fear, lack of socialization, or improper training. It is essential to address aggression promptly and appropriately to prevent potential harm. Here are some types of aggression that may occur:

Fear Aggression: Italian Greyhounds that have had negative experiences or lack socialization may exhibit fear-based aggression. They may display defensive behaviors, such as growling, barking, or snapping when they feel threatened or cornered.

Dog-Dog Aggression: Some Italian Greyhounds may show aggression towards other dogs. This can occur due to fear, lack of socialization, or territorial instincts. It is important to manage these interactions carefully and gradually introduce positive experiences with other dogs.

Human Aggression: Although rare, Italian Greyhounds may display aggression towards humans. This can stem from fear, previous traumatic experiences, or inadequate socialization. Professional help and behavior modification techniques are recommended to address this type of aggression.

Strategies to Manage Resource Guarding and Aggression:

Prevention and Early Intervention: Recognizing and addressing resource guarding and aggression early on is crucial. Implement positive reinforcement training methods from an early age to establish a positive association with sharing resources and interacting with others.

Professional Guidance: Seek guidance from a professional dog trainer or behaviorist experienced in handling resource guarding and aggression issues. They can provide a tailored training plan and techniques specific to your Italian Greyhound's needs.

Desensitization and Counterconditioning: Gradual desensitization and counterconditioning can help change your Italian Greyhound's emotional response to situations that trigger resource guarding or aggression. This involves exposing them to controlled and positive experiences, gradually increasing the difficulty level while ensuring their comfort and security.

1Behavior Modification: Implement behavior modification techniques to address resource guarding and aggression. This may involve teaching the "leave it" and "drop it" commands, encouraging a positive exchange for items, and rewarding calm and non-aggressive behaviors.

Fun and Games with Your Italian Greyhound

Unleashing the Joy: Fun and Games with Your Italian Greyhound

Italian Greyhounds are playful and energetic companions, always ready for an adventure or a good game. Engaging in interactive activities not only provides physical exercise but also strengthens the bond between you and your Italian Greyhound. From outdoor pursuits to indoor brain games, there are plenty of exciting ways to have fun together. Below we will explore various fun and games you can enjoy with your Italian Greyhound, promoting their well-being and ensuring an enjoyable companionship.

Outdoor Adventures:

Italian Greyhounds thrive on outdoor exploration and physical activities. Here are some outdoor games that can ignite their joy and energy:

Fetch: Italian Greyhounds possess a natural prey drive and excel at chasing. Playing fetch with a ball or a favorite toy is an excellent way to engage their athleticism and provide a satisfying mental and physical workout. Ensure you have a secure area and use appropriate toys for their small size.

Agility: Italian Greyhounds are agile and quick on their feet. Setting up a mini agility course in your backyard or attending agility classes can stimulate their minds and challenge their physical abilities. Activities such as jumping through hoops, navigating tunnels, and weaving through poles can be exhilarating for both of you.

Long Walks and Hikes: Italian Greyhounds enjoy long walks and hikes in different environments. Exploring nature trails, parks, or beaches allows them to experience new sights, smells, and textures. Ensure they are on a secure leash or harness to prevent any mishaps.

Water Fun: If your Italian Greyhound enjoys water, consider water activities such as swimming or playing in a shallow pool. However, always prioritize their safety and supervise them closely to prevent accidents.

Indoor Brain Games:

While Italian Greyhounds have a natural inclination for physical activities, mental stimulation is equally important. Here are some indoor brain games to challenge their minds:

Puzzle Toys: Provide your Italian Greyhound with puzzle toys that require problem-solving skills. These toys often involve hiding treats or kibble inside compartments, encouraging them to figure out how to access the rewards. It keeps their minds engaged and provides a stimulating challenge.

Hide and Seek: Hide and seek is a fun game that taps into your Italian Greyhound's natural hunting instincts. Start by having them sit and stay while you hide in another room or behind furniture. Then call them and let them use their senses to find you. Reward them with praise or treats when they succeed.

Interactive Treat Dispensers: Invest in interactive treat dispensing toys that require your Italian Greyhound to manipulate the toy to release treats. This keeps them occupied and mentally engaged as they work to access the rewards.

Trick Training: Italian Greyhounds are intelligent and eager to please. Teach them new tricks and commands through positive reinforcement training. Tricks such as "sit," "stay," "shake hands," or even more advanced tricks like "roll over" can be a rewarding experience for both of you.

Bonding Activities:

Spending quality time together is vital for building a strong bond with your Italian Greyhound. Here are some activities that promote bonding and create cherished memories:

Massage and Grooming: Italian Greyhounds enjoy physical contact and the comfort of touch. Gently massaging their muscles or providing a relaxing grooming session not only enhances their physical well-being but also strengthens the emotional connection between you.

1Cuddle Time: Dedicate regular cuddle sessions with your Italian Greyhound. These moments of affection and closeness help them feel secure and loved. Curl up together on the couch, under a cozy blanket, and enjoy the simple pleasure of each other's company.

Interactive Toys and Puzzles

Unleashing the Mind: Interactive Toys and Puzzles for Italian Greyhounds

Italian Greyhounds are intelligent and inquisitive dogs that thrive on mental stimulation. Interactive toys and puzzles not only provide entertainment but also engage their minds, prevent boredom, and promote problem-solving skills. These interactive toys challenge their intellect, keeping them mentally sharp and satisfied. Below we will explore a variety of interactive toys and puzzles suitable for Italian Greyhounds, enhancing their cognitive abilities and ensuring hours of engaging playtime.

Treat-Dispensing Toys:

Treat-dispensing toys are excellent for engaging Italian Greyhounds mentally and rewarding them with tasty treats. Here are some popular options:

Kong Classic: The Kong Classic is a versatile and durable toy that can be stuffed with treats or peanut butter. Its unpredictable bounce and the challenge of getting the treats out make it an engaging toy for Italian Greyhounds.

Nina Ottosson Puzzle Toys: Nina Ottosson is renowned for her innovative puzzle toys. These toys require Italian Greyhounds to manipulate different components to access hidden treats. The range includes toys like the Dog Tornado and Dog Brick, which provide varying levels of difficulty to match your dog's abilities.

Busy Buddy Twist 'n Treat: This toy allows you to adjust the difficulty level by twisting it tighter or looser to control the treat dispensing. Italian Greyhounds must figure out how to manipulate the toy to release the treats, providing mental stimulation and entertainment.

Interactive Feeding Toys:

Interactive feeding toys turn mealtime into a mentally stimulating experience for Italian Greyhounds. These toys slow down eating and make mealtime more engaging. Here are some options:

Slow Feeder Bowls: Slow feeder bowls feature ridges, mazes, or obstacles that require Italian Greyhounds to work around them to access their food. These bowls promote slower eating, prevent bloating, and engage their problem-solving skills during mealtime.

Snuffle Mats: Snuffle mats are fabric mats with various layers of fabric strips or folds. Sprinkle your Italian Greyhound's kibble or treats among the fabric strips, and they'll have to use their nose and paws to find the hidden food. This mimics foraging behavior and provides a mentally stimulating feeding experience.

Puzzle Toys:

Puzzle toys challenge Italian Greyhounds to solve problems to access hidden rewards. These toys come in different shapes and designs and offer varying levels of difficulty. Here are some examples:

Outward Hound Dog Brick Puzzle Toy: The Dog Brick puzzle toy features sliding blocks and removable bones that conceal treats. Italian Greyhounds must slide and lift the components to retrieve the hidden rewards.

Trixie Flip Board: The Trixie Flip Board is a multi-compartment puzzle toy that requires Italian Greyhounds to flip open lids, lift cones, and slide disks to access treats. It offers different difficulty levels and keeps them engaged and mentally stimulated.

Dog Casino Interactive Treat Puzzle: The Dog Casino puzzle toy consists of drawers that Italian Greyhounds must pull open using ropes or knobs to reveal treats. It provides a fun and challenging experience as they figure out how to access the hidden rewards.

Interactive Plush Toys:

Interactive plush toys combine play and mental stimulation by incorporating interactive elements within a soft, plush toy. These toys often include squeakers, crinkle sounds, and hidden compartments for treats. Here are some examples:

Hide-A-Squirrel Plush Toy: The Hide-A-Squirrel toy features a plush tree trunk with squeaky squirrel toys that can be hidden inside. Italian Greyhounds must remove the squirrels from the trunk, providing entertainment and mental engagement.

Fetch and Retrieval Games

Unleashing the Fun: Fetch and Retrieval Games for Italian Greyhounds

Italian Greyhounds are energetic and agile dogs that love to chase and retrieve objects. Engaging in fetch and retrieval games not only provides physical exercise but also stimulates their natural instincts and strengthens the bond between you and your Italian Greyhound. Below we will explore the excitement and benefits of fetch and retrieval games specifically tailored for Italian Greyhounds, ensuring a fun and fulfilling experience for both you and your furry companion.

Choosing the Right Toys:

Selecting suitable toys for fetch and retrieval games is crucial to ensure safety and enjoyment. Consider the following factors when choosing toys for your Italian Greyhound:

Size: Italian Greyhounds are small in stature, so opt for toys that are appropriately sized for their mouth and body. Avoid toys that are too large or heavy, as they may pose a risk of injury or discomfort.

Durability: Look for toys that are durable and able to withstand the intensity of play. Italian Greyhounds can be enthusiastic chewers, so choose toys made from strong materials such as rubber or nylon.

Texture: Italian Greyhounds may have sensitive teeth and gums, so choose toys with a soft or gentle texture. Avoid toys with sharp edges or rough surfaces that may cause irritation or injury.

Basic Fetch:

Basic fetch is a classic game that taps into your Italian Greyhound's natural chasing and retrieving instincts. Here's how to play:

Start in a safe and enclosed area, such as a backyard or a fenced park. This ensures that your Italian Greyhound remains within a controlled space.

Begin by showing the toy or ball to your Italian Greyhound, encouraging their interest and attention. Use a clear and enthusiastic voice to command "Fetch" or a similar cue to initiate the game.

Toss the toy or ball a short distance away from you. As your Italian Greyhound chases after it, encourage them with verbal praise and gestures.

Once your Italian Greyhound retrieves the toy, encourage them to return to you by using a cue like "Come" or "Bring it back." Reward them with treats or praise when they return the toy to your hand.

Repeat the process, gradually increasing the distance of the throws as your Italian Greyhound becomes more proficient in the game.

Retrieval Training:

Retrieval training takes fetch to the next level by introducing more advanced skills and commands. It enhances your Italian Greyhound's ability to retrieve specific objects and respond to commands. Here are some steps to follow:

Begin with the basic fetch game as described earlier to establish a foundation for retrieving.

Introduce specific objects that your Italian Greyhound can learn to retrieve, such as a designated retrieving toy or a soft cloth.

Use a consistent cue, such as "Fetch" or "Get it," when you want your Italian Greyhound to retrieve the object. Repeat the cue each time you initiate the game to reinforce their understanding.

Gradually incorporate additional commands, such as "Drop it" or "Give," to teach your Italian Greyhound to release the object on command.

Reward your Italian Greyhound with treats, praise, or playtime each time they successfully retrieve and release the object.

Practice retrieving in different environments to generalize the skill and ensure that your Italian Greyhound can retrieve objects regardless of the surroundings.

Hiking and Exploring

Embarking on Adventures: Hiking and Exploring with Italian Greyhounds

Italian Greyhounds are lively and adventurous companions, always ready to explore the great outdoors. Hiking and exploring not only provide physical exercise but also stimulate their senses and fulfill their natural curiosity. Below we will delve into the joys and considerations of hiking and exploring with Italian Greyhounds, ensuring a safe and enjoyable experience for both you and your furry friend.

Preparing for the Adventure:

Before embarking on a hiking or exploring trip with your Italian Greyhound, it's important to make adequate preparations. Consider the following factors:

Fitness Level: Assess your Italian Greyhound's fitness level to ensure they can handle the physical demands of the activity. Start with shorter hikes or walks and gradually increase the intensity and duration over time.

Check Local Regulations: Research local regulations and guidelines regarding hiking trails and outdoor areas. Some areas may have specific rules regarding dogs, such as leash requirements or restricted access.

Weather Conditions: Check the weather forecast before heading out. Extreme heat, cold, or inclement weather can pose risks to your Italian Greyhound's well-being. Adjust your plans accordingly to ensure their safety and comfort.

Pack Essentials: Carry essentials such as water, collapsible bowls, a first-aid kit, poop bags, and a leash. It's also advisable to have identification tags with up-to-date contact information in case your Italian Greyhound becomes separated from you.

Choosing Suitable Trails:

When selecting hiking trails or outdoor areas for exploration, consider the following factors to ensure a positive experience for your Italian Greyhound:

Length and Difficulty: Choose trails suitable for your Italian Greyhound's fitness level and stamina. Start with shorter, less strenuous trails and gradually progress to longer and more challenging ones.

Terrain: Opt for trails with terrain that is safe and comfortable for your Italian Greyhound. Avoid trails with sharp rocks, steep cliffs, or dense vegetation that may pose hazards or cause discomfort.

Shade and Water Sources: Select trails that provide shade and access to water sources, especially during hot weather. Italian Greyhounds are prone to heat sensitivity, so it's essential to prevent overheating and dehydration.

Dog-Friendly Trails: Seek out trails that are dog-friendly and allow dogs off-leash, if permitted. These trails often provide a more enjoyable experience for your Italian Greyhound, allowing them to explore and roam freely.

Safety Measures:

While hiking and exploring, prioritize your Italian Greyhound's safety by following these measures:

Leash Etiquette: Observe leash regulations and guidelines. In areas where leashes are required, keep your Italian Greyhound on a leash to prevent them from wandering off or encountering potential dangers.

1Wildlife Awareness: Be mindful of the local wildlife and keep your Italian Greyhound away from wild animals. Avoid areas known for encounters with predators or other potentially aggressive animals.

Tick Prevention: Apply tick prevention measures to protect your Italian Greyhound from tick-borne diseases. Check them for ticks after each outing and promptly remove any ticks you find.

Paw Protection: Italian Greyhounds have delicate paws that may be susceptible to rough or hot surfaces. Consider using paw wax or protective booties to safeguard their paws from sharp rocks, hot pavement, or harsh terrain.

Enjoying the Experience:

Make the most of your hiking and exploring adventures with your Italian Greyhound by incorporating these elements:

Exploration and Sniffing Time: Allow your Italian Greyhound ample time to explore and sniff their surroundings. This not only satisfies their natural curiosity but also provides mental stimulation.

Breaks and Rests: Take frequent breaks and allow your Italian Greyhound to rest and hydrate. This helps prevent exhaustion and ensures their comfort throughout the excursion.

Italian Greyhound Legends and Stories

Elegant and Enigmatic: Italian Greyhound Legends and Stories

Italian Greyhounds have captivated hearts for centuries with their graceful appearance and endearing nature. These beloved dogs have not only found a place in our homes but also in the realms of legend and folklore. Below we will delve into the enchanting world of Italian Greyhound legends and stories, exploring their historical significance and cultural impact.

An Ancient Heritage:

Italian Greyhounds have a long and storied history that dates back thousands of years. It is believed that their lineage can be traced to ancient Egypt, where depictions of small greyhound-like dogs resembling Italian Greyhounds have been found. These elegant canines were often associated with nobility and were highly regarded for their beauty and companionship.

Roman Royalty:

One of the most prominent Italian Greyhound legends stems from ancient Rome. It is said that Roman emperors, such as Julius Caesar and Alexander the Great, were smitten by these small greyhounds. Legend has it that these regal figures would carry Italian Greyhounds in their robes and even let them sleep in their beds. These tales of Roman royalty's fondness for Italian Greyhounds further elevated their status as coveted companions.

Symbol of Aristocracy:

During the Renaissance period in Europe, Italian Greyhounds became symbols of aristocracy and opulence. They were often depicted in the artwork of renowned painters, such as Titian and Giotto, as cherished pets of the wealthy and influential. Their graceful presence in paintings and sculptures added to their allure and cemented their reputation as dogs of high social standing.

The Story of Lubya:

A legendary tale from Russia tells the story of Lubya, a brave Italian Greyhound who served as a companion to Grand Duchess Olga Nikolaevna, daughter of Tsar Nicholas II. According to the story, Lubya accompanied the duchess during her imprisonment and exile. Despite the hardships they faced, Lubya remained loyal and provided comfort and companionship to the duchess until the end. This heartwarming story highlights the unwavering bond between Italian Greyhounds and their human companions.

Symbolism in Literature:

Italian Greyhounds have made their way into literature, where they often symbolize loyalty, beauty, and grace. In Charles Dickens' novel "David Copperfield," the character Miss Rosa Dartle is accompanied by her faithful Italian Greyhound named Jip, representing her unwavering devotion and protective nature. The inclusion of Italian Greyhounds in literature adds depth and symbolism to the stories in which they appear.

Cultural Significance:

Italian Greyhounds have also found a place in various cultural traditions and superstitions. In Italy, it is believed that having an Italian Greyhound in the home brings good luck and ensures a harmonious household. They are often associated with love, loyalty, and protection, and are even believed to possess the power to ward off evil spirits. These cultural beliefs showcase the enduring fascination and reverence for Italian Greyhounds across different societies.

Contemporary Popularity:

In modern times, Italian Greyhounds continue to captivate the hearts of dog lovers worldwide. Their elegant appearance, affectionate nature, and unique personalities have earned them a dedicated following. Italian Greyhound enthusiasts often share stories and anecdotes about their beloved companions through online communities and social media platforms, further highlighting the ongoing fascination with these remarkable dogs.

Italian Greyhound legends and stories serve as testaments to the enduring allure and significance of these enchanting dogs throughout history. Whether as symbols of royalty and nobility or as loyal and devoted companions, Italian Greyhounds have left an indelible mark on our cultural consciousness.

Famous Italian Greyhounds

Awe-Inspiring and Legendary: Famous Italian Greyhounds

Italian Greyhounds have not only won the hearts of countless dog lovers but have also left their mark in the realms of fame and celebrity. These charming and elegant dogs have found themselves in the company of notable figures from various walks of life, whether in the world of entertainment, politics, or even royalty. Below we will explore the stories of some famous Italian Greyhounds who have achieved fame and left a lasting legacy.

Bambi:

Bambi, an Italian Greyhound, gained fame as the beloved companion of actress and icon Audrey Hepburn. Hepburn's love for animals was well-known, and Bambi became an inseparable part of her life. The pair often graced the covers of magazines and were seen together on various public outings. Bambi's presence in the life of such an influential figure further elevated the status of Italian Greyhounds as cherished pets.

Lorenzo the Magnificent:

Lorenzo the Magnificent, also known as Lorenzo de' Medici, was a prominent figure during the Italian Renaissance. This powerful ruler and patron of the arts had a deep affinity for Italian Greyhounds. It is said that he owned a large number of these elegant dogs and kept them as companions and status symbols. Lorenzo's love for Italian Greyhounds not only enhanced their popularity but also immortalized them in the annals of history.

Miss Scarlet:

Miss Scarlet, a beloved Italian Greyhound, captured the hearts of many as the loyal companion of fashion designer and icon Valentino Garavani. Miss Scarlet was often seen accompanying Valentino during interviews, fashion shows, and social events. Her elegant presence and undeniable charm made her a beloved figure in the fashion world and helped solidify Italian Greyhounds as symbols of sophistication and style.

Isabella:

Isabella, an Italian Greyhound owned by Queen Victoria, played a significant role in popularizing the breed in Victorian England. Queen Victoria was an avid dog lover, and Isabella became one of her most cherished companions. The queen's fondness for Italian Greyhounds helped establish them as fashionable and desirable pets among the upper class. Isabella's influence on the breed's popularity in the 19th century cannot be overstated.

Kinski:

Kinski, an Italian Greyhound, rose to fame in the modern era through his appearance in popular films and television shows. Known for his striking looks and charismatic presence, Kinski became a beloved pet of renowned director and actor Werner Herzog. He appeared in Herzog's films "Fitzcarraldo" and "Aguirre, the Wrath of God," captivating audiences with his on-screen charm. Kinski's involvement in the world of cinema showcased the versatility and star quality of Italian Greyhounds.

Gherkin:

Gherkin, an Italian Greyhound owned by comedian and talk show host Ellen DeGeneres, gained fame through his regular appearances on her television show. Gherkin became an instant hit with the audience, winning hearts with his adorable antics and playful personality. His presence on the show helped introduce Italian Greyhounds to a broader audience and showcased their lovable and entertaining nature.

Eusapia:

Eusapia, an Italian Greyhound belonging to the legendary painter and sculptor Michelangelo, holds a special place in history. It is believed that Michelangelo was so fond of Eusapia that he created a marble sculpture in her likeness. The sculpture, known as "Eusapia," portrays the grace and beauty of Italian Greyhounds and serves as a testament to the bond between the artist and his beloved companion.

Inspirational Stories of Italian Greyhounds

The Unbreakable Spirit: Inspirational Stories of Italian Greyhounds

Italian Greyhounds are not only known for their elegance and charm but also for their indomitable spirit and unwavering determination. These small but mighty dogs have shown incredible resilience and bravery in the face of adversity, inspiring people around the world. Below we will explore some remarkable and inspirational stories of Italian Greyhounds that highlight their courage, strength, and ability to overcome challenges.

Lily: The Miracle Survivor

One extraordinary Italian Greyhound named Lily captured the hearts of many with her incredible survival story. Lily was found severely injured and malnourished, abandoned on the streets. She had multiple fractures and was in desperate need of medical attention. With the help of a compassionate rescuer and a dedicated team of veterinarians, Lily underwent surgeries and intensive care. Despite the odds stacked against her, Lily's determination and will to live triumphed. She made a remarkable recovery and went on to become an ambassador for rescue organizations, inspiring others to never give up hope.

Jasper: From Shelter to Service Dog

Jasper, an Italian Greyhound, began his journey as a rescue dog in a shelter. His path took an extraordinary turn when he was selected to undergo training as a service dog. Despite his challenging start in life, Jasper displayed a remarkable aptitude for learning and a deep desire to help others. With his gentle nature and intelligence, Jasper excelled in his training and eventually became a certified service dog, providing assistance and companionship to a person with disabilities. His transformation from a shelter dog to a dedicated service companion is a testament to the resilience and potential of Italian Greyhounds.

Bella: Overcoming Physical Limitations

Bella, an Italian Greyhound born with a congenital disability, defied all odds and became an inspiration to many. Due to her condition, Bella faced physical challenges and had difficulty walking. However, with the love and support of her dedicated owner, Bella underwent physical therapy and rehabilitation. Through sheer determination and perseverance, Bella not only regained her mobility but also participated in agility competitions, showcasing her strength and agility despite her initial limitations. Bella's story serves as a reminder that with the right support and determination, anything is possible.

Max: A Therapy Dog's Healing Touch

Max, an Italian Greyhound with a gentle and affectionate nature, became a therapy dog and touched the lives of many. Max and his owner regularly visited hospitals and nursing homes, bringing comfort and joy to patients and residents. Max had an innate ability to sense emotions and provide a calming presence to those in need. His unwavering love and companionship offered solace to individuals facing challenging circumstances. Max's therapeutic impact and ability to bring smiles to people's faces demonstrate the special bond between Italian Greyhounds and those they comfort.

Rocky: A Canine Athlete's Triumph

Rocky, an Italian Greyhound with a passion for agility, overcame numerous obstacles to achieve greatness. Despite his small stature, Rocky displayed remarkable agility and speed on the agility course. He faced challenges, such as height restrictions and skepticism due to his breed's size. However, with his extraordinary athleticism and relentless determination, Rocky defied expectations and earned numerous accolades in competitive agility. His story is a testament to the fact that Italian Greyhounds, regardless of their size, can excel in various endeavors when given the opportunity and support.

These inspirational stories of Italian Greyhounds remind us of the incredible strength and resilience found within these remarkable dogs. From overcoming adversity to providing comfort and joy, Italian Greyhounds continue to inspire and touch the lives of people around the world.

Italian Greyhounds in Pop Culture

Italian Greyhounds have captivated the hearts of dog lovers for centuries with their elegance, beauty, and gentle nature. These remarkable dogs have not only found their way into the homes of countless families but have also made appearances in the world of pop culture. Below we will explore the presence of Italian Greyhounds in various forms of entertainment, including films, television shows, and even fashion, highlighting their influence and enduring popularity.

Film Stars:

Italian Greyhounds have graced the silver screen in numerous films, becoming icons of style and sophistication. Their sleek and graceful appearance adds an element of elegance to any scene. In the movie "The Royal Tenenbaums," an Italian Greyhound named Buckley steals the show with his understated charm. This film showcased the breed's regal presence and showcased them as desirable and fashionable pets.

Television Companions:

Italian Greyhounds have also found their way into our living rooms through television shows. In the hit series "Sex and the City," the character Charlotte York is often seen walking her Italian Greyhound, Elizabeth Taylor. This portrayal helped cement the breed's image as a chic and fashionable accessory, making them even more sought after by dog enthusiasts.

Fashion Icons:

Italian Greyhounds have made a significant impact on the fashion industry, with their graceful appearance inspiring designers and appearing in high-end campaigns. Designers like Valentino Garavani and Versace have been known to include Italian Greyhounds in their fashion shows and advertisements, further enhancing the breed's association with style and glamour. Their presence on runways and in fashion magazines has solidified their position as fashion icons.

Social Media Influencers:

In the digital age, Italian Greyhounds have amassed a significant following on social media platforms. Their photogenic looks and charming personalities have made them popular subjects for viral videos and adorable photos. Many Italian Greyhounds have become influencers in their own right, attracting thousands of followers and sharing their daily lives with an engaged online community. These social media stars have helped introduce the breed to a broader audience and showcase their endearing qualities.

Artistic Inspirations:

Italian Greyhounds have been a favorite subject of artists throughout history. Paintings and sculptures featuring Italian Greyhounds can be found in renowned art collections around the world. These artworks celebrate the breed's elegance and grace, immortalizing them in the realm of fine art. Italian Greyhounds have inspired artists to capture their beauty and unique characteristics, further perpetuating their image as timeless and beloved companions.

Literary Characters:

Italian Greyhounds have also made appearances in literature, becoming beloved characters in various stories. In the book "The Story of Edgar Sawtelle" by David Wroblewski, a courageous Italian Greyhound named Almondine plays a significant role in the protagonist's journey. Through her loyalty and unwavering support, Almondine showcases the breed's devotion and companionship.

The presence of Italian Greyhounds in pop culture reflects their enduring appeal and impact on our collective imagination. Whether through films, television shows, fashion, art, or literature, Italian Greyhounds have left an indelible mark as symbols of elegance, style, and companionship. Their representation in various forms of entertainment has elevated their status and reinforced their position as beloved pets in the hearts of dog lovers worldwide.

Italian Greyhound Art, Photography, and Collectibles

Italian Greyhounds, with their graceful appearance and charming demeanor, have long been a source of inspiration for artists and photographers. Their delicate features and slender form make them ideal subjects for various forms of artistic expression. Below we will explore the rich world of Italian Greyhound art, photography, and collectibles, highlighting their enduring appeal and the unique ways in which they have been celebrated in the realm of creativity.

Fine Art:

Italian Greyhounds have been celebrated in the world of fine art for centuries. Renowned painters, such as Sir Joshua Reynolds and Thomas Gainsborough, depicted these elegant dogs in their works, capturing their beauty and gentle nature. The artistry and attention to detail in these paintings showcase the breed's elegance and have helped immortalize the Italian Greyhound as an artistic muse.

Sculptures and Statues:

Italian Greyhounds have also been immortalized in three-dimensional art forms. Sculptures and statues featuring Italian Greyhounds can be found in public spaces, parks, and private collections around the world. These art pieces showcase the breed's delicate features, capturing their grace and charm in intricate detail. Italian Greyhound sculptures serve as tangible representations of the breed's timeless beauty.

Photography:

The unique charm of Italian Greyhounds has made them popular subjects for photographers. Their expressive eyes, sleek coat, and graceful movements lend themselves well to capturing captivating images. Professional photographers and enthusiasts alike have used their skills to capture the essence of Italian Greyhounds through stunning photographs. From playful shots to poised portraits, Italian Greyhound photography showcases the breed's elegance and personality.

Collectibles and Memorabilia:

Italian Greyhound enthusiasts can indulge in a wide range of collectibles and memorabilia dedicated to their favorite breed. From figurines and ornaments to calendars and coffee table books, there is a plethora of items available that feature Italian Greyhounds. These collectibles allow admirers of the breed to display their passion and appreciation for Italian Greyhounds in their homes or personal collections.

Artistic Merchandise:

Italian Greyhound-themed merchandise extends beyond collectibles and includes various artistic creations. Artists and designers have incorporated Italian Greyhound motifs into clothing, accessories, and home decor items. These artistic products allow people to showcase their love for Italian Greyhounds in a fashionable and creative way, spreading awareness and admiration for the breed.

Online Communities and Social Media:

The digital age has provided a platform for Italian Greyhound enthusiasts to connect and share their love for the breed. Online communities and social media platforms have become spaces where artists, photographers, and collectors can come together to showcase their Italian Greyhound-related work. These platforms offer a vibrant and interactive space for individuals to appreciate and celebrate the breed's artistic representation.

Italian Greyhound art, photography, and collectibles serve as a testament to the breed's enduring appeal and the artistic talent it has inspired. Whether through paintings, sculptures, photographs, or collectible items, these creations capture the elegance, grace, and unique personality of Italian Greyhounds. They allow admirers of the breed to bring a piece of their beauty and charm into their everyday lives.

Portraits and Artwork

The Artistry of Italian Greyhound Portraits and Artwork

Italian Greyhounds, with their sleek lines, graceful movements, and expressive features, have captivated artists throughout history. From ancient times to the present day, these elegant dogs have been the subjects of numerous portraits and artwork, showcasing their beauty, charm, and unique character. Below we will delve into the world of Italian Greyhound portraits and artwork, exploring the rich history, diverse styles, and enduring appeal of these artistic representations.

Historical Portraits:

Italian Greyhound portraits date back centuries, reflecting the breed's long history and cultural significance. In ancient Egyptian, Greek, and Roman civilizations, Italian Greyhounds were often depicted in artwork, symbolizing beauty, nobility, and companionship. These early portraits showcased the breed's distinct physical characteristics and their close association with royalty and aristocracy.

Renaissance and Baroque Art:

During the Renaissance and Baroque periods, Italian Greyhound portraits became more prominent in European art. Artists such as Titian and Velázquez included Italian Greyhounds in their paintings, often as companions to their human subjects. These portraits highlighted the breed's elegance and refinement, portraying them as cherished companions of the elite.

Contemporary Art:

Italian Greyhound portraits continue to be created by contemporary artists, reflecting the breed's enduring appeal. Artists use various mediums, including oil paintings, watercolors, drawings, and digital art, to capture the essence of Italian Greyhounds. These modern interpretations explore different styles and techniques, ranging from realistic to abstract, showcasing the versatility and creativity of artists.

Personalized Portraits:

Many Italian Greyhound owners commission personalized portraits of their beloved pets. These commissioned artworks capture the unique characteristics and personality of individual dogs. Artists work closely with owners to ensure the portrayal of their Italian Greyhounds is accurate and emotionally resonant, resulting in treasured keepsakes that celebrate the bond between human and canine.

Sculptures and Statues:

In addition to portraits, Italian Greyhounds have also been immortalized in sculptures and statues. These three-dimensional artworks capture the breed's physical form and capture their grace and elegance. From small figurines to larger public installations, Italian Greyhound sculptures allow art enthusiasts and dog lovers to appreciate the breed's beauty in a tangible and lasting form.

Artistic Interpretations:

Italian Greyhound artwork goes beyond traditional portraiture and explores creative interpretations of the breed. Artists experiment with various styles, colors, and compositions to evoke emotions and tell stories. This can include abstract representations, impressionistic renderings, and even mixed media pieces. These artistic interpretations showcase the breed's versatility as a muse for artistic expression.

Digital Art and Photography:

With the advent of digital technology, Italian Greyhounds have become popular subjects in digital art and photography. Artists and photographers use advanced software and editing techniques to create stunning digital illustrations and capture captivating images of Italian Greyhounds. These digital creations offer a modern and unique perspective on the breed.

Italian Greyhound portraits and artwork not only celebrate the breed's physical beauty but also capture their unique personality, spirit, and connection with humans. They allow us to appreciate the elegance and charm of these dogs, creating a lasting tribute to their presence in our lives.

Photography Tips and Tricks

Capturing the Essence: Photography Tips and Tricks for Italian Greyhounds

Italian Greyhounds, with their graceful movements and expressive features, make captivating subjects for photography. Whether you're a professional photographer or an enthusiastic dog lover with a camera, capturing the essence of these elegant dogs can be a rewarding experience. Below we will explore some tips and tricks to help you capture stunning photographs of Italian Greyhounds, highlighting their beauty, personality, and unique traits.

Understand the Breed:

To capture the essence of Italian Greyhounds in your photographs, it's important to understand their breed characteristics. Learn about their physical features, such as their slender build, long legs, and expressive eyes. Familiarize yourself with their unique traits, such as their gentle and affectionate nature. This knowledge will guide you in capturing their distinctive qualities in your photographs.

Patience is Key:

Italian Greyhounds are known for their energy and agility, which can make it challenging to photograph them. However, patience is key. Allow them to get comfortable with your presence and the camera before starting the photo session. Be prepared to take multiple shots to capture the perfect moment when they are still or displaying their characteristic movements.

Natural Lighting:

Take advantage of natural lighting to enhance your Italian Greyhound photographs. Natural light provides a soft and flattering illumination, highlighting the dog's features and bringing out their natural colors. Avoid using flash, as it can cause red-eye and create harsh shadows. Instead, photograph them near windows or outdoors during the golden hours of early morning or late afternoon for beautiful and warm lighting.

Focus on the Eyes:

The eyes are the windows to the soul, and this holds true for Italian Greyhounds. Focus on their eyes to capture their expressiveness and create a connection between the viewer and the subject. Ensure that the eyes are sharp and in focus, as they can convey the emotions and personality of the dog.

Composition and Background:

Pay attention to the composition of your photographs. Use the rule of thirds to create a visually pleasing composition, placing the Italian Greyhound off-center to add interest to the image. Consider the background and choose one that complements the dog's color and fur. Simple and uncluttered backgrounds allow the focus to remain on the dog, while textured or outdoor environments can add depth and context to the photograph.

Candid Moments:

Capture candid moments that showcase the Italian Greyhound's natural behavior and personality. Allow them to engage in their favorite activities, such as playing or running, and capture their genuine expressions and movements. These candid shots can reveal the spirit and liveliness of the breed.

Get Down to Their Level:

Italian Greyhounds are small dogs, so it's important to get down to their eye level when photographing them. This perspective allows you to capture the world from their point of view, resulting in more intimate and engaging photographs. Kneel down or lie on the ground to capture their unique perspective and showcase their perspective of the world.

Use Props and Accessories:

Consider using props and accessories to add interest and personality to your Italian Greyhound photographs. This could include colorful toys, decorative scarves, or unique settings that reflect their personality. However, ensure that the props and accessories are safe and comfortable for the dog.

Patience, Treats, and Rewards:

Photographing Italian Greyhounds requires patience, treats, and rewards. Use positive reinforcement to keep them engaged and cooperative during the photo session. Reward them with treats and praise for their good behavior, which will help create a positive association with the photography experience.

Collectibles and Memorabilia

Treasures and Tributes: Exploring Italian Greyhound Collectibles and Memorabilia

Italian Greyhounds, with their elegance and charm, have inspired a range of collectibles and memorabilia that celebrate their unique beauty and personality. From figurines and artwork to clothing and accessories, these items provide a way for Italian Greyhound enthusiasts to showcase their love for the breed and create a lasting tribute. Below we will delve into the world of Italian Greyhound collectibles and memorabilia, exploring the fascinating array of items available and the significance they hold for enthusiasts.

Figurines and Sculptures:

One of the most popular forms of Italian Greyhound collectibles is figurines and sculptures. These intricately crafted pieces capture the grace and beauty of the breed in various materials, such as porcelain, resin, or bronze. From lifelike representations to stylized interpretations, these figurines showcase the unique features and characteristics of Italian Greyhounds, making them highly sought after by collectors.

Artwork and Prints:

Artwork and prints featuring Italian Greyhounds are another cherished form of collectibles. Paintings, drawings, and prints capture the essence of the breed's elegance and capture moments frozen in time. These pieces can range from realistic portraits to abstract interpretations, allowing art enthusiasts to appreciate the breed from different artistic perspectives.

Clothing and Accessories:

For Italian Greyhound enthusiasts who want to display their love for the breed, clothing and accessories offer a way to do so in style. T-shirts, hoodies, and hats featuring Italian Greyhound designs allow individuals to proudly showcase their admiration for the breed. Additionally, accessories like jewelry, keychains, and tote bags adorned with Italian Greyhound motifs add a touch of elegance and personalization to everyday items.

Books and Publications:

Books and publications dedicated to Italian Greyhounds provide invaluable resources for breed enthusiasts. These materials offer a wealth of information on topics such as breed history, care, training, and health. From breed-specific guides to memoirs and training manuals, these publications cater to the diverse interests and needs of Italian Greyhound owners and enthusiasts.

Collectible Cards and Trading Cards:

Collectible cards and trading cards featuring Italian Greyhounds have gained popularity among collectors. These cards often showcase individual dogs or memorable moments in the breed's history. They can be collected and traded among enthusiasts, creating a sense of community and camaraderie.

Home Décor and Household Items:

Italian Greyhound-themed home décor and household items allow enthusiasts to infuse their living spaces with their passion for the breed. From throw pillows and blankets to mugs and coasters, these items add a touch of whimsy and charm to any room. Additionally, Italian Greyhound-inspired kitchenware, such as aprons and cutting boards, allow enthusiasts to incorporate their love for the breed into their culinary endeavors.

Calendars and Stationery:

Calendars and stationery featuring Italian Greyhounds are practical yet delightful collectibles. Calendars adorned with captivating photographs of Italian Greyhounds not only serve as functional tools but also bring joy and inspiration throughout the year. Italian Greyhound-themed stationery, including notepads, greeting cards, and journals, provide an elegant way to express one's love for the breed and add a personal touch to correspondence.

Vintage Collectibles:

Vintage Italian Greyhound collectibles hold a special allure for enthusiasts. These items, such as antique figurines, vintage prints, or collectible breed-specific items from the past, offer a glimpse into the breed's history and serve as a nostalgic reminder of its enduring appeal. Collecting vintage Italian Greyhound memorabilia allows enthusiasts to connect with the breed's past and appreciate its continued popularity.

Italian Greyhound Rescue and Adoption

Saving Lives and Finding Forever Homes: Italian Greyhound Rescue and Adoption

Italian Greyhounds, with their delicate beauty and gentle nature, have captured the hearts of dog lovers worldwide. Unfortunately, not all Italian Greyhounds have the privilege of a loving home from the start. Many find themselves in need of rescue and adoption due to various circumstances. Below we will explore the world of Italian Greyhound rescue and adoption, shedding light on the important work carried out by organizations and individuals dedicated to saving and rehoming these precious dogs.

The Need for Rescue:

Italian Greyhounds, like any other breed, may find themselves in need of rescue for various reasons. Some are surrendered by their owners due to life changes or inability to care for them, while others are found as strays or rescued from abusive situations. Additionally, puppy mills and irresponsible breeding practices contribute to the population of Italian Greyhounds in need of rescue. These dogs often require medical attention, rehabilitation, and emotional support before they can find their forever homes.

Rescue Organizations:

Rescue organizations play a vital role in saving and rehoming Italian Greyhounds. These non-profit organizations are dedicated to rescuing, rehabilitating, and finding suitable homes for Italian Greyhounds in need. They provide medical care, socialization, and training to prepare these dogs for their new lives. Additionally, they often educate the public about responsible dog ownership and the specific needs of Italian Greyhounds.

Adoption Process:

The adoption process for Italian Greyhounds typically involves several steps to ensure a suitable match between the dog and the adoptive family. Prospective adopters usually need to complete an application, undergo a screening process, and provide references. Home visits may be conducted to assess the safety and suitability of the environment for the dog. Adoption fees are often required to help cover the costs of rescue, rehabilitation, and ongoing care.

Foster Homes:

Foster homes play a crucial role in Italian Greyhound rescue. These temporary homes provide a safe and nurturing environment for dogs in transition. Foster families offer love, care, and socialization to help the dogs heal and adjust to a home environment. They also assess the dog's temperament, behavior, and compatibility with other animals, which helps in finding the right permanent home.

Breed-specific Rescue vs. General Rescue:

Some rescue organizations specialize in Italian Greyhound rescue, focusing solely on this breed. These breed-specific rescues have extensive knowledge and experience with Italian Greyhounds, allowing them to provide targeted care and support. On the other hand, general rescue organizations may also rescue Italian Greyhounds along with other breeds. Both types of organizations contribute to the welfare of Italian Greyhounds, and potential adopters can explore both options when searching for a new furry family member.

Benefits of Rescue and Adoption:

Rescuing and adopting an Italian Greyhound can be a rewarding experience for both the dog and the adoptive family. By adopting, individuals provide a second chance at life and a loving home for a dog in need. Furthermore, rescued Italian Greyhounds often demonstrate immense gratitude and resilience, forming deep bonds with their adoptive families. Adopting from a rescue organization also helps combat puppy mills and supports ethical breeding practices.

Education and Support:

Italian Greyhound rescue organizations offer educational resources and support to adopters. They provide information about the breed's specific needs, behavior, and health issues. Adopters receive guidance on training, socialization, and nutrition to ensure the well-being of their new companion. Some organizations also offer post-adoption support, including behavioral consultations and networking opportunities with other adopters.

The Importance of Rescue Organizations

Lifesavers and Guardians: The Importance of Rescue Organizations for Italian Greyhounds

Rescue organizations play a pivotal role in the welfare and well-being of Italian Greyhounds, providing them with a second chance at life and finding them loving forever homes. These dedicated organizations tirelessly work to rescue, rehabilitate, and rehome Italian Greyhounds in need. Below we will explore the significance of rescue organizations in the context of Italian Greyhounds, highlighting their vital contributions and the impact they have on the lives of these remarkable dogs.

Saving Lives:

Rescue organizations are a lifeline for Italian Greyhounds facing challenging circumstances. They step in to save dogs from neglect, abuse, abandonment, or situations where their owners can no longer care for them. Without the intervention of rescue organizations, these dogs would be left vulnerable and at risk. By providing immediate rescue and safe shelter, these organizations ensure the physical and emotional well-being of Italian Greyhounds in need.

Rehabilitation and Medical Care:

Italian Greyhounds that come into rescue organizations often require specialized care and rehabilitation. Many have suffered neglect or abuse, resulting in physical and emotional trauma. Rescue organizations work diligently to address these issues, providing essential medical care, vaccinations, spaying or neutering, and addressing any health concerns. Additionally, they offer behavioral rehabilitation, socialization, and training to help these dogs overcome their past experiences and develop into well-adjusted companions.

Matching Dogs with Suitable Homes:

One of the core responsibilities of rescue organizations is to find suitable forever homes for the Italian Greyhounds in their care. This process involves comprehensive adoption applications, interviews, and home visits to ensure that potential adopters are prepared and equipped to meet the needs of an Italian Greyhound. By carefully matching dogs with responsible and committed families, rescue organizations strive to create successful and lasting human-canine relationships.

Breed Knowledge and Expertise:

Rescue organizations specializing in Italian Greyhounds possess valuable breed-specific knowledge and expertise. They understand the unique characteristics, temperament, and care requirements of Italian Greyhounds, allowing them to provide tailored care and support. This specialized knowledge helps ensure that Italian Greyhounds find homes where their specific needs will be met and that adopters receive accurate information about the breed.

Fostering:

Fostering is a crucial component of rescue organizations' work. Foster homes provide temporary care and support to Italian Greyhounds before they are placed in their permanent homes. Fosters offer a loving and nurturing environment, helping dogs transition from their previous circumstances and gain vital socialization and behavioral skills. Foster homes also provide valuable insights into the dog's personality, temperament, and compatibility with other animals, aiding in the placement process.

Education and Outreach:

Rescue organizations play a vital role in educating the public about Italian Greyhounds, responsible dog ownership, and the importance of adoption. They raise awareness about the breed's unique qualities, care requirements, and potential challenges. Through outreach programs, educational materials, and community events, rescue organizations strive to dispel myths, promote ethical breeding practices, and encourage the adoption of Italian Greyhounds rather than purchasing from irresponsible sources.

Networking and Collaboration:

Rescue organizations actively network and collaborate with other organizations, animal shelters, and breed-specific groups to increase their reach and impact. They work together to share resources, information, and expertise, ensuring the best possible outcomes for Italian Greyhounds in need. Collaboration helps facilitate the transfer of dogs from high-kill shelters, coordinate medical interventions, and provide support in emergency situations.

Preparing for an Adopted Italian Greyhound

A New Beginning: Preparing for an Adopted Italian Greyhound

Adopting an Italian Greyhound is an exciting and fulfilling decision. These elegant and affectionate dogs bring joy and companionship to their new families. However, preparing for the arrival of an adopted Italian Greyhound requires careful planning and consideration. Below we will explore the essential steps to take in preparing for the arrival of your adopted Italian Greyhound, ensuring a smooth transition and a happy life together.

Home Environment:

Creating a safe and welcoming home environment is crucial for your newly adopted Italian Greyhound. Start by designating a comfortable and secure space where your dog can rest and feel at ease. Provide a cozy bed, blankets, and a crate if you plan to crate train. Ensure that your home is free of hazards such as toxic plants, loose electrical cords, and small objects that could be swallowed. Secure any areas that you want to keep off-limits using baby gates or closed doors.

Basic Supplies:

Before bringing your Italian Greyhound home, gather the necessary supplies. These include food and water bowls, a collar or harness, a leash, and identification tags. Purchase high-quality dog food suitable for Italian Greyhounds, considering their specific nutritional needs. Have a few toys and chew bones available to keep your new companion entertained and mentally stimulated.

Veterinary Care:

Schedule a visit to the veterinarian soon after adopting your Italian Greyhound. A comprehensive physical examination will ensure that your dog is in good health and identify any underlying issues. Discuss vaccinations, parasite prevention, and spaying or neutering if it hasn't been done already. Establish a regular preventive care routine, including regular check-ups and dental care, to keep your Italian Greyhound healthy and happy.

House Training:

House training is an essential aspect of preparing for your adopted Italian Greyhound. Establish a consistent routine for bathroom breaks, using positive reinforcement to reward your dog's desired behavior. Set up a designated bathroom area in your yard, and establish a regular schedule for outdoor potty breaks. Patience and consistency are key during the house training process, as it may take time for your Italian Greyhound to adjust to the new routine.

Socialization:

Italian Greyhounds, like all dogs, benefit from socialization with people and other animals. Introduce your Italian Greyhound to various environments, sounds, and experiences in a positive and controlled manner. Take them on outings to meet other dogs and people, ensuring that the interactions are calm and positive. Gradually expose them to new environments, such as parks or pet-friendly establishments, to help build their confidence and promote positive social behaviors.

Training and Obedience:

Training is an essential part of helping your Italian Greyhound become a well-behaved and obedient companion. Enroll in obedience classes or seek the assistance of a professional dog trainer to guide you in teaching basic commands and leash manners. Positive reinforcement techniques, such as treats and praise, work well with Italian Greyhounds, as they respond positively to rewards and gentle guidance. Consistency and patience are vital during the training process.

Establishing Routines:

Italian Greyhounds thrive on routine and structure. Establishing consistent daily routines for feeding, exercise, playtime, and rest will help your dog feel secure and reduce anxiety. Create a regular schedule for meals and stick to it. Designate specific times for walks and play sessions, providing both physical and mental stimulation. A predictable routine will help your Italian Greyhound adjust quickly and feel more secure in their new home.

Success Stories and Testimonials

Triumph and Transformation: Inspiring Success Stories and Testimonials of Italian Greyhounds

Italian Greyhounds have the power to transform lives and bring immeasurable joy to their adoptive families. Many heartwarming success stories and testimonials demonstrate the remarkable impact these gentle and graceful dogs have on their human companions. Below we will explore a collection of inspiring success stories and testimonials related to Italian Greyhounds, highlighting their ability to uplift spirits, foster resilience, and create lifelong bonds.

From Neglect to Nurturing:

Some Italian Greyhounds have endured neglect or abuse before finding their forever homes. Their success stories reflect the incredible resilience of these dogs and the transformative power of love and care. These once-timid and fearful dogs blossom into confident and affectionate companions when given a nurturing environment. Adopters recount the journey of watching their Italian Greyhounds heal emotionally, gradually overcoming their past traumas and learning to trust again.

Therapy and Emotional Support:

Italian Greyhounds have a special way of providing comfort and emotional support to their human companions. Many success stories revolve around the therapeutic bond between Italian Greyhounds and individuals facing physical or emotional challenges. These dogs have shown a remarkable ability to intuitively sense and respond to their human's needs, offering solace, companionship, and a source of joy during difficult times.

Rescued and Rescuer:

Rescue stories highlight the incredible bond that forms between an Italian Greyhound and their adoptive family. These stories often involve a mutual transformation, where the dog rescues the family just as much as they are rescued. Adopters describe the profound impact of their Italian Greyhound's presence, crediting their four-legged companion with bringing laughter, love, and a renewed sense of purpose to their lives.

Overcoming Challenges:

Italian Greyhounds are not exempt from facing their own challenges, including health issues or physical disabilities. However, their success stories showcase their resilience and the determination of their adoptive families to provide them with the best possible care. These stories depict Italian Greyhounds thriving despite obstacles, inspiring others with their indomitable spirit and ability to embrace life to the fullest.

Lifelong Companionship:

Success stories and testimonials often emphasize the enduring bond and companionship that Italian Greyhounds bring to their adoptive families. From creating cherished memories to providing unwavering loyalty, these dogs become cherished members of the family. Adopters recount the joy of sharing adventures, celebrations, and even quiet moments with their Italian Greyhounds, solidifying a lifelong connection that enriches their lives.

Therapy and Service Work:

Italian Greyhounds have also made significant contributions as therapy dogs and service animals. Their gentle and empathetic nature, combined with their compact size, make them well-suited for therapy work, bringing comfort to individuals in hospitals, nursing homes, and other care facilities. Success stories in this realm highlight the positive impact Italian Greyhounds have on individuals in need, offering companionship and emotional support in therapeutic settings.

Community Engagement:

Italian Greyhounds and their adoptive families often become active participants in community events and activities. Success stories detail the involvement of Italian Greyhounds in fundraisers, awareness campaigns, and dog-friendly gatherings. These dogs become ambassadors for the breed, captivating the hearts of those they encounter and educating the public about the unique qualities and care requirements of Italian Greyhounds.

Inspiration and Advocacy:

The success stories of Italian Greyhounds inspire others to consider adoption, promoting the importance of giving these dogs a second chance. Testimonials often express gratitude for the positive impact the Italian Greyhound has had on their lives and encourage others to experience the unconditional love and joy these dogs bring.

Italian Greyhounds in the Show Ring

Grace and Elegance: Italian Greyhounds in the Show Ring

Italian Greyhounds, with their slender physique and graceful movements, have captured the attention of dog enthusiasts around the world. These remarkable dogs not only make wonderful companions but also excel in the show ring. Below we will explore the captivating world of Italian Greyhounds in the show ring, shedding light on the dedication, training, and beauty that defines their participation in dog shows.

Breed Standards and Conformation:

Italian Greyhounds participate in dog shows that assess their adherence to breed standards and conformation. The American Kennel Club (AKC) and other kennel clubs outline specific criteria that judges evaluate, including size, proportion, coat color and texture, head shape, eyes, ears, and overall structure. Dogs that come closest to meeting these standards are recognized for their exceptional conformation.

Selecting Show Prospects:

Breeding and show enthusiasts carefully select Italian Greyhounds with the potential to excel in the show ring. They consider various factors, such as pedigree, physical attributes, and temperament. Show prospects must possess the ideal traits outlined in the breed standard and exhibit the grace and elegance characteristic of Italian Greyhounds. Breeders evaluate puppies based on their structure, movement, and overall presence to determine their show potential.

Training and Conditioning:

Preparing an Italian Greyhound for the show ring involves diligent training and conditioning. Show dogs undergo training to learn how to walk, stand, and move gracefully. They must become comfortable with being examined by judges, allowing them to assess their physical attributes. Handlers focus on teaching dogs to show their best side and highlight their breed-specific features. Additionally, conditioning exercises, such as regular exercise and proper nutrition, help maintain the dog's physical fitness and overall health.

Handling and Presentation:

Handlers play a crucial role in showcasing Italian Greyhounds in the show ring. They must present the dog's conformation and movement in the most favorable light. Handlers work on developing a harmonious partnership with the dog, using subtle cues and commands to guide their movements and maintain the desired show posture. Skilled handlers understand how to accentuate the dog's strengths and minimize any potential flaws.

Ring Etiquette and Sportsmanship:

Dog shows adhere to a strict code of ring etiquette and sportsmanship. Handlers and exhibitors must demonstrate professionalism, respect, and fair play throughout the competition. They maintain a calm demeanor, present their dogs in a positive light, and refrain from any actions that could disrupt the show environment. Exhibitors are encouraged to support and appreciate the achievements of their fellow competitors, fostering a sense of camaraderie within the show community.

Competitive Classes:

Italian Greyhounds compete in various classes based on age, sex, and experience. Classes include Puppy, Bred-by-Exhibitor, Open, and Specials. In each class, dogs are assessed against others of the same sex and age group. The winners of each class then compete for Best of Breed, where the best Italian Greyhound is selected from those that have competed. The top dogs may then progress to compete for Group placements and ultimately Best in Show.

Breeders and Breed Promotion:

Participation in dog shows is not only a chance to showcase individual Italian Greyhounds but also an opportunity for breeders to promote their breeding programs and the overall betterment of the breed. Responsible breeders aim to produce Italian Greyhounds that exemplify the breed standard, possess good health, and demonstrate desirable temperament. Their dedication to preserving the breed's heritage and improving its qualities is highlighted through their show dogs.

Breed Standards and Judging Criteria

The Art of Assessment: Breed Standards and Judging Criteria for Italian Greyhounds

In the world of dog shows, breed standards and judging criteria provide a blueprint for evaluating and recognizing excellence in various breeds. Italian Greyhounds, with their graceful and elegant demeanor, are no exception. Below we will explore the intricacies of breed standards and judging criteria specific to Italian Greyhounds, uncovering the qualities and characteristics that judges assess to determine the epitome of the breed.

Breed Standards:

Breed standards serve as a benchmark for evaluating the ideal representation of a particular breed. These standards define the specific physical and behavioral traits that define the breed's essence. The American Kennel Club (AKC) and other kennel clubs outline the Italian Greyhound breed standard, which acts as a guide for breeders, exhibitors, and judges. Breed standards encompass various aspects, including size, proportion, head shape, eyes, ears, coat color and texture, and overall structure.

Size and Proportion:

Italian Greyhounds possess a distinct size and proportion that contribute to their unique charm. According to breed standards, Italian Greyhounds should ideally stand between 13 and 15 inches at the shoulder, with males slightly larger than females. They should have a well-balanced and proportionate body, with a slender build and long, graceful legs. Judges evaluate dogs to ensure they conform to these specific size and proportion requirements.

Head and Expression:

The head of an Italian Greyhound is a defining feature that reflects the breed's elegance and intelligence. The breed standard describes the ideal head shape, which should be long and narrow, with a slight stop and a well-defined jawline. Judges examine the head for proper proportions and evaluate the expression, seeking a sweet and intelligent expression in the dog's eyes. They also assess the nose pigment, which should be black or dark in color.

Eyes and Ears:

Italian Greyhounds have expressive eyes that reflect their sensitivity and attentiveness. Breed standards specify that the eyes should be medium-sized, oval-shaped, and dark in color. Judges examine the eyes to ensure they are bright and alert. The shape and placement of the eyes contribute to the overall expression of the dog. Ears, which are thin and fine, should be set high on the head, with a fold that brings them forward.

Coat Color and Texture:

Italian Greyhounds showcase a variety of coat colors, which are carefully evaluated in the show ring. Breed standards outline permissible colors, including solid colors such as black, blue, fawn, and red, as well as various shades of brindle. The coat should be short, glossy, and fine in texture, accentuating the sleek and elegant appearance of the breed. Judges assess the coat color and texture to ensure adherence to breed standards.

Structure and Movement:

The structure and movement of Italian Greyhounds are critical components of breed standards. Judges evaluate the dog's overall structure, looking for a well-balanced body with a level topline, a deep chest, and a strong yet refined bone structure. The front and rear angulation should be moderate, allowing for efficient and fluid movement. When assessing movement, judges seek a free, flowing gait that showcases the breed's elegance and grace.

Temperament and Behavior:

Although temperament and behavior are not explicitly outlined in breed standards, they play a significant role in assessing Italian Greyhounds in the show ring. Judges observe the dogs' overall demeanor, seeking a gentle, affectionate, and intelligent temperament. Italian Greyhounds should display confidence and a willingness to engage with the handler. Dogs that exhibit fear, aggression, or excessive shyness are typically penalized in the show ring.

Preparing Your Italian Greyhound for the Show Ring

Striving for Success: Preparing Your Italian Greyhound for the Show Ring

Entering your Italian Greyhound into the show ring can be an exciting and rewarding experience. However, it requires careful preparation to showcase your dog's beauty, grace, and adherence to breed standards. Below we will explore the essential steps in preparing your Italian Greyhound for the show ring, ensuring that they are in top form and ready to make a lasting impression.

Understand Breed Standards:

Before embarking on the show ring journey, familiarize yourself with the Italian Greyhound breed standards established by kennel clubs such as the American Kennel Club (AKC). Study the guidelines regarding size, proportion, head shape, eyes, ears, coat color and texture, and overall structure. Understanding these standards will allow you to assess your Italian Greyhound objectively and present them in the best possible light.

Physical Conditioning:

Physical conditioning plays a crucial role in preparing your Italian Greyhound for the show ring. Regular exercise helps maintain their overall health, stamina, and muscle tone. Engage in activities that promote cardiovascular fitness, such as brisk walks, jogs, or play sessions. Conditioning exercises, such as trotting or running on different terrains, help improve their movement and balance. Consult with a veterinarian or a professional trainer for a tailored exercise regimen.

Grooming and Coat Care:

Grooming your Italian Greyhound is essential to showcase their coat's beauty and texture. Regular brushing removes loose hairs and keeps the coat smooth and glossy. Pay particular attention to sensitive areas such as the ears, paws, and tail. Bathing should be done as needed, using a gentle dog shampoo. Maintain the nails at a proper length and ensure that the teeth are clean and free from plaque buildup. Professional grooming assistance may be beneficial to achieve show-ready presentation.

Socialization and Behavioral Training:

Socialization is a crucial aspect of preparing your Italian Greyhound for the show ring. Expose them to different environments, sounds, and experiences to build their confidence and ensure they remain calm and composed during the show. Arrange playdates and interactions with other dogs to encourage positive social behaviors. Basic obedience training, including commands such as "sit," "stay," and "heel," helps establish control and cooperation in the show ring.

Ring Training and Handling:

Ring training familiarizes your Italian Greyhound with the show ring environment and prepares them for the expectations of a show. Practice walking in a straight line, trotting, and standing still, allowing the judge to examine them. Teach your dog to respond to handling, including being touched and examined by strangers. Collaborate with a professional handler or attend handling classes to learn techniques specific to Italian Greyhounds and refine your presentation skills.

Attire and Accessories:

Choosing appropriate attire and accessories enhances your Italian Greyhound's appearance in the show ring. Select a well-fitted and clean show lead that complements your dog's coat color. Opt for simple and elegant attire that does not distract from your dog's presentation. Avoid excessive accessories or decorations that may take away from the focus on your Italian Greyhound's conformation and movement.

Practice and Rehearsal:

Consistent practice and rehearsal are essential for both you and your Italian Greyhound. Establish a routine that includes ring training sessions, where you simulate the show ring environment and practice gaiting, stacking, and standing still. Focus on maintaining a calm and relaxed atmosphere, ensuring that your dog is comfortable and responsive to your commands. Monitor their behavior and make adjustments as necessary to achieve the desired presentation.

Tips for Success in Competitions Breeding Italian Greyhounds

Achieving Excellence: Tips for Success in Competitively Breeding Italian Greyhounds

Breeding Italian Greyhounds is both an art and a science, requiring dedication, knowledge, and a passion for the breed. Competitions play a crucial role in evaluating breeding stock and maintaining the breed's integrity. Below we will explore essential tips for success in competitively breeding Italian Greyhounds, providing insights into the factors to consider, the breeding process, and the significance of competitions in advancing the breed.

Understand the Breed Standard:

A deep understanding of the Italian Greyhound breed standard is fundamental to successful breeding. Familiarize yourself with the specific criteria outlined by kennel clubs such as the American Kennel Club (AKC). Study the ideal size, proportion, structure, coat color and texture, head shape, eyes, ears, and temperament. Breeding decisions should be guided by the goal of producing Italian Greyhounds that conform to these standards and exemplify the breed's unique characteristics.

Select Quality Breeding Stock:

Selecting high-quality breeding stock is paramount in achieving success. Evaluate potential breeding dogs based on their adherence to the breed standard, health clearances, temperament, and genetic background. Look for dogs with proven lineage, including show champions or dogs that have excelled in various competitive venues. Consult with experienced breeders, mentors, and professionals to assist in identifying suitable breeding partners that complement each other's strengths.

Health Testing:

Maintaining the health and genetic integrity of the breed is of utmost importance in competitive breeding. Conduct thorough health tests to screen for potential hereditary conditions and genetic abnormalities. Common health tests for Italian Greyhounds include hip evaluations, eye examinations, and DNA tests for specific genetic disorders. Breeding dogs with good health clearances reduces the risk of passing on genetic issues and contributes to the overall well-being of the breed.

Pedigree Analysis:

Analyzing pedigrees helps assess the genetic potential and compatibility of breeding dogs. Study the pedigrees of prospective mating partners, considering the strengths, weaknesses, and common ancestors within the lineage. Look for dogs with consistent performance, conformation, and health attributes throughout their ancestry. A well-planned pedigree analysis enhances the likelihood of producing offspring that embody the desired traits and characteristics.

Breeding Management:

Effective breeding management is essential in maximizing breeding success. Pay attention to the timing of breeding to optimize fertility and increase the chances of conception. Consult with a veterinarian for guidance on the reproductive cycle and the most opportune time for mating. Consider factors such as the age and health of the dogs, as well as the overall goals of the breeding program. Ensure proper nutrition, regular veterinary care, and a safe and comfortable breeding environment.

Puppy Socialization and Early Development:

Early socialization and development are crucial for the well-being and success of the puppies produced. Implement a comprehensive socialization program that exposes the puppies to various environments, people, sounds, and experiences. This helps them become well-rounded and adaptable companions. Additionally, provide appropriate mental and physical stimulation to promote their learning and growth during the early stages of development.

Competing in Shows and Performance Events:

Competitions, such as conformation shows and performance events, are valuable platforms for evaluating breeding stock and showcasing the breed's qualities. Participate in reputable shows and events to receive feedback from experienced judges and breeders. These competitions provide opportunities to compare breeding stock with others, assess their adherence to the breed standard, and identify areas for improvement. Successful participation in competitions helps validate breeding choices and advances the breed's quality.

Responsible Breeding Practices

Upholding Excellence: Responsible Breeding Practices for Italian Greyhounds

Responsible breeding practices form the foundation of maintaining and improving the integrity of dog breeds. For Italian Greyhounds, a breed known for its elegance and grace, responsible breeding is essential to preserve their unique qualities and ensure their overall health and well-being. Below we will explore the principles and practices that contribute to responsible breeding for Italian Greyhounds, highlighting the importance of ethical decisions, health considerations, and responsible ownership.

Knowledge and Understanding:

Responsible breeders possess a deep knowledge and understanding of the Italian Greyhound breed. They familiarize themselves with the breed standard, studying the desired size, proportions, structure, coat color and texture, head shape, eyes, ears, and temperament. Breeders continually educate themselves about the breed's history, genetic traits, and potential health issues. This knowledge allows them to make informed decisions that align with the breed's integrity and well-being.

Breed Preservation:

Preserving the unique qualities and characteristics of Italian Greyhounds is a primary goal of responsible breeding. Breeders carefully select breeding pairs that complement each other, working toward maintaining the breed standard and enhancing desirable traits. They prioritize producing healthy, well-tempered puppies that embody the breed's elegance, intelligence, and overall conformation. Through responsible breeding practices, Italian Greyhounds can continue to flourish and thrive for generations to come.

Health Testing and Screening:

Responsible breeders prioritize the health and well-being of their Italian Greyhounds. They conduct thorough health testing and screening to minimize the risk of hereditary diseases and genetic abnormalities. Health tests may include hip evaluations, eye examinations, cardiac evaluations, and DNA tests for specific genetic disorders. By screening breeding dogs, breeders can make informed decisions to reduce the incidence of inherited health issues and improve the overall health of the breed.

Genetic Diversity:

Maintaining genetic diversity is a crucial aspect of responsible breeding. Breeders strive to avoid excessive inbreeding or linebreeding, as it can lead to an increased risk of inherited disorders and reduced overall vigor. Responsible breeders carefully analyze pedigrees and genetic backgrounds to ensure a diverse gene pool for future generations. They may collaborate with other breeders to introduce new bloodlines and broaden the genetic diversity within the Italian Greyhound population.

Selective Breeding:

Selective breeding is an essential component of responsible breeding practices. Breeders carefully select breeding dogs based on their adherence to the breed standard, health clearances, temperament, and genetic background. They aim to improve upon the existing qualities of the breed, focusing on conformation, temperament, and overall health. Selective breeding helps ensure that future generations of Italian Greyhounds maintain the desired traits while minimizing the risk of inherited disorders.

Responsible Ownership:

Responsible breeding extends beyond the breeding program itself. Breeders emphasize responsible ownership, ensuring that the Italian Greyhounds they produce are placed in suitable, loving homes. They carefully screen potential buyers, taking into account their knowledge of the breed, their ability to provide a suitable environment, and their commitment to the dog's lifelong care. Responsible breeders prioritize the well-being and happiness of their puppies, emphasizing responsible ownership as a cornerstone of their breeding practices.

Ethical Sales and Contracts:

Responsible breeders maintain high ethical standards when it comes to selling their Italian Greyhound puppies. They provide potential buyers with accurate information about the breed, including its needs, temperament, and potential health concerns. They ensure that puppies are properly socialized, dewormed, and vaccinated before they go to their new homes. Responsible breeders also use contracts to protect the welfare of their puppies, including provisions for returning the dog if the buyer is unable to keep it.

Genetic Testing and Health Considerations

Preserving Well-being: Genetic Testing and Health Considerations for Italian Greyhounds

Genetic testing and health considerations play a vital role in ensuring the well-being and longevity of dog breeds, including the beloved Italian Greyhound. These proactive measures help identify potential health risks, prevent inherited disorders, and promote responsible breeding practices. Below we will explore the significance of genetic testing and health considerations in relation to Italian Greyhounds, highlighting the importance of informed decisions and the overall welfare of the breed.

Understanding Genetic Testing:

Genetic testing involves analyzing an individual's DNA to identify specific genetic mutations or markers associated with certain diseases or traits. For Italian Greyhounds, genetic testing helps breeders and owners make informed decisions about breeding, early disease detection, and overall health management. Advances in veterinary genetics have made it possible to identify various inherited disorders and traits specific to the breed.

Health Conditions in Italian Greyhounds:

Italian Greyhounds are generally a healthy breed, but like any other, they can be susceptible to specific health conditions. Responsible breeders prioritize the health of their breeding dogs and utilize genetic testing to screen for potential issues. Some common health conditions in Italian Greyhounds include patellar luxation, progressive retinal atrophy (PRA), primary lens luxation (PLL), and autoimmune thyroiditis. Genetic testing helps identify carriers of these conditions and allows breeders to make informed breeding decisions to reduce the risk of passing on these disorders.

Hip Evaluations:

Hip dysplasia is a common orthopedic condition that can affect dogs, including Italian Greyhounds. Responsible breeders often conduct hip evaluations to assess the quality of the hip joint and determine if dysplasia is present. Radiographs are taken and evaluated by veterinary professionals using standardized scoring systems, such as the Orthopedic Foundation for Animals (OFA) or the PennHIP method. Breeders can use these evaluations to make informed decisions about breeding dogs and reduce the risk of passing on hip dysplasia.

Eye Examinations:

Regular eye examinations are essential for Italian Greyhounds to identify and manage potential ocular disorders. Conditions such as progressive retinal atrophy (PRA) and cataracts can impact vision and quality of life. Breeders should have their dogs' eyes examined by a veterinary ophthalmologist to detect any abnormalities. Regular eye examinations also help ensure the overall health of the breed and reduce the incidence of hereditary eye diseases.

DNA Testing for Specific Genetic Disorders:

Advancements in DNA testing have made it possible to detect specific genetic disorders in Italian Greyhounds. Responsible breeders use DNA tests to identify carriers and affected individuals for conditions such as progressive retinal atrophy (PRA), primary lens luxation (PLL), and von Willebrand's disease (vWD). DNA testing allows breeders to make informed breeding decisions and reduce the risk of passing on these disorders to future generations.

Responsible Breeding Decisions:

Genetic testing and health considerations enable responsible breeders to make informed decisions when selecting breeding pairs. By screening potential breeding dogs for genetic disorders, breeders can reduce the risk of producing offspring affected by inherited conditions. They can use the test results to select mates that are genetically compatible, minimizing the chance of producing puppies with these disorders. Responsible breeding decisions prioritize the health and well-being of the breed and work towards reducing the overall incidence of genetic disorders.

Improved Breed Health:

Through genetic testing and health considerations, breeders contribute to the overall health and longevity of the Italian Greyhound breed. By selectively breeding dogs with clear health test results and low-risk genetic profiles, breeders help reduce the prevalence of inherited diseases within the breed.

Whelping and Puppy Care

Welcoming New Life: Whelping and Puppy Care for Italian Greyhounds

The arrival of a litter of puppies is an exciting and joyous occasion for both breeders and owners. Proper whelping and puppy care are crucial in ensuring the health, well-being, and successful development of Italian Greyhound puppies. Below we will explore the essential aspects of whelping and puppy care specific to Italian Greyhounds, shedding light on the whelping process, newborn care, socialization, and early development.

Preparing for Whelping:

Whelping refers to the process of giving birth to puppies. Before the expected due date, breeders should create a safe and comfortable whelping area. This area should be quiet, warm, and free from drafts. Provide a whelping box with low sides to prevent the puppies from wandering off and ensure the mother's comfort during labor. Stock up on essential supplies such as clean towels, sterile scissors, lubricant, and an emergency contact number for a veterinarian.

Signs of Labor:

Recognizing the signs of labor is crucial in ensuring a smooth whelping process. The pregnant Italian Greyhound may exhibit restlessness, nesting behavior, loss of appetite, and a drop in body temperature prior to labor. As labor begins, the mother may pant, show discomfort, and exhibit contractions. Monitoring the mother closely during this time helps breeders provide support and timely intervention if needed.

Assisting the Whelping Process:

Italian Greyhounds generally handle the whelping process without much assistance. However, breeders should be present to provide comfort, reassurance, and assistance if complications arise. It is important to maintain a calm and quiet environment, allowing the mother to focus on the task at hand. Breeders should monitor the progress of each puppy's delivery, ensuring they are breathing and responding. In case of difficulties, such as prolonged labor or a stuck puppy, consult with a veterinarian for guidance.

Newborn Care:

After the puppies are born, breeders should attend to their immediate needs. Clear the puppies' airways by gently wiping their noses and mouths with a clean towel. Ensure that each puppy is nursing and receiving colostrum, which provides vital antibodies for their immune system. Monitor the puppies' weight gain to ensure they are thriving. Keep the whelping area clean and warm, and observe the puppies for any signs of illness or distress.

Nutrition and Feeding:

Proper nutrition is essential for the growth and development of Italian Greyhound puppies. The mother's milk provides optimal nutrition during the first few weeks of life. Breeders should ensure that the mother receives a balanced diet to support milk production. As the puppies grow, breeders may introduce a gradual transition to a high-quality, age-appropriate puppy food. Consult with a veterinarian for guidance on feeding schedules, portion sizes, and suitable food options.

Socialization and Handling:

Early socialization and gentle handling are critical for Italian Greyhound puppies' development. Breeders should introduce the puppies to various sights, sounds, and experiences to build their confidence and prepare them for future interactions. Regular handling helps puppies become comfortable with human touch and promotes their overall socialization. It is important to provide positive and age-appropriate stimuli while being mindful of the puppies' limitations and individual temperaments.

Vaccinations and Veterinary Care:

Vaccinations and veterinary care are essential components of responsible puppy care. Breeders should follow a veterinarian-recommended vaccination schedule to protect the puppies against common diseases. Regular veterinary check-ups ensure that the puppies are growing and developing appropriately. Veterinarians can provide advice on parasite prevention, dental care, and any specific health concerns related to Italian Greyhounds.

Living in Harmony with Your Italian Greyhound

A Serene Partnership: Living in Harmony with Your Italian Greyhound

Italian Greyhounds, with their elegance, grace, and affectionate nature, make wonderful companions. Living in harmony with your Italian Greyhound requires understanding their unique characteristics, meeting their physical and emotional needs, and establishing a strong bond based on trust and respect. Below we will explore the essential elements of living in harmony with your Italian Greyhound, focusing on their temperament, exercise requirements, training, grooming, and health considerations.

Understanding the Temperament:

Italian Greyhounds possess a gentle and sensitive temperament. They are known for their loyalty and devotion to their human companions. Understanding their temperament helps create a harmonious living environment. Italian Greyhounds thrive on companionship and may develop separation anxiety if left alone for long periods. Being aware of their emotional needs and providing them with love, attention, and companionship fosters a strong and harmonious bond.

Exercise and Mental Stimulation:

Although Italian Greyhounds are a small breed, they have a surprising amount of energy. Regular exercise and mental stimulation are essential to keep them physically and mentally healthy. Daily walks, interactive play sessions, and opportunities for off-leash exploration in a safe and secure area allow Italian Greyhounds to expend their energy. Engage in activities that provide mental stimulation, such as puzzle toys or obedience training, to prevent boredom and promote a harmonious living environment.

Positive Reinforcement Training:

Training is an integral part of living in harmony with your Italian Greyhound. Positive reinforcement training techniques, such as reward-based methods and clicker training, are highly effective with this breed. Italian Greyhounds are intelligent and eager to please, making them responsive to positive and gentle guidance. Use praise, treats, and playtime as rewards to reinforce desired behaviors. Consistency, patience, and positive reinforcement foster a harmonious and cooperative relationship with your Italian Greyhound.

Grooming and Coat Care:

Maintaining a regular grooming routine contributes to the overall well-being and appearance of your Italian Greyhound. Their short, fine coat requires minimal grooming but benefits from weekly brushing to remove loose hairs and keep the coat shiny. Pay special attention to dental care, as Italian Greyhounds are prone to dental issues. Regular teeth brushing and professional dental cleanings help prevent periodontal disease and maintain good oral hygiene. Keep the nails trimmed and check the ears regularly for cleanliness and signs of infection.

Healthy Diet and Veterinary Care:

Providing a healthy diet and regular veterinary care are essential components of living in harmony with your Italian Greyhound. Consult with a veterinarian to determine the most appropriate diet for your dog's age, size, and specific nutritional needs. Italian Greyhounds can be prone to certain health conditions, such as dental disease, patellar luxation, and autoimmune thyroiditis. Regular veterinary check-ups, vaccinations, preventive care, and appropriate health screenings help maintain their well-being and detect any potential health issues early.

Establishing Boundaries and Consistency:

Establishing boundaries and maintaining consistency in expectations and routines create a harmonious living environment for both you and your Italian Greyhound. Set clear rules and boundaries from the beginning and consistently reinforce them. Use positive reinforcement to reward desirable behaviors and redirect or ignore undesirable ones. Consistency in training, daily routines, and expectations helps Italian Greyhounds understand their place in the household and fosters a sense of security and balance.

Environmental Enrichment:

Providing environmental enrichment is crucial to prevent boredom and destructive behaviors. Italian Greyhounds are intelligent and curious, requiring mental stimulation beyond physical exercise. Offer interactive toys, puzzle games, and treat-dispensing toys to engage their minds. Rotate toys and provide new challenges to keep them mentally engaged.

Creating a Safe and Comfortable Environment

A Haven of Comfort: Creating a Safe and Comfortable Environment for Your Italian Greyhound

Creating a safe and comfortable environment for your Italian Greyhound is essential for their overall well-being and happiness. Italian Greyhounds are sensitive, affectionate, and love to be close to their human companions. Below we will explore the key elements of creating a safe and comfortable environment for your Italian Greyhound, focusing on the importance of a secure living space, adequate shelter, temperature regulation, a balanced diet, and mental stimulation.

Secure Living Space:

Providing a secure living space is paramount for the safety of your Italian Greyhound. Ensure that your home and outdoor areas are securely fenced to prevent accidental escapes. Italian Greyhounds have a natural prey drive, and their slender build allows them to fit through small openings. Regularly inspect the fencing for any gaps or weak spots that could pose a risk. Supervise outdoor activities to ensure their safety and prevent encounters with potential hazards or other animals.

Adequate Shelter:

Italian Greyhounds thrive when they have a designated space within the home that they can call their own. Provide a comfortable and cozy area for your Italian Greyhound to rest and relax. Consider providing a dog bed or a soft blanket in a quiet corner of your home where they can retreat when they need their own space. This not only gives them a sense of security but also helps prevent unwanted behaviors that may arise from anxiety or stress.

Temperature Regulation:

Italian Greyhounds are sensitive to extreme temperatures, both hot and cold. Ensure that your Italian Greyhound is protected from temperature extremes in your home. During the hot summer months, provide access to a cool and shaded area, and avoid prolonged exposure to the sun. In colder weather, consider providing them with a warm and cozy sweater or jacket when outdoors. Inside the home, maintain a comfortable temperature to keep your Italian Greyhound at ease.

Balanced Diet and Fresh Water:

A balanced diet is vital for the health and well-being of your Italian Greyhound. Provide them with a high-quality, nutritionally balanced dog food that suits their specific needs. Consult with a veterinarian to determine the appropriate portion sizes and feeding schedule based on your dog's age, weight, and activity level. Ensure that fresh, clean water is always available for your Italian Greyhound to stay hydrated throughout the day.

Mental Stimulation:

Italian Greyhounds are intelligent dogs that require mental stimulation to prevent boredom and destructive behaviors. Engage your Italian Greyhound in activities that challenge their minds and provide outlets for their natural instincts. Interactive toys, puzzle games, and treat-dispensing toys can keep them mentally engaged and entertained. Regular walks, play sessions, and training exercises also help provide mental stimulation while strengthening the bond between you and your Italian Greyhound.

Safe Households Items and Plants:

Ensure that your home is free from potential hazards for your Italian Greyhound. Keep household cleaning chemicals, toxic plants, and small objects that could be swallowed out of reach. Secure electrical cords and keep them hidden or covered to prevent chewing or tripping hazards. Be cautious of common household foods that can be toxic to dogs, such as chocolate, grapes, and onions. Taking these precautions helps create a safe environment and reduces the risk of accidents or injuries.

Regular Exercise:

Italian Greyhounds require regular exercise to maintain their physical and mental well-being. Daily walks, playtime, and opportunities for off-leash exercise in safe areas help satisfy their natural need for physical activity. Engaging in regular exercise not only keeps them fit and healthy but also helps prevent behavioral issues that may arise from excess energy.

Establishing Routines and Boundaries

Finding Harmony: Establishing Routines and Boundaries for Your Italian Greyhound

Establishing routines and boundaries is essential for creating a harmonious and well-balanced environment for your Italian Greyhound. These practices help provide structure, predictability, and a sense of security for your furry friend. Below we will explore the importance of routines and boundaries, focusing on daily routines, training, setting boundaries, and promoting positive behaviors.

Daily Routines:

Consistency in daily routines is crucial for Italian Greyhounds. Establish a regular schedule for feeding, exercise, playtime, and rest. Dogs thrive on predictability, so try to feed your Italian Greyhound at the same time each day to regulate their digestive system. Designate specific times for walks or play sessions to provide them with regular physical and mental stimulation. Incorporate downtime and rest periods into their routine to ensure they receive adequate rest and relaxation.

Training:

Training plays a vital role in establishing boundaries and promoting desirable behaviors. Italian Greyhounds are intelligent and eager to please, making them highly trainable. Begin training early on and focus on positive reinforcement techniques such as rewards, treats, and praise. Use consistent commands and establish clear expectations to teach basic obedience skills, such as sit, stay, come, and leash walking. Incorporate regular training sessions into your daily routine to reinforce good behavior and strengthen the bond between you and your Italian Greyhound.

Setting Boundaries:

Setting boundaries helps your Italian Greyhound understand what is acceptable behavior and what is not. Establish boundaries within your home by designating certain areas as off-limits or creating barriers to prevent access. For example, you may want to keep your Italian Greyhound out of certain rooms or prevent them from jumping on furniture. Use positive reinforcement and redirect their attention to appropriate behaviors when they approach restricted areas. Consistency is key to reinforcing boundaries and preventing confusion.

Promoting Positive Behaviors:

Italian Greyhounds respond well to positive reinforcement and thrive on praise and rewards. Encourage positive behaviors by rewarding good actions with treats, verbal praise, or playtime. This approach helps reinforce desired behaviors and encourages your Italian Greyhound to repeat them. For example, if your Italian Greyhound sits calmly when visitors arrive instead of jumping up, reward them with a treat and praise. Consistently rewarding positive behaviors helps shape their behavior and fosters a harmonious household environment.

Socialization:

Socialization is crucial for Italian Greyhounds to become well-adjusted and confident dogs. Expose your Italian Greyhound to a variety of people, animals, and environments from a young age. This helps them develop good social skills and reduces the likelihood of fear or aggression towards unfamiliar situations. Take your Italian Greyhound on regular outings, introduce them to other friendly dogs, and provide positive experiences to help build their confidence and sociability.

Consistency and Clear Communication:

Consistency and clear communication are fundamental when establishing routines and boundaries. Use consistent commands, gestures, and cues to convey your expectations to your Italian Greyhound. Avoid mixed messages or conflicting signals, as this can lead to confusion. Additionally, ensure that all family members and household members are on the same page regarding rules and boundaries. Consistency in training and communication helps your Italian Greyhound understand what is expected of them and promotes a harmonious living environment.

Patience and Understanding:

Lastly, it is essential to approach the establishment of routines and boundaries with patience and understanding. Each Italian Greyhound is unique and may require different approaches and timelines for learning and adapting to routines. Be patient with their progress, celebrate small victories, and understand that setbacks may occur. Positive reinforcement, consistency, and a gentle approach will yield the best results.

Enrichment and Mental Stimulation

Unleashing Potential: Enrichment and Mental Stimulation for Italian Greyhounds

Italian Greyhounds are not only graceful and elegant but also intelligent and curious companions. As a responsible owner, it is essential to provide them with adequate mental stimulation and enrichment to keep their minds engaged and their spirits high. Below we will explore the importance of enrichment and mental stimulation for Italian Greyhounds, discuss various activities and strategies to promote mental engagement, and highlight the benefits of incorporating these practices into their daily lives.

Understanding the Need for Mental Stimulation:

Italian Greyhounds have active minds and a strong desire to explore and learn. Mental stimulation is crucial to prevent boredom, frustration, and the development of behavioral issues. Engaging their minds through various activities not only provides entertainment but also promotes problem-solving skills, boosts confidence, and strengthens the bond between you and your Italian Greyhound.

Puzzle Toys and Interactive Feeders:

Puzzle toys and interactive feeders are excellent tools to challenge your Italian Greyhound's problem-solving abilities while making mealtime more exciting. These toys are designed to dispense treats or kibble gradually, requiring your dog to figure out how to access the food. The mental effort involved keeps them engaged, encourages persistence, and provides a satisfying reward once they solve the puzzle. It also helps slow down fast eaters and promotes healthier eating habits.

Scent Games and Nose Work:

Italian Greyhounds have an exceptional sense of smell, and engaging in scent games or nose work activities taps into their natural abilities. Hide treats or toys around the house or in a designated area and encourage your Italian Greyhound to use their nose to locate them. You can gradually increase the difficulty by hiding the items in more challenging spots. This activity not only stimulates their senses but also provides a sense of accomplishment when they successfully find the hidden treasures.

Training and Trick Learning:

Training sessions provide mental stimulation while reinforcing obedience and building a stronger bond with your Italian Greyhound. Teach them new tricks, such as "sit," "stay," "roll over," or more advanced commands like "fetch" or "play dead." The process of learning and mastering these skills keeps their minds active and engaged. Positive reinforcement methods, including treats and praise, help motivate your Italian Greyhound and make the training sessions enjoyable for both of you.

Interactive Play and Games:

Engage your Italian Greyhound in interactive play and games that require mental engagement. Play hide-and-seek by hiding behind furniture and calling their name, or hide their favorite toys and encourage them to search for them. Tug-of-war, when played in a controlled manner, can also provide mental stimulation while reinforcing the bond between you and your Italian Greyhound. Rotate toys regularly to keep their interest piqued and introduce new textures, sounds, and shapes to keep playtime exciting.

Outings and Exploration:

Taking your Italian Greyhound on regular outings and providing opportunities for exploration can stimulate their minds and senses. Visit new places, such as parks, dog-friendly hiking trails, or beaches, and allow them to explore their surroundings. Expose them to different sights, sounds, and smells, which will stimulate their senses and provide mental enrichment. However, always ensure their safety and follow local regulations regarding leash laws and public spaces.

Food Dispensing Toys and Treat Dispensers:

Food dispensing toys and treat dispensers provide mental stimulation while satisfying your Italian Greyhound's natural instinct to forage for food. These toys are designed to hold kibble or treats that are released gradually as the dog interacts with the toy. The challenge of extracting the food keeps them mentally engaged and entertained. Additionally, it helps prevent gulping food too quickly and promotes a healthier eating pace.

Common Italian Greyhound Health Myths and Misconceptions

Unveiling the Truth: Common Italian Greyhound Health Myths and Misconceptions

Italian Greyhounds are charming and delicate dogs known for their slender build and affectionate nature. However, like any breed, they are not immune to health concerns. Unfortunately, misinformation and misconceptions about Italian Greyhound health often circulate, leading to confusion and unnecessary worry among owners. Below we will debunk some common myths and misconceptions surrounding Italian Greyhound health, providing accurate and factual information to help owners better understand and care for their beloved companions.

Myth 1: Italian Greyhounds are Fragile and Prone to Frequent Injuries

Fact: While Italian Greyhounds may appear delicate due to their slim physique, they are generally sturdy and resilient dogs. While they do have a higher risk of certain injuries due to their thin bones, such as fractures or sprains, they are not overly fragile. With proper care, a balanced diet, regular exercise, and a safe environment, Italian Greyhounds can lead healthy and active lives.

Myth 2: Italian Greyhounds are Highly Susceptible to Dental Problems

Fact: Dental health is important for all dogs, and Italian Greyhounds are no exception. However, it is not accurate to say that they are more prone to dental problems than other breeds. Regular dental care, including daily brushing, professional cleanings as needed, and providing appropriate dental chews or toys, can help maintain good oral hygiene for Italian Greyhounds, just like any other dog breed.

Myth 3: Italian Greyhounds Have a Short Lifespan

Fact: Italian Greyhounds, on average, have a lifespan of 12 to 15 years, which is comparable to many small to medium-sized dog breeds. With proper nutrition, regular veterinary care, a healthy lifestyle, and a nurturing environment, Italian Greyhounds can live long and fulfilling lives. Individual variations in lifespan can occur due to factors such as genetics, overall health, and the quality of care provided.

Myth 4: All Italian Greyhounds Suffer from Separation Anxiety

Fact: Separation anxiety can affect dogs of any breed, including Italian Greyhounds. However, it is not accurate to assume that all Italian Greyhounds will experience separation anxiety. While they are known for their close bond with their owners, proper socialization, training, and gradually acclimating them to being alone can help prevent or minimize separation anxiety in Italian Greyhounds, just as with any other breed.

Myth 5: Italian Greyhounds are Prone to Hypothermia

1Fact: Italian Greyhounds have a thin coat and minimal body fat, which can make them more sensitive to cold weather. However, this does not mean they are prone to hypothermia under normal circumstances. With appropriate measures such as providing warm clothing or blankets, limiting exposure to extreme cold, and monitoring their comfort during colder seasons, Italian Greyhounds can comfortably navigate cooler temperatures.

Myth 6: Italian Greyhounds Should Be Fed a Special Diet to Prevent Health Issues

Fact: While proper nutrition is vital for Italian Greyhounds' overall health and well-being, there is no specific diet required to prevent health issues unique to this breed. A balanced diet that meets their nutritional needs, provides appropriate portions, and is suitable for their age and activity level is sufficient. Consulting with a veterinarian can help determine the best diet for an individual Italian Greyhound based on their specific needs.

Debunking Popular Myths

Unraveling the Truth: Debunking Popular Myths About Italian Greyhounds

Italian Greyhounds, with their graceful appearance and gentle disposition, have become beloved companions for many dog enthusiasts. However, like any popular breed, they have become the subject of numerous myths and misconceptions. Below we will delve into some common myths surrounding Italian Greyhounds, providing accurate information to dispel these misconceptions and provide a clearer understanding of these delightful dogs.

Myth 1: Italian Greyhounds Need Excessive Exercise Due to Their Athletic Build

Fact: While Italian Greyhounds do possess an athletic build, they are not high-energy dogs that require excessive exercise. They are sprinters by nature and enjoy short bursts of intense activity rather than endurance exercises. A daily walk or moderate playtime is generally sufficient to meet their exercise needs. Over-exercising Italian Greyhounds can actually put them at risk of injury due to their slender bone structure. It is important to strike a balance between exercise and rest to maintain their health and well-being.

Myth 2: Italian Greyhounds Are High-Maintenance Dogs Due to Their Fragile Nature

Fact: While Italian Greyhounds may appear delicate with their slender bodies, they are not inherently high-maintenance dogs. With proper care, Italian Greyhounds can lead healthy and fulfilling lives. They require regular grooming to maintain their coat, which is short and easy to manage. Additionally, providing a balanced diet, regular veterinary check-ups, and a safe environment can help prevent health issues and ensure their well-being. Like any dog, Italian Greyhounds benefit from love, attention, and companionship, but they are not overly fragile or high-maintenance.

Myth 3: Italian Greyhounds Cannot Be Trusted Off-Leash Due to Their Prey Drive

Fact: While Italian Greyhounds have a strong prey drive, it is not accurate to assume that they cannot be trusted off-leash. With proper training, socialization, and recall exercises, Italian Greyhounds can learn to respond reliably to commands and enjoy off-leash time in secure areas. It is important to provide a safe and controlled environment and ensure that they are trained and supervised in open spaces. Every dog is an individual, and training methods may vary, but it is possible to have an Italian Greyhound that can be trusted off-leash.

Myth 4: Italian Greyhounds Are Not Good with Children or Other Pets

Fact: Italian Greyhounds can be wonderful companions for children and get along well with other pets when properly socialized and trained. They are generally gentle and affectionate dogs that can form strong bonds with their human family members. Early socialization, positive experiences, and teaching children how to interact respectfully with dogs are key to fostering a harmonious relationship. As with any dog breed, supervision is important when Italian Greyhounds are interacting with children or other pets to ensure everyone's safety and well-being.

Myth 5: Italian Greyhounds Are Yappy and Excessive Barkers

1Fact: While some Italian Greyhounds may be more vocal than others, it is incorrect to assume that all Italian Greyhounds are yappy or excessive barkers. Barking behavior can be influenced by various factors, including individual temperament, training, and environment. With proper socialization and training, Italian Greyhounds can learn appropriate barking behavior and respond to commands to curb excessive barking. It is essential to understand that each dog is unique and may have different barking tendencies.

Fact vs. Fiction: Italian Greyhound Health Issues

Unmasking the Truth: Fact vs. Fiction - Italian Greyhound Health Issues

Italian Greyhounds are beloved companions known for their elegance and affectionate nature. As with any breed, there are both factual health concerns and fictionalized notions surrounding their well-being. Below we will separate fact from fiction, providing accurate information about Italian Greyhound health issues and debunking common misconceptions. By dispelling myths, we aim to foster a better understanding of the breed's health and help owners provide optimal care for their Italian Greyhounds.

Fiction: Italian Greyhounds are extremely fragile and prone to injuries.

Fact: While Italian Greyhounds are delicate in appearance, they are not excessively fragile. Their slender frames may make them more susceptible to certain injuries, such as fractures or sprains, but with proper care and supervision, they can lead active and healthy lives. It's important to provide a safe environment, avoid rough play or excessive jumping, and handle them gently to reduce the risk of injuries.

Fiction: Italian Greyhounds are prone to severe dental problems.

Fact: Dental care is important for all dogs, and Italian Greyhounds are no exception. However, it is inaccurate to claim that they are inherently more prone to dental issues than other breeds. Regular dental care, including brushing their teeth, providing dental treats, and scheduling professional cleanings as needed, can help maintain good oral hygiene and prevent dental problems in Italian Greyhounds.

Fiction: Italian Greyhounds have a short lifespan.

Fact: While individual lifespans can vary, Italian Greyhounds typically have a lifespan of 12 to 15 years. With proper nutrition, regular veterinary care, and a healthy lifestyle, they can live long and fulfilling lives. Owners can contribute to their longevity by providing a balanced diet, regular exercise, mental stimulation, and a loving environment.

Fiction: All Italian Greyhounds suffer from separation anxiety.

Fact: Separation anxiety can affect dogs of any breed, including Italian Greyhounds. However, it is incorrect to assume that all Italian Greyhounds will experience separation anxiety. Proper socialization, gradual acclimation to being alone, and providing mental stimulation can help prevent or minimize separation anxiety in Italian Greyhounds. Each dog is an individual, and their tendency to experience separation anxiety may vary.

Fiction: Italian Greyhounds are prone to hypothermia.

1Fact: Italian Greyhounds have thin coats and minimal body fat, which can make them more sensitive to cold weather. However, they are not inherently prone to hypothermia under normal circumstances. By providing appropriate protection, such as dog sweaters or coats, and limiting exposure to extreme cold, Italian Greyhounds can comfortably navigate colder temperatures. It's important to monitor their comfort and take precautions to keep them warm.

Fiction: Italian Greyhounds require a specialized diet.

Fact: While proper nutrition is essential for Italian Greyhound health, there is no specific diet required solely for this breed. A balanced and high-quality diet appropriate for their age, size, and activity level is sufficient. Consultation with a veterinarian can help determine the best diet for an individual Italian Greyhound based on their specific needs and any existing health conditions.

Fiction: Italian Greyhounds are highly prone to allergies.

Fact: While Italian Greyhounds, like any breed, can develop allergies, they are not inherently more prone to allergies compared to other dogs. Allergies can be triggered by various factors, including food, environmental allergens, or flea bites. Identifying and managing allergies may require working closely with a veterinarian to develop a suitable treatment plan, which may include dietary adjustments, medication, or environmental modifications.

Promoting Accurate Information and Awareness

Empowering Knowledge: Promoting Accurate Information and Awareness about Italian Greyhounds

In a world overflowing with information, it is crucial to ensure that accurate and reliable knowledge is readily available to promote the well-being of our beloved Italian Greyhounds. Misinformation and misconceptions can lead to confusion, improper care, and unnecessary worry among owners. Below we will explore the importance of promoting accurate information and awareness about Italian Greyhounds, discuss the role of education, reputable sources, and community involvement in dispelling myths, and highlight the benefits of fostering a knowledgeable and informed community of Italian Greyhound enthusiasts.

The Role of Education:

Education plays a pivotal role in promoting accurate information and awareness about Italian Greyhounds. Educating current and prospective owners about the breed's unique characteristics, health considerations, and proper care is essential. This can be accomplished through various means, such as breed-specific seminars, workshops, online resources, and collaboration with reputable breed organizations. By providing educational opportunities, owners can gain a deeper understanding of their Italian Greyhounds' needs and ensure they receive the best possible care.

Reputable Sources:

Access to reliable and reputable sources of information is vital in dispelling myths and promoting accurate knowledge about Italian Greyhounds. Encouraging owners to consult trustworthy sources, such as veterinary professionals, reputable breed organizations, and peer-reviewed publications, helps ensure they receive accurate and up-to-date information. Emphasizing the importance of critically evaluating online resources and distinguishing credible information from speculative or anecdotal sources is also crucial in fostering a well-informed community.

Community Involvement:

Building a community of informed Italian Greyhound enthusiasts plays a significant role in promoting accurate information and awareness. Encouraging open dialogue, sharing experiences, and fostering a supportive environment can facilitate the exchange of knowledge and debunk myths. Online forums, social media groups, and breed-specific clubs provide platforms for individuals to connect, learn from one another, and collectively disseminate accurate information. Active participation in these communities contributes to a shared commitment to the well-being of Italian Greyhounds.

Collaboration with Veterinary Professionals:

Collaboration between Italian Greyhound owners and veterinary professionals is paramount in promoting accurate information and awareness. Veterinary professionals are a valuable source of expertise and can provide evidence-based guidance tailored to individual Italian Greyhounds. Regular veterinary check-ups, open communication, and proactive discussions about breed-specific health concerns help ensure that owners receive accurate information, preventative care, and timely interventions when needed.

Responsible Breeding Practices:

Promoting responsible breeding practices is essential for the well-being of Italian Greyhounds and the dissemination of accurate information. Responsible breeders prioritize the health and temperament of the breed, conduct appropriate health screenings, and provide comprehensive support to puppy buyers. They actively educate potential owners about the breed's characteristics, potential health issues, and responsible ownership. By supporting responsible breeders and discouraging unethical practices, we can contribute to a healthier and better-informed Italian Greyhound population.

Encouraging Research and Collaboration:

Encouraging research initiatives and collaboration among experts in veterinary medicine, genetics, and Italian Greyhound-specific health concerns fosters a deeper understanding of the breed and promotes accurate information. Continued research into breed-specific health conditions, genetic screening, and advancements in veterinary care contributes to the development of evidence-based recommendations and the dissemination of accurate information. Supporting and participating in research studies can help uncover new insights and ensure that accurate knowledge continues to evolve.

Individual Responsibility:

Each individual has a responsibility to promote accurate information and awareness about Italian Greyhounds. It starts with being critical consumers of information and fact-checking before accepting and sharing it. By cultivating a habit of seeking accurate information, verifying sources, and engaging in respectful conversations, individuals can contribute to the dissemination of reliable knowledge.

Italian Greyhounds and Special Needs

Inclusive Companions: Italian Greyhounds and Special Needs

Italian Greyhounds are known for their grace, beauty, and affectionate nature, making them wonderful companions for individuals of all abilities. Their gentle demeanor, adaptability, and intuitive nature enable them to provide comfort, support, and companionship to individuals with special needs. Below we will explore the unique qualities of Italian Greyhounds that make them suitable for individuals with special needs, discuss their role as therapy dogs, and highlight the positive impact they can have on the lives of those facing challenges.

Gentle and Calm Nature:

Italian Greyhounds possess a gentle and calm nature, which can be particularly beneficial for individuals with special needs. Their patient and understanding demeanor allows them to adapt to different personalities and comfort levels. They have an innate ability to sense emotions and respond with empathy, providing a soothing presence to those experiencing anxiety, stress, or sensory sensitivities.

Size and Portability:

Italian Greyhounds are small in size, making them easily portable and suitable for individuals with mobility challenges or limited physical strength. Their compact build allows them to be comfortably held, carried, or accommodated in various settings, including homes, schools, or healthcare facilities. This size advantage facilitates increased accessibility and the ability to form close bonds with individuals with special needs.

Sensory Support:

Italian Greyhounds can offer valuable sensory support to individuals with special needs. Their soft fur, comforting presence, and willingness to be touched or cuddled can provide sensory stimulation and promote relaxation. For individuals with sensory processing disorders, the tactile experience of stroking or petting an Italian Greyhound can have a calming effect and assist in self-regulation.

Emotional Support and Companionship:

Italian Greyhounds excel in providing emotional support and companionship to individuals with special needs. Their unwavering loyalty and unconditional love create a strong bond that can alleviate feelings of loneliness, anxiety, or depression. The presence of an Italian Greyhound can offer a sense of security and emotional stability, acting as a constant source of comfort and companionship.

Therapy Dog Work:

Italian Greyhounds can also serve as therapy dogs, assisting individuals with special needs in various therapeutic settings. As therapy dogs, they undergo specialized training to provide comfort, support, and companionship to individuals in hospitals, schools, or rehabilitation centers. Their calm temperament, patience, and ability to connect with people make them excellent candidates for therapy work, contributing to emotional healing and enhanced well-being.

Assistance in Physical Therapy:

Italian Greyhounds can assist individuals with special needs in physical therapy sessions. Their size and agility make them ideal partners for activities such as walking, balance exercises, or targeted movements. Incorporating Italian Greyhounds into physical therapy sessions can increase motivation, engagement, and enjoyment, leading to improved outcomes for individuals undergoing rehabilitation.

Support for Autism Spectrum Disorders:

Italian Greyhounds have shown to be particularly beneficial for individuals on the autism spectrum. Their calm and predictable nature can help create a structured and soothing environment. The presence of an Italian Greyhound can assist in reducing anxiety, improving social interactions, and providing emotional support for individuals with autism. Additionally, the responsibility of caring for a pet can teach important life skills and promote independence.

Sensitivity to Medical Conditions:

Italian Greyhounds have demonstrated an exceptional ability to sense changes in their owners' health. They can detect subtle shifts in body language, scent, or behavior, allowing them to alert individuals with medical conditions such as diabetes or seizures. This sensitivity can be life-saving, as Italian Greyhounds can provide early warnings and prompt individuals to seek appropriate medical attention.

Italian Greyhounds Assisting Individuals with Disabilities

Supporting Independence: Italian Greyhounds Assisting Individuals with Disabilities

Italian Greyhounds, with their gentle nature and loyal disposition, have proven to be incredible companions for individuals with disabilities. Their adaptability and intuitive nature allow them to provide support, companionship, and assistance in various ways. Below we will explore how Italian Greyhounds can assist individuals with disabilities, discuss their role as service dogs, and highlight the positive impact they have on enhancing independence and quality of life.

Mobility Assistance:

Italian Greyhounds can provide valuable mobility assistance to individuals with physical disabilities. Through specialized training, they can be taught to retrieve items, open doors, or assist in tasks that require manual dexterity. For individuals with mobility challenges, having an Italian Greyhound by their side can enhance their independence and enable them to perform daily activities more easily.

Balance and Stability Support:

Italian Greyhounds can also assist individuals with balance and stability issues. By walking beside or slightly in front of their handlers, they can provide a supportive base and help individuals maintain their balance while walking. This support is particularly beneficial for individuals with conditions such as Parkinson's disease or balance disorders, allowing them to navigate their surroundings with increased confidence and stability.

Alerting to Medical Conditions:

Italian Greyhounds have shown remarkable abilities to detect changes in their owners' medical conditions. They can be trained to alert individuals with conditions such as diabetes, epilepsy, or allergies to specific scents or behavioral cues. By alerting their handlers to potential health emergencies, Italian Greyhounds help individuals take necessary precautions or seek timely medical assistance, promoting their safety and well-being.

Psychiatric Support:

Italian Greyhounds can provide invaluable emotional support and assistance to individuals with psychiatric disabilities. They can offer comfort during anxiety or panic attacks, provide a grounding presence during stressful situations, and offer a non-judgmental source of companionship. Their presence can help reduce symptoms of anxiety, depression, and post-traumatic stress disorder, enhancing emotional well-being and overall quality of life.

Retrieval of Items:

For individuals with limited mobility or reach, Italian Greyhounds can be trained to retrieve items on command. Whether it's picking up dropped objects, fetching medications, or assisting with daily tasks, their dexterity and willingness to help make them reliable assistants. This support can significantly improve independence and reduce reliance on others for simple tasks.

Social Interaction and Communication Aid:

Italian Greyhounds can serve as social facilitators and communication aids for individuals with disabilities. Their presence often sparks interest and positive interactions from others, facilitating social connections and easing feelings of isolation. In addition, Italian Greyhounds can provide a topic of conversation or act as a bridge to initiate social interactions, fostering a sense of belonging and inclusion.

Senses and Sensory Support:

Italian Greyhounds have keen senses that can benefit individuals with sensory processing disorders or other sensory-related challenges. Their gentle and comforting presence can help soothe sensory overload, providing a calming effect. In addition, Italian Greyhounds can be trained to respond to specific sensory cues or provide deep pressure stimulation, promoting relaxation and assisting individuals in regulating their sensory experiences.

Personal Assistance and Independence:

Italian Greyhounds can be trained to perform a wide range of tasks that promote independence and self-reliance for individuals with disabilities. Whether it's turning lights on and off, carrying small items, or assisting with dressing and undressing, their small size and adaptability make them well-suited for these tasks. By supporting individuals in their daily activities, Italian Greyhounds contribute to increased autonomy and a sense of accomplishment.

Training and Certification Requirements

A Path to Success: Training and Certification Requirements for Italian Greyhounds

Training and certification are vital components in the process of preparing Italian Greyhounds to become reliable and capable service dogs. These requirements ensure that the dogs possess the necessary skills, behavior, and temperament to assist individuals with disabilities effectively. Below we will explore the training and certification requirements for Italian Greyhounds, including the skills they must acquire, the importance of professional guidance, and the benefits of a well-trained and certified service dog.

Professional Guidance:

Training Italian Greyhounds to become service dogs should ideally be conducted under the guidance of professional trainers with experience in service dog training. These trainers have the knowledge and expertise to develop training programs tailored to the specific needs of Italian Greyhounds and the individuals they will assist. Their guidance ensures that the training process is efficient, effective, and focused on the skills necessary for service dog work.

Basic Obedience:

Before advancing to specialized service dog training, Italian Greyhounds must first master basic obedience skills. These skills include commands such as sit, stay, come, heel, and down. Basic obedience training lays the foundation for more advanced training, teaching dogs to respond reliably to commands and exhibit good behavior in various settings. It also promotes effective communication between the dog and the handler.

Task Training:

Task training is a crucial aspect of service dog preparation. Italian Greyhounds are trained to perform specific tasks that assist individuals with disabilities, such as retrieving items, opening doors, or alerting to medical conditions. Task training requires repetition, consistency, and positive reinforcement to ensure that Italian Greyhounds understand and perform their tasks reliably and accurately. The training focuses on honing the dog's abilities and developing their problem-solving skills.

Public Access Training:

Service dogs, including Italian Greyhounds, must be comfortable and well-behaved in public settings. Public access training exposes the dogs to various environments, distractions, and situations they may encounter while accompanying individuals with disabilities. It includes teaching the dog to walk calmly on a leash, ignore distractions, and exhibit appropriate behavior in public places. Public access training ensures that service dogs are well-prepared to navigate different environments and provide assistance without causing disruptions.

Socialization:

Socialization is a critical aspect of training for Italian Greyhounds. It involves exposing the dogs to various people, animals, and environments from a young age. Proper socialization helps Italian Greyhounds develop good manners, adaptability, and confidence in different situations. It also ensures that they remain calm and composed when faced with new or unfamiliar experiences. Well-socialized Italian Greyhounds are more likely to be reliable, well-behaved service dogs.

Public Access Test:

To become certified service dogs, Italian Greyhounds must pass a public access test. This test evaluates their ability to behave appropriately in public settings, follow commands, and maintain focus despite distractions. The specific requirements may vary depending on the certifying organization or jurisdiction. The test typically includes scenarios such as walking through crowds, navigating busy streets, and responding to commands in public spaces.

Health and Vaccination Requirements:

Service dogs, including Italian Greyhounds, must meet specific health and vaccination requirements to ensure the safety and well-being of both the dog and the individuals they assist. Regular veterinary check-ups, vaccinations, and preventive treatments are necessary to maintain the dog's health and prevent the spread of diseases. Additionally, service dogs should be free from conditions that may compromise their ability to perform their tasks effectively and safely.

The Benefits of Italian Greyhound Assistance Dogs

Unleashing Independence: The Benefits of Italian Greyhound Assistance Dogs

Italian Greyhounds, with their gentle demeanor and loyal nature, are well-suited to serve as assistance dogs for individuals with disabilities. These remarkable dogs provide invaluable support, companionship, and assistance, enhancing the independence and quality of life for those they serve. Below we will explore the benefits of Italian Greyhound assistance dogs, including their ability to promote physical and emotional well-being, increase social interactions, and foster a sense of empowerment.

Physical Assistance:

Italian Greyhound assistance dogs offer a range of physical assistance to individuals with disabilities. They can perform tasks such as retrieving objects, opening doors, turning on lights, or providing stability and balance support. These tasks reduce the physical strain on individuals, enabling them to navigate their surroundings more easily and independently. By assisting with everyday tasks, Italian Greyhound assistance dogs enhance mobility and promote greater self-reliance.

Alerting and Medical Assistance:

Italian Greyhounds possess a remarkable ability to detect changes in their owner's medical condition. They can be trained to alert individuals with conditions such as diabetes, epilepsy, or allergies to potential health emergencies. These early warnings allow individuals to take necessary precautions or seek medical assistance promptly. Italian Greyhound assistance dogs act as a reliable safety net, providing a sense of security and peace of mind.

Emotional Support:

Italian Greyhound assistance dogs excel in providing emotional support to individuals with disabilities. Their calming presence, loyalty, and unconditional love have a profound impact on emotional well-being. These dogs offer comfort during times of anxiety, stress, or emotional distress, providing a constant source of companionship and reassurance. Italian Greyhound assistance dogs help alleviate feelings of loneliness, depression, and anxiety, contributing to improved mental health and overall emotional stability.

Social Interaction and Confidence Building:

Italian Greyhound assistance dogs serve as social facilitators, opening doors to increased social interactions for individuals with disabilities. The presence of these dogs often sparks positive conversations and interest from others, promoting social connections and reducing social isolation. Italian Greyhound assistance dogs provide individuals with a shared interest and a topic of conversation, fostering a sense of belonging and increasing confidence in social settings.

Increased Independence:

Perhaps one of the most significant benefits of Italian Greyhound assistance dogs is the enhanced independence they bring to individuals with disabilities. By providing physical assistance, emotional support, and alerting to medical conditions, these dogs enable individuals to accomplish tasks that may have previously required assistance from others. The increased independence fosters a sense of empowerment, self-confidence, and a greater ability to participate fully in daily activities.

Enhanced Safety and Security:

Italian Greyhound assistance dogs offer a heightened level of safety and security to individuals with disabilities. Their alertness and ability to sense potential dangers contribute to a safer living environment. Whether it's alerting to approaching individuals, providing stability to prevent falls, or acting as a deterrent to potential threats, these dogs act as a reliable companion, ensuring the well-being and safety of their owners.

Improved Quality of Life:

The presence of an Italian Greyhound assistance dog has a transformative effect on the overall quality of life for individuals with disabilities. These dogs bring joy, unconditional love, and a sense of purpose to their owners. They provide constant companionship, reduce feelings of isolation, and promote a positive outlook on life. Italian Greyhound assistance dogs empower individuals to overcome challenges, engage in activities they enjoy, and live a more fulfilling life.

The Future of the Italian Greyhound Breed

Unleashing the Potential: The Future of the Italian Greyhound Breed

The Italian Greyhound, a breed renowned for its elegance, gentle nature, and affectionate personality, has captured the hearts of dog enthusiasts around the world. As we look to the future, it is essential to consider the evolving landscape of the breed and the steps necessary to ensure its continued well-being and preservation. Below we will explore the future of the Italian Greyhound breed, including the importance of responsible breeding practices, health considerations, breed standards, and the role of education in safeguarding the breed's future.

Responsible Breeding Practices:

The foundation of a bright future for the Italian Greyhound breed lies in responsible breeding practices. Breeders play a crucial role in preserving the breed's unique characteristics, maintaining health standards, and promoting genetic diversity. Responsible breeders prioritize the health and temperament of their dogs, conduct appropriate health screenings, and carefully select breeding pairs to minimize the risk of hereditary conditions. By adhering to ethical breeding practices, breeders contribute to the overall well-being and long-term sustainability of the Italian Greyhound breed.

Health Considerations:

Maintaining the health of the Italian Greyhound breed is of paramount importance for its future. Breed-specific health concerns, such as dental issues, luxating patellas, or progressive retinal atrophy, must be addressed through diligent health testing and responsible breeding practices. Collaborative efforts among breeders, veterinarians, and genetic researchers can help identify potential health risks, develop preventive measures, and ensure that the breed continues to thrive in terms of physical well-being.

Preservation of Breed Standards:

Preserving and adhering to breed standards is essential in maintaining the distinctive qualities of the Italian Greyhound breed. Breed standards outline the ideal characteristics, structure, and temperament that define the breed. By evaluating breeding stock against these standards, breeders can work towards producing Italian Greyhounds that conform to the desired breed type. Preserving breed standards ensures that the Italian Greyhound's unique attributes are retained and appreciated for generations to come.

Genetic Diversity:

Promoting genetic diversity is crucial for the long-term health and sustainability of the Italian Greyhound breed. A limited gene pool increases the risk of inherited health conditions and reduces overall genetic resilience. Breeders should collaborate and exchange information to expand the genetic diversity of the breed. Responsible breeding practices, such as outcrossing or careful selection of genetically diverse breeding stock, can help maintain genetic vigor and minimize the risk of inherited disorders.

Education and Awareness:

Education and awareness play a vital role in safeguarding the future of the Italian Greyhound breed. Breeders, owners, and enthusiasts must stay informed about the breed's history, characteristics, health concerns, and responsible breeding practices. By disseminating accurate and up-to-date information, educating prospective owners, and encouraging open dialogue, the Italian Greyhound community can promote responsible ownership, proper care, and ethical breeding practices.

Collaboration and Networking:

Collaboration and networking within the Italian Greyhound community are essential for the breed's future. Breed clubs, associations, and online forums provide platforms for breeders, owners, and enthusiasts to share knowledge, exchange ideas, and work towards common goals. Collaborative efforts can include health research, mentorship programs for new breeders, and initiatives to promote responsible ownership. By pooling resources and expertise, the Italian Greyhound community can tackle challenges and ensure the breed's continued success.

Competitive Activities:

Participation in competitive activities, such as conformation shows, lure coursing, or obedience trials, not only showcases the Italian Greyhound's unique qualities but also serves as a means to evaluate breeding stock against breed standards. These activities encourage breeders to strive for excellence, breed for purpose, and preserve the breed's working abilities.

Advances in Canine Health Research

Unveiling the Future: Advances in Canine Health Research and the Impact on Italian Greyhounds

Canine health research has made significant strides in recent years, leading to a better understanding of various health conditions and the development of innovative treatments. These advancements have not only improved the well-being of dogs but also hold great promise for breeds like the Italian Greyhound. Below we will explore the latest advances in canine health research, their implications for Italian Greyhounds, and how these breakthroughs can contribute to the breed's overall health and longevity.

Genetic Testing and Screening:

One of the most significant advances in canine health research is the development of genetic testing and screening for various hereditary conditions. With advancements in DNA analysis, researchers have identified genetic markers associated with specific diseases, allowing breeders to make informed decisions and reduce the prevalence of these conditions. For Italian Greyhounds, genetic testing can help identify and manage breed-specific health concerns such as progressive retinal atrophy, epilepsy, or primary lens luxation.

Precision Medicine:

The advent of precision medicine has revolutionized the field of veterinary care, offering tailored treatment options based on an individual dog's genetic makeup. Precision medicine involves using genetic information to predict how a dog may respond to certain medications or therapies, optimizing treatment plans for better outcomes. This approach has the potential to benefit Italian Greyhounds by providing personalized treatment options that target their specific health needs, ultimately improving their quality of life.

Regenerative Medicine:

Regenerative medicine, which focuses on harnessing the body's natural healing processes, has shown great promise in the field of veterinary care. Stem cell therapy, for example, has been used to promote tissue regeneration and repair in dogs with conditions such as osteoarthritis or soft tissue injuries. The application of regenerative medicine in Italian Greyhounds can potentially alleviate age-related degenerative conditions and enhance their overall mobility and well-being.

Immunotherapy:

Immunotherapy has emerged as a groundbreaking treatment approach in both human and veterinary medicine. This innovative technique harnesses the power of the immune system to target and eliminate cancer cells. Immunotherapy holds potential for Italian Greyhounds, as this breed is predisposed to certain types of cancer, such as osteosarcoma or hemangiosarcoma. Research in immunotherapy can lead to novel treatments that specifically target cancer cells, offering hope for improved outcomes and prolonged survival.

Nutrigenomics:

Nutrigenomics, the study of how diet influences gene expression, has gained attention in recent years. By understanding the interactions between diet and genetics, researchers can develop specialized dietary recommendations that promote optimal health and address specific conditions. In the case of Italian Greyhounds, who may be prone to dental issues or food sensitivities, nutrigenomics research can guide the development of tailored diets that support dental health and optimize nutrient absorption.

Behavioral Health:

Canine behavioral health is an essential aspect of overall well-being, and advancements in this field have improved our understanding of canine behavior and mental health. Research into behavior modification techniques, stress reduction strategies, and the impact of environmental factors on dogs' emotional well-being can contribute to better mental health outcomes for Italian Greyhounds. By addressing behavior-related challenges, such as separation anxiety or noise phobias, researchers can improve the overall quality of life for Italian Greyhounds and their owners.

Telemedicine and Remote Monitoring:

The integration of technology into veterinary care has given rise to telemedicine and remote monitoring, offering convenient access to veterinary expertise and improved monitoring of a dog's health. These tools allow veterinarians to remotely assess Italian Greyhounds' health, provide guidance, and monitor chronic conditions, all from the comfort of the dog's home.

Ethical Breeding and Preservation of the Breed

Preserving the Legacy: Ethical Breeding and the Future of the Italian Greyhound Breed

Ethical breeding practices are the cornerstone of preserving the integrity and well-being of dog breeds, including the beloved Italian Greyhound. These practices prioritize the breed's health, temperament, and adherence to breed standards. Below we will explore the importance of ethical breeding, the challenges it faces, and the strategies that can be employed to ensure the preservation of the Italian Greyhound breed for future generations.

Breed Preservation:

Ethical breeding is essential for preserving the unique characteristics that define the Italian Greyhound breed. Breed standards outline the ideal physical attributes, temperament, and behavior that embody the breed. By adhering to these standards, responsible breeders ensure that the distinctive qualities of Italian Greyhounds are maintained, fostering the breed's legacy and preventing it from losing its identity over time.

Health Considerations:

One of the primary objectives of ethical breeding is to prioritize the health and well-being of the breed. Responsible breeders conduct health screenings and genetic testing to identify and reduce the incidence of hereditary conditions within the Italian Greyhound population. By selecting breeding pairs based on their health clearances, breeders can minimize the risk of passing on genetic diseases, promote healthier bloodlines, and enhance the overall health of future generations.

Genetic Diversity:

Preserving genetic diversity is a crucial aspect of ethical breeding. A diverse gene pool reduces the prevalence of inherited diseases and promotes the overall resilience of the breed. Breeders must carefully select breeding pairs to maintain genetic diversity while adhering to breed standards. Collaboration between breeders, genetic researchers, and breed organizations can help prevent the loss of genetic variation within the Italian Greyhound breed.

Responsible Ownership:

Ethical breeding extends beyond breeders to encompass responsible ownership. Prospective owners should be well-informed about the breed's characteristics, potential health concerns, and responsible care requirements. Ethical breeders educate potential owners about the responsibilities involved in Italian Greyhound ownership, including socialization, proper nutrition, regular veterinary care, and providing a safe and nurturing environment. Responsible owners contribute to the breed's preservation by providing lifelong care and support to their Italian Greyhounds.

Breeder Education and Mentorship:

Continued education and mentorship for breeders are vital to ensuring ethical breeding practices. Breeders should stay informed about advancements in veterinary medicine, genetics, and best breeding practices. Engaging in educational programs, attending seminars or workshops, and seeking guidance from experienced mentors allows breeders to expand their knowledge and make informed decisions that benefit the breed's long-term health and preservation.

Selective Breeding:

Selective breeding is a fundamental principle of ethical breeding. Breeders carefully evaluate potential breeding pairs, taking into consideration health clearances, temperament, conformation, and genetic diversity. By selecting dogs that complement each other's strengths and weaknesses, breeders can work towards producing Italian Greyhounds that meet breed standards, exhibit desirable traits, and maintain good overall health. Selective breeding also helps reduce the risk of passing on genetic disorders and promotes the breed's overall quality.

Collaboration and Responsible Breeding Networks:

Collaboration among breeders, breed organizations, and veterinary professionals is crucial in promoting ethical breeding and breed preservation. Breed clubs and organizations provide a platform for breeders to exchange information, share best practices, and collaborate on health research. Responsible breeding networks promote transparency, accountability, and the sharing of knowledge and resources. By working together, breeders can tackle challenges, support each other, and collectively ensure the welfare and preservation of the Italian Greyhound breed.

Italian Greyhounds in the 21st Century and Beyond

Unleashing the Potential: Italian Greyhounds in the 21st Century and Beyond

Italian Greyhounds, with their grace, elegance, and gentle nature, have captivated the hearts of dog lovers for centuries. As we enter the 21st century and beyond, the future holds exciting possibilities for this beloved breed. Below we will explore the evolving landscape of Italian Greyhounds, including their role as family companions, therapy dogs, and competitive athletes, as well as the potential impact of technology and advancements in veterinary care on their well-being and future.

Family Companions:

Italian Greyhounds have long been cherished as beloved family companions, and their popularity continues to grow in the 21st century. Their small size, adaptability, and affectionate nature make them well-suited for various living environments, including apartments or urban settings. As family pets, Italian Greyhounds bring joy, companionship, and a sense of playfulness to their owners, creating lasting bonds and enriching the lives of individuals and families.

Therapy Dogs:

The therapeutic benefits of the Italian Greyhound breed have gained recognition in recent years. Their calm demeanor, sensitivity, and willingness to provide comfort make them excellent therapy dogs. Italian Greyhounds can offer emotional support to individuals in hospitals, nursing homes, schools, or rehabilitation centers. Their presence can help reduce stress, promote relaxation, and uplift the spirits of those they interact with, making a positive impact on overall well-being.

Competitive Activities:

Italian Greyhounds have a rich history as competitive athletes, particularly in lure coursing and other dog sports. In the 21st century, these activities continue to provide opportunities for Italian Greyhounds to showcase their speed, agility, and natural hunting instincts. Participating in events such as conformation shows, agility trials, or obedience competitions allows Italian Greyhounds to demonstrate their unique talents and skills, promoting the breed's versatility and athleticism.

Advancements in Veterinary Care:

Advancements in veterinary care have the potential to revolutionize the well-being of Italian Greyhounds in the 21st century and beyond. Improved diagnostic techniques, such as advanced imaging technology or genetic testing, can aid in the early detection and treatment of health conditions. Additionally, advancements in surgical techniques, pain management, and regenerative medicine can enhance the quality of life for Italian Greyhounds facing health challenges.

Telemedicine and Remote Monitoring:

The integration of technology into veterinary care, such as telemedicine and remote monitoring, offers new possibilities for Italian Greyhound owners. Telemedicine allows for virtual veterinary consultations, enabling timely access to professional advice and guidance. Remote monitoring devices can track a dog's vital signs, activity levels, and behavior, providing valuable insights into their overall health and well-being. These advancements improve convenience, allow for proactive health management, and enhance the bond between Italian Greyhound owners and their veterinary care teams.

Responsible Ownership and Advocacy:

Responsible ownership and advocacy play a vital role in shaping the future of Italian Greyhounds. As awareness of responsible pet ownership continues to grow, so does the importance of advocating for the breed's welfare. Responsible owners prioritize the breed's health, temperament, and well-being. They provide proper nutrition, regular veterinary care, mental and physical stimulation, and a loving environment. By sharing knowledge, promoting ethical breeding practices, and advocating for the breed, Italian Greyhound enthusiasts can ensure a bright future for the breed.

Training Resources and Techniques

Unlocking Potential: Training Resources and Techniques for Italian Greyhounds

Training is a crucial aspect of raising a well-behaved and happy Italian Greyhound. Effective training not only ensures that these graceful and intelligent dogs develop good manners but also strengthens the bond between dogs and their owners. Below we will explore a variety of training resources and techniques specifically designed for Italian Greyhounds, highlighting the importance of positive reinforcement, socialization, and utilizing professional guidance to maximize training success.

Positive Reinforcement:

Positive reinforcement is a powerful training technique that focuses on rewarding desired behaviors rather than punishing unwanted behaviors. This method involves using treats, praise, and other rewards to motivate and reinforce good behavior. Italian Greyhounds respond well to positive reinforcement, as they are eager to please and enjoy the interaction and rewards associated with training. By rewarding desired behaviors, such as sitting, staying, or walking on a leash, Italian Greyhounds learn to associate obedience with positive outcomes, leading to consistent and reliable responses.

Socialization:

Socialization is a critical aspect of training for Italian Greyhounds. Early and ongoing socialization exposes dogs to various people, animals, environments, and stimuli, helping them become well-adjusted and confident companions. It is important to introduce Italian Greyhounds to new experiences gradually and positively, ensuring that they associate these encounters with positive outcomes. Well-socialized Italian Greyhounds are more likely to exhibit appropriate behavior, handle new situations with ease, and enjoy positive interactions with both humans and other animals.

Basic Obedience Training:

Basic obedience training lays the foundation for a well-behaved Italian Greyhound. Training sessions should focus on teaching essential commands such as sit, stay, come, and leash walking. Consistency, patience, and positive reinforcement are key to successful obedience training. Short, frequent training sessions using clear and consistent commands help Italian Greyhounds understand and respond appropriately. Obedience training not only promotes good manners but also ensures the safety and well-being of both the dog and their owner.

Crate Training:

Crate training is a valuable tool for Italian Greyhounds, providing them with a safe and comfortable space of their own. Introducing the crate gradually and positively helps Italian Greyhounds view it as a positive and secure environment. Crate training aids in house training, prevents destructive behaviors, and serves as a place of relaxation and retreat. When done correctly, crate training can become an integral part of an Italian Greyhound's routine and contribute to their overall well-being.

Leash Training:

Leash training is essential for Italian Greyhounds to ensure safe and enjoyable walks. Introducing a leash and collar or harness gradually, using positive reinforcement, helps Italian Greyhounds associate the leash with pleasant experiences. Training sessions should focus on loose leash walking, where the dog walks calmly by the owner's side without pulling. Consistency, patience, and positive reinforcement play a crucial role in teaching Italian Greyhounds to walk politely on a leash.

Advanced Training:

Italian Greyhounds are intelligent dogs capable of learning advanced commands and tricks. Advanced training can include activities such as agility, obedience trials, or scent work. These activities engage Italian Greyhounds mentally and physically, providing both mental stimulation and opportunities for bonding with their owners. Advanced training enhances their problem-solving abilities, builds confidence, and strengthens the owner-dog relationship.

Professional Guidance:

Seeking professional guidance is beneficial for Italian Greyhound owners, especially when faced with challenging training situations or specific goals. Professional dog trainers with experience in working with Italian Greyhounds can provide valuable insights, tailor training programs to individual needs, and offer guidance in overcoming behavioral issues. Their expertise ensures that training is conducted effectively, safely, and with the dog's best interests in mind.

Positive Reinforcement and Reward-Based Training

Pawsitive Progress: Positive Reinforcement and Reward-Based Training for Italian Greyhounds

Positive reinforcement and reward-based training methods have gained popularity in recent years as effective and humane approaches to teaching and shaping behavior in dogs. These methods focus on encouraging and rewarding desired behaviors rather than punishing unwanted ones. When applied to Italian Greyhounds, known for their sensitive nature and eagerness to please, positive reinforcement and reward-based training can unlock their potential and strengthen the bond between dogs and their owners. Below we will explore the principles of positive reinforcement, the benefits of reward-based training for Italian Greyhounds, and how these techniques can contribute to successful training outcomes.

Principles of Positive Reinforcement:

Positive reinforcement involves rewarding a dog for exhibiting desired behaviors, thereby increasing the likelihood of those behaviors being repeated. The rewards used can vary and may include treats, praise, play, or any other positive stimuli that motivate the dog. The key principles of positive reinforcement include timing, consistency, and the use of meaningful rewards. By providing rewards immediately after the desired behavior occurs, Italian Greyhounds can associate the behavior with the positive outcome, reinforcing the desired response.

Tailoring Rewards to Individual Dogs:

Italian Greyhounds, like any other dog breed, have unique preferences and motivations. It is important to identify what rewards are most appealing to them. Some dogs may be highly food-motivated and respond well to treats, while others may be more motivated by praise, play, or a combination of rewards. Understanding and utilizing the rewards that are most meaningful to Italian Greyhounds can enhance the effectiveness of positive reinforcement training.

Building a Positive Association:

Positive reinforcement training focuses on creating a positive association with training sessions and desired behaviors. By incorporating rewards, Italian Greyhounds learn to associate training with enjoyable experiences. This creates a positive learning environment, encouraging dogs to actively participate and engage in the training process. Positive associations promote enthusiasm, motivation, and a willingness to learn, making training sessions enjoyable for both dogs and their owners.

Encouraging Calm Behavior:

Italian Greyhounds, known for their sensitive nature, can benefit greatly from positive reinforcement training methods. These dogs respond well to gentle and encouraging approaches, as opposed to harsh or punitive methods. Positive reinforcement training helps Italian Greyhounds develop self-confidence, trust, and a sense of security. By focusing on rewarding calm and desired behaviors, Italian Greyhounds learn to exhibit appropriate behavior in various situations, promoting a harmonious relationship with their owners.

Enhancing Communication and Bonding:

Positive reinforcement training strengthens the communication and bond between Italian Greyhounds and their owners. Dogs learn to understand and respond to verbal cues and commands, facilitating effective communication. Additionally, the positive interaction during training sessions fosters a sense of trust, respect, and cooperation. The bond between dogs and their owners grows stronger as they work together towards shared goals, leading to a more fulfilling and rewarding relationship.

Addressing Behavioral Challenges:

Positive reinforcement training techniques are particularly effective in addressing behavioral challenges in Italian Greyhounds. Undesirable behaviors, such as excessive barking, jumping, or pulling on the leash, can be effectively modified through positive reinforcement methods. By rewarding alternative, desirable behaviors and redirecting their focus, Italian Greyhounds learn to make positive choices. This approach not only improves behavior but also reduces stress, anxiety, and frustration in dogs.

Long-Term Training Success:

Positive reinforcement and reward-based training methods are known for their long-term effectiveness. By focusing on rewarding desired behaviors, Italian Greyhounds learn to offer the desired response consistently. The training becomes a positive habit, making it more likely for the behaviors to generalize to different environments and situations.

Clicker Training and Marker Techniques

Clicking for Success: Clicker Training and Marker Techniques for Italian Greyhounds

Clicker training and marker techniques have emerged as popular and effective training methods for dogs, including the intelligent and eager-to-learn Italian Greyhound. These techniques utilize the use of a clicker or a verbal marker to communicate and reinforce desired behaviors. Below we will explore the principles of clicker training and marker techniques, their benefits for Italian Greyhounds, and how these methods can be applied to achieve training success.

Understanding Clicker Training:

Clicker training is a form of operant conditioning that relies on the use of a handheld device called a clicker. The clicker emits a distinct sound when pressed, serving as a marker to indicate the exact moment a desired behavior is performed. The sound of the clicker is immediately followed by a reward, such as a treat or praise, which reinforces the behavior. Italian Greyhounds quickly associate the sound of the clicker with positive outcomes and learn to repeat the behavior that elicits the click.

Marker Techniques with Verbal Cues:

Marker techniques can also be used with verbal cues instead of a clicker. In this approach, a specific word or phrase, such as "yes" or "good," is used as a marker to signal to the dog that they have performed the desired behavior correctly. Like clicker training, the verbal marker is immediately followed by a reward. The consistency and timing of the marker are crucial in effectively communicating the desired behavior to Italian Greyhounds.

Advantages of Clicker Training and Marker Techniques:

Clicker training and marker techniques offer several advantages for training Italian Greyhounds:

Precise Communication: The click or marker word provides clear and precise communication to the dog, indicating the exact moment the desired behavior is performed. This clarity helps Italian Greyhounds understand and learn faster, resulting in more efficient training.

b. Timing and Consistency: The click or marker word allows for precise timing and consistency in training. It bridges the time gap between the desired behavior and the delivery of the reward, reinforcing the connection between the behavior and the positive outcome.

c. Positive Association: The click or marker word creates a positive association with training and the desired behaviors. Italian Greyhounds learn to associate the sound with rewards, making training sessions enjoyable and motivating.

Mental Stimulation: Clicker training and marker techniques engage Italian Greyhounds mentally, challenging them to think and problem-solve. This mental stimulation promotes cognitive development, enhances focus, and strengthens the bond between dogs and their owners.

Versatility: Clicker training and marker techniques can be used to teach a wide range of behaviors, from basic commands such as sit and stay to more complex tricks and tasks. This versatility allows Italian Greyhound owners to tailor training to their dog's individual needs and interests.

Getting Started with Clicker Training:

To begin clicker training with an Italian Greyhound, follow these steps:

Conditioning the Click: Start by associating the sound of the clicker with positive rewards. Click the device and immediately offer a treat or praise. Repeat this process several times until the dog associates the click with something positive.

Shaping Behaviors: Once the dog understands the clicker as a signal for a reward, use it to capture and reinforce desired behaviors. Click the moment the dog performs the behavior and follow it with a reward. Gradually shape the behavior by requiring more specific criteria before clicking and rewarding.

Timing and Consistency: Click at the exact moment the behavior is performed to communicate precisely what you want from the Italian Greyhound. Consistency in timing and criteria is crucial to avoid confusion and maintain clear communication.

Online and In-Person Training Resources

Unleashing the Possibilities: Online and In-Person Training Resources for Italian Greyhounds

Training is an essential component of raising a well-behaved and balanced Italian Greyhound. Fortunately, in today's digital age, there are a wide array of training resources available to Italian Greyhound owners, both online and in-person. These resources provide valuable guidance, support, and techniques to help owners effectively train their dogs. Below we will explore the benefits of online and in-person training resources, how they can be utilized for Italian Greyhounds, and the considerations to keep in mind when choosing the most suitable training approach.

Online Training Resources:

Online training resources have gained immense popularity and offer convenience and flexibility to Italian Greyhound owners. These resources include websites, instructional videos, webinars, and online courses specifically tailored to dog training. Some benefits of online training resources include:

Access to Expertise: Online training resources provide access to expert trainers and behaviorists who share their knowledge and techniques through instructional videos and webinars. Italian Greyhound owners can benefit from the expertise of professionals without the constraints of geographical location.

b. Self-Paced Learning: Online training resources allow owners to learn at their own pace and convenience. Training materials can be accessed and reviewed as needed, providing flexibility to accommodate busy schedules and individual learning preferences.

c. Cost-Effective: Online training resources are often more cost-effective compared to in-person training sessions. They eliminate the need for travel expenses and can be a more affordable option for Italian Greyhound owners seeking training guidance on a budget.

Variety of Topics: Online training resources cover a wide range of topics, including basic obedience, problem-solving, behavior modification, and specialized training activities. Italian Greyhound owners can find resources that address specific needs or interests, allowing them to tailor their training approach to their dog's individual requirements.

In-Person Training Resources:

In-person training resources provide a hands-on and interactive approach to training Italian Greyhounds. These resources include professional trainers, obedience classes, and behavior consultations. Some advantages of in-person training resources include:

Personalized Attention: In-person training resources offer the opportunity for personalized attention from experienced trainers. Trainers can assess the Italian Greyhound's behavior, address specific concerns, and provide tailored guidance to meet individual training goals.

Socialization Opportunities: In-person training resources, such as obedience classes, provide Italian Greyhounds with opportunities to socialize with other dogs and people in a controlled environment. This promotes proper socialization, helps develop good canine manners, and builds confidence.

Immediate Feedback: With in-person training, owners receive immediate feedback from trainers on their techniques and their Italian Greyhound's progress. This allows for real-time adjustments and fine-tuning of training methods, leading to more effective and efficient training outcomes.

Accountability and Support: In-person training resources provide accountability and ongoing support from trainers. Regular classes or sessions encourage consistency in training efforts and offer guidance in overcoming challenges that may arise during the training process.

Considerations When Choosing a Training Approach:

When selecting between online and in-person training resources for Italian Greyhounds, consider the following factors:

Training Goals and Needs: Assess the specific training goals and needs of your Italian Greyhound. Determine if you require general obedience training, behavior modification, or specialized training for activities such as agility or therapy work. Different resources may cater to specific goals and needs.

Learning Style and Preferences: Consider your preferred learning style and the Italian Greyhound's individual temperament. Some owners may thrive in a self-paced online learning environment, while others may benefit from the guidance and hands-on support of in-person training.

Emergency Preparedness and Your Italian Greyhound

Safeguarding Your Furry Companion: Emergency Preparedness and Your Italian Greyhound

In the face of unexpected emergencies or disasters, being prepared can make all the difference for the safety and well-being of your Italian Greyhound. Just as humans need emergency plans, supplies, and procedures, our canine companions also require specific preparations. Below we will explore the importance of emergency preparedness for Italian Greyhounds, the key considerations for safeguarding their welfare, and how to effectively navigate emergency situations to ensure the best possible outcomes for our furry friends.

Identification and Documentation:

Identification is crucial during emergencies to ensure a swift and safe reunion with your Italian Greyhound if separated. Ensure your Italian Greyhound wears a collar with up-to-date identification tags containing your contact information. Microchipping is an additional and permanent form of identification that can greatly aid in reuniting you with your pet. Keep a record of your Italian Greyhound's identification information, including microchip details, vaccination records, and any relevant medical history in a readily accessible location.

Emergency Contact Information:

Maintain a list of emergency contact numbers, including your veterinarian's office, local animal shelters, and pet-friendly hotels or accommodations. In the event of an emergency evacuation, this information will help you access the necessary resources and support for your Italian Greyhound.

Emergency Supplies:

Assemble an emergency kit specifically tailored for your Italian Greyhound. This kit should include:

Food and Water: Pack a sufficient supply of your Italian Greyhound's regular food and fresh water in airtight containers. Ensure the food remains fresh and rotated periodically.

b. Medications and Medical Supplies: Include any necessary medications your Italian Greyhound requires, along with a copy of their prescriptions. Additionally, include basic medical supplies such as bandages, antiseptic solution, and any specific first aid items recommended by your veterinarian.

c. Comfort Items: Familiar items such as blankets, toys, and bedding can provide comfort and reduce stress for your Italian Greyhound during emergency situations. These items can help create a sense of security and familiarity amidst the chaos.

Leash, Collar, and Harness: Have an extra leash, collar, and harness readily available in your emergency kit. These items are essential for keeping your Italian Greyhound secure and under control during evacuations or in unfamiliar environments.

Sanitation Supplies: Include waste bags, paper towels, and disinfectant wipes for cleaning up after your Italian Greyhound. Maintaining cleanliness and hygiene is crucial during emergencies to prevent the spread of disease.

Evacuation Planning:

Develop a comprehensive evacuation plan that takes your Italian Greyhound's specific needs into account. Identify pet-friendly accommodations, shelters, or friends and family who can provide a safe haven in case of evacuation. Ensure you have a reliable means of transportation and pre-plan evacuation routes to avoid unnecessary delays or confusion during emergencies.

Familiarization with Carriers and Crates:

Train your Italian Greyhound to become comfortable with carriers or crates in case they need to be transported during an emergency. Gradually introduce and associate positive experiences with the carrier or crate to alleviate anxiety and stress. This familiarity will ease the process of evacuation and ensure your Italian Greyhound's safety during transportation.

Emergency Training:

Train your Italian Greyhound in essential commands and behaviors that can be crucial during emergencies. Teach commands such as "come," "stay," and "leave it" to ensure their responsiveness and ability to follow directions in potentially hazardous situations. These commands can help keep your Italian Greyhound out of harm's way and aid in managing unpredictable circumstances.

Creating a Pet Emergency Plan

Guardianship in Crisis: Creating a Pet Emergency Plan for Your Italian Greyhound

Disasters and emergencies can strike at any moment, leaving little time for preparation. As responsible pet owners, it is our duty to ensure the safety and well-being of our Italian Greyhounds during these challenging times. Creating a comprehensive pet emergency plan is crucial to protect your beloved companion. Below we will explore the essential steps to creating a pet emergency plan specifically tailored for Italian Greyhounds, ensuring their welfare in times of crisis.

Emergency Contacts:

Compile a list of emergency contacts specific to your Italian Greyhound. Include the contact information for your veterinarian, local animal shelters, and any nearby friends or family who could assist in an emergency. Ensure this list is easily accessible, both digitally and in hard copy, so it can be readily available when needed.

Identification and Documentation:

Proper identification is vital to the swift and safe return of your Italian Greyhound in case of separation during an emergency. Ensure your pet wears a collar with up-to-date identification tags displaying your contact information. Additionally, microchipping your Italian Greyhound provides a permanent form of identification that greatly increases the chances of being reunited if lost. Keep a copy of your pet's identification records, including microchip details, medical history, and vaccination records, in a waterproof container or a cloud-based storage system.

Emergency Kit:

Prepare an emergency kit specifically for your Italian Greyhound. This kit should contain essential supplies to sustain your pet's well-being for at least three days. Include the following items:

Food and Water: Pack a sufficient amount of your Italian Greyhound's regular food in a sealed container. Store it alongside bottled water to sustain your pet's hydration needs. Remember to rotate the food and water supply periodically to maintain freshness.

b. Medications and Medical Records: Include a supply of any necessary medications your Italian Greyhound requires, as well as a copy of their prescriptions. Keep medical records, including vaccination certificates and any pertinent health information, in a waterproof bag.

c. Comfort Items: Familiar items such as bedding, blankets, toys, and a familiar-scented item, like a t-shirt, can provide comfort and reduce anxiety for your Italian Greyhound during times of stress and uncertainty.

Leash, Collar, and Harness: Pack an extra leash, collar, and harness to ensure you have a backup in case of loss or damage. These items are essential for safely restraining and controlling your Italian Greyhound during an emergency situation.

Sanitation Supplies: Include waste bags, disposable litter trays (if applicable), and pet-safe disinfectant wipes for maintaining cleanliness and hygiene.

Safe Haven:

Identify safe havens for your Italian Greyhound in case of evacuation or temporary relocation. Research pet-friendly hotels, boarding facilities, or the homes of friends or family members who are willing to accommodate your pet during emergencies. It is important to establish these arrangements in advance to ensure a smooth transition and the well-being of your Italian Greyhound.

Transportation:

Plan for safe and secure transportation for your Italian Greyhound during emergencies. If you have a personal vehicle, ensure it is well-maintained and always keep the gas tank at least half full. If you do not have access to a vehicle, identify alternative modes of transportation, such as public transportation or arrangements with friends or neighbors, to ensure you can evacuate your Italian Greyhound safely if needed.

Assembling a Canine First Aid Kit

Safety First: Assembling a Canine First Aid Kit for Your Italian Greyhound

Accidents and injuries can occur unexpectedly, and having a well-stocked canine first aid kit is essential for providing immediate care to your Italian Greyhound in times of need. By assembling a comprehensive first aid kit, you can effectively address minor injuries and potentially stabilize your dog until professional veterinary assistance is available. Below we will explore the key components to include in a canine first aid kit specifically tailored for Italian Greyhounds, ensuring their well-being and prompt attention during emergencies.

Essential Supplies:

Sterile Dressings and Bandages: Include a variety of sterile dressings, such as non-stick pads, gauze pads, and adhesive bandages, to address wounds or cuts. These supplies will help stop bleeding and protect wounds from contamination.

b. Adhesive Tape and Self-Adhering Bandages: These items are crucial for securing dressings in place and providing support to injured limbs. Opt for non-stick, breathable, and self-adhering bandages that won't stick to your Italian Greyhound's fur.

c. Antiseptic Solution or Wipes: Use antiseptic solution or wipes to clean wounds and minimize the risk of infection. Choose a pet-safe antiseptic solution, such as chlorhexidine, to avoid any adverse reactions.

Saline Solution: Saline solution can be used to flush eyes or clean wounds. It provides a gentle and soothing cleansing method that is safe for your Italian Greyhound.

Tweezers and Tick Remover: These tools are essential for safely removing splinters, thorns, or ticks from your Italian Greyhound's skin. Ensure they have a fine tip for precision and are sanitized before use.

Scissors: Include a pair of blunt-edged scissors to safely trim fur around wounds or to cut bandages or tape. Blunt-edged scissors reduce the risk of accidental injuries.

Digital Thermometer: A digital thermometer specifically designed for pets can help you monitor your Italian Greyhound's body temperature, which is crucial in identifying fever or hypothermia. Use a water-based lubricant or petroleum jelly for easy insertion.

Emergency Blanket: An emergency blanket provides insulation and can help regulate body temperature in cases of hypothermia or shock. It is lightweight and compact, making it easy to include in your first aid kit.

Medications and Topical Treatments:

Hydrogen Peroxide: Hydrogen peroxide can be used to induce vomiting in cases of ingestion of toxins or foreign objects. However, consult with your veterinarian or a poison control hotline before administering hydrogen peroxide.

Sterile Saline Eye Drops: Sterile saline eye drops can be used to flush foreign objects or irritants from your Italian Greyhound's eyes. They provide a gentle and safe method of eye irrigation.

c. Antibiotic Ointment: Antibiotic ointment, such as triple antibiotic or chlorhexidine, can be applied to minor wounds or cuts after cleaning to prevent infection.

d. Antihistamine: Consult your veterinarian for the appropriate antihistamine to include in your first aid kit. Antihistamines can help alleviate allergic reactions or insect bites, but the dosage should be determined by a professional.

Styptic Powder: Styptic powder is useful for stopping bleeding in cases of minor nail injuries or cuts. It promotes blood clotting and can be applied directly to the affected area.

Recognizing and Responding to Emergencies

Urgency Unveiled: Recognizing and Responding to Emergencies with Your Italian Greyhound

Being prepared for emergencies is crucial for the safety and well-being of your Italian Greyhound. Accidents and unexpected incidents can happen at any time, and the ability to recognize and respond promptly can make all the difference in preserving your dog's health and potentially saving their life. Below we will explore the importance of recognizing and responding to emergencies specifically related to Italian Greyhounds, equipping you with the knowledge and confidence to handle critical situations effectively.

Respiratory Distress:

Choking: If your Italian Greyhound is choking, they may exhibit signs such as pawing at the mouth, gasping for breath, or making choking sounds. Open their mouth and carefully remove any visible obstructions if you can safely do so. If the object cannot be dislodged, perform the Heimlich maneuver by applying gentle pressure to the abdomen just below the ribcage.

b. Difficulty Breathing: Rapid or labored breathing, wheezing, or excessive panting may indicate respiratory distress. Ensure your Italian Greyhound has access to fresh air and a cool environment. Seek immediate veterinary attention to address the underlying cause.

Heatstroke:

a. Heat Exhaustion: Signs of heat exhaustion include excessive panting, drooling, rapid breathing, weakness, and collapse. Move your Italian Greyhound to a cool, shaded area, provide water, and wet their coat with cool (not cold) water. Contact your veterinarian for further guidance.

Heatstroke: Heatstroke is a life-threatening emergency characterized by high body temperature, rapid heartbeat, vomiting, diarrhea, and disorientation. Immediately move your Italian Greyhound to a cool area, apply cool water to their body, and seek immediate veterinary assistance.

Seizures:

Generalized Seizure: During a seizure, your Italian Greyhound may experience uncontrollable shaking, loss of consciousness, drooling, or urination. Ensure their safety by removing any nearby objects that could cause injury. Do not attempt to restrain or hold down your dog. After the seizure, keep them calm and seek veterinary attention.

Status Epilepticus: Status epilepticus refers to prolonged or recurring seizures. If your Italian Greyhound experiences consecutive seizures without regaining consciousness, seek immediate veterinary care.

Allergic Reactions:

Insect Bites or Stings: Swelling, redness, hives, difficulty breathing, or collapse may indicate an allergic reaction to an insect bite or sting. If you can identify the stinger, carefully remove it. Administer an antihistamine if advised by your veterinarian and seek prompt veterinary attention.

Food or Medication Allergies: Signs of an allergic reaction to food or medication may include itching, swelling, hives, vomiting, or diarrhea. Contact your veterinarian if you suspect an allergic reaction, as prompt medical attention may be necessary.

Poisoning:

Ingestion of Toxins: If you suspect your Italian Greyhound has ingested a toxic substance, contact a veterinarian or poison control hotline immediately. Be prepared to provide information on the type of toxin, quantity ingested, and your dog's weight. Do not induce vomiting without professional guidance.

Antifreeze: Antifreeze poisoning can be life-threatening. Symptoms may include excessive thirst, vomiting, increased urination, depression, seizures, or coma. If you suspect antifreeze ingestion, seek veterinary assistance urgently.

Celebrating Your Italian Greyhound

Elegant Euphoria: Celebrating the Charms of Your Italian Greyhound

Italian Greyhounds are a unique and enchanting breed, capturing the hearts of many with their grace, beauty, and endearing personalities. As proud owners of these remarkable companions, it's important to celebrate and cherish the special qualities that make Italian Greyhounds so beloved. Below we will explore the joys of celebrating your Italian Greyhound, highlighting their distinctive characteristics, and offering ideas for creating memorable moments that honor their presence in your life.

Embracing Their Elegance:

Beauty in Motion: Italian Greyhounds are known for their elegant and graceful movement. Organize a gathering with fellow Italian Greyhound enthusiasts to showcase their agility and speed through activities such as lure coursing or organized playdates. These events provide opportunities for your Italian Greyhound to showcase their innate talents and for you to connect with other passionate owners.

b. Fashion Forward: With their sleek and slender build, Italian Greyhounds can rock a fashionable wardrobe. Embrace their stylish nature by dressing them in chic and comfortable clothing. From cozy sweaters to trendy accessories, there is no shortage of fashionable options to suit your Italian Greyhound's personality.

Intellectual Stimulation:

a. Puzzle Games: Italian Greyhounds are intelligent and thrive on mental stimulation. Engage their minds with puzzle toys or interactive games that challenge their problem-solving skills. These activities provide mental exercise while strengthening the bond between you and your Italian Greyhound.

Canine Enrichment: Create an enriching environment for your Italian Greyhound by offering sensory experiences such as scent games, treat-dispensing toys, or even a dedicated digging area in your backyard. Enrichment activities engage their senses and provide them with opportunities to explore and express their natural instincts.

Capturing Memories:

Professional Photoshoot: Hire a professional pet photographer to capture stunning portraits of your Italian Greyhound. These photographs can immortalize their unique personality and serve as cherished mementos for years to come. Consider including yourself in the photos to document the bond you share.

Scrapbooking: Create a personalized scrapbook filled with photographs, stories, and mementos that showcase your Italian Greyhound's journey with you. Include milestones, achievements, and memorable moments that reflect their vibrant presence in your life. This creative project allows you to reminisce and celebrate the joy your Italian Greyhound brings.

Sharing Adventures:

Exploring Nature: Italian Greyhounds love to explore the world around them. Take them on hikes, beach outings, or nature walks where they can revel in new scents and sights. Ensure their safety by using a secure harness or leash designed for their delicate structure.

Travel Companions: Italian Greyhounds can be wonderful travel companions. Plan pet-friendly vacations or day trips where you can explore new places together. From visiting dog-friendly parks to exploring pet-friendly attractions, these adventures create lasting memories and strengthen the bond between you and your Italian Greyhound.

Community Connections:

Dog Clubs and Meetups: Engage with the Italian Greyhound community by joining dog clubs or attending breed-specific meetups. These gatherings provide opportunities to connect with other Italian Greyhound owners, share experiences, and learn from one another.

Volunteering and Therapy Work: Italian Greyhounds have a gentle and affectionate nature that makes them ideal candidates for therapy work. Consider enrolling your Italian Greyhound in therapy dog training programs, allowing them to bring joy and comfort to others in hospitals, nursing homes, or schools.

Birthday Parties and Special Occasions

Pawsitively Paw-some: Birthday Parties and Special Occasions for Your Italian Greyhound

Birthdays and special occasions provide the perfect opportunity to celebrate the joy and love that Italian Greyhounds bring into our lives. Just like any cherished family member, Italian Greyhounds deserve to be honored and showered with affection on these special days. Below we will explore the delights of organizing birthday parties and other special occasions for your Italian Greyhound, offering ideas and tips to make these moments memorable and enjoyable for both you and your beloved companion.

Planning the Perfect Party:

Guest List: Invite fellow dog-loving friends, family members, and their well-behaved dogs to join the celebration. Ensure the guest dogs are sociable and compatible with your Italian Greyhound's temperament.

b. Venue Selection: Choose a venue that provides a safe and secure environment for the party. Consider hosting the celebration in your backyard, a local dog-friendly park, or a spacious indoor area. Be mindful of the weather conditions and provide shade or shelter if necessary.

c. Decorations: Create a festive atmosphere with themed decorations that reflect your Italian Greyhound's personality. Incorporate colors, patterns, or motifs that resonate with their character. Balloons, banners, and personalized signage can add a special touch to the ambiance.

Party Supplies: Provide water bowls, interactive toys, and comfortable resting areas for your Italian Greyhound and their furry guests. Ensure there are designated waste disposal stations and plenty of poop bags available for cleanliness.

Delicious Delights:

Birthday Cake: Treat your Italian Greyhound to a dog-friendly birthday cake made with wholesome ingredients. There are numerous recipes available that cater to canine dietary needs. Decorate the cake with dog-friendly frosting or personalized treats for an extra special touch.

Treat Bar: Set up a treat bar with a variety of snacks and goodies for both dogs and humans. Include homemade dog treats, pupcakes, and a selection of human-friendly snacks. Ensure all treats are safe and appropriate for consumption by dogs.

Hydration Station: Keep your Italian Greyhound and their furry friends well-hydrated with a hydration station. Provide fresh water in easily accessible bowls or consider setting up a dog-friendly beverage station with flavored waters or frozen treats.

Games and Activities:

Lure Coursing: Italian Greyhounds excel in lure coursing, a sport that mimics the chase of prey. Set up a safe and supervised lure coursing activity for the party, allowing your Italian Greyhound and their friends to showcase their natural abilities and have a blast.

Canine Games: Engage your Italian Greyhound and their guests in games tailored to their size and abilities. From treasure hunts to agility courses, these activities provide mental stimulation and opportunities for friendly competition.

Dressing for Success:

Party Attire: Dress up your Italian Greyhound in a special party outfit befitting the occasion. Choose comfortable and lightweight clothing that allows freedom of movement and doesn't restrict their natural grace.

Party Favors: Provide party favors for the canine guests to take home. These can include small toys, personalized bandanas, or treats. Ensure that any toys or treats given are safe and appropriate for the guests' individual needs.

Charity and Giving Back:

Donation Drive: Incorporate a charitable element into your Italian Greyhound's special occasion by organizing a donation drive for a local animal shelter or rescue organization. Encourage guests to bring pet food, blankets, or toys to contribute to the cause.

Customized Gifts and Keepsakes

Tailored Treasures: Customized Gifts and Keepsakes for Your Italian Greyhound

Italian Greyhounds hold a special place in our hearts, captivating us with their elegance and affectionate nature. When it comes to expressing our love and appreciation for these magnificent companions, personalized gifts and keepsakes can be the perfect way to commemorate their presence in our lives. Below we will explore the enchanting world of customized gifts and keepsakes for Italian Greyhounds, showcasing a range of delightful options to celebrate their unique personalities and create lasting memories.

Personalized Accessories:

Engraved ID Tags: A personalized ID tag adds a touch of style and uniqueness while ensuring the safety of your Italian Greyhound. Consider having a tag engraved with their name, your contact information, or a special message that holds significance to you and your dog.

b. Customized Collars and Leashes: Opt for collars and leashes that can be customized with your Italian Greyhound's name or embroidered with a special pattern or design. This not only adds a personal touch but also enhances their overall appearance.

c. Monogrammed Clothing: Dress your Italian Greyhound in personalized clothing, such as sweaters or hoodies, adorned with their initials or a customized monogram. This adds a sophisticated and exclusive touch to their wardrobe.

Artistic Expressions:

Custom Pet Portraits: Commission a professional artist to create a stunning, lifelike portrait of your Italian Greyhound. A personalized artwork capturing their unique features and personality will become a cherished heirloom and a beautiful centerpiece in your home.

Digital Illustrations: With advancements in technology, you can have digital illustrations created from photographs of your Italian Greyhound. These artistic renderings can be transformed into prints, phone cases, or even custom-made puzzles.

Paw Prints and Nose Casts: Capture your Italian Greyhound's unique paw prints or nose casts as a sentimental keepsake. There are various DIY kits available that allow you to create molds or prints, or you can visit a professional who specializes in these personalized creations.

Customized Jewelry:

Pet-themed Charm Bracelets: Design a charm bracelet that showcases your Italian Greyhound's image or features dog-themed charms. Each charm can symbolize a special memory or represent a unique aspect of your pet's personality.

Engraved Pendants: Personalize a pendant or locket with your Italian Greyhound's name or picture. These wearable pieces of art can be cherished and worn close to your heart.

Photo Books and Albums:

Personalized Photo Books: Compile a collection of your favorite photographs of your Italian Greyhound in a customized photo book. Add captions, stories, and memories to create a unique keepsake that celebrates the special moments you've shared together.

Scrapbooks: Create a personalized scrapbook filled with photographs, drawings, and mementos that document your Italian Greyhound's life journey. Include significant milestones, achievements, and unforgettable memories that bring joy and warmth to your heart.

Customized Home Décor:

1Customized Throw Pillows and Blankets: Personalize decorative throw pillows or cozy blankets with images of your Italian Greyhound. These customized home accessories add a touch of warmth and personality to your living space.

Wall Art: Display your Italian Greyhound's image or a customized portrait as a captivating piece of wall art. From canvas prints to framed posters, these creations become stunning focal points in your home.

Italian Greyhound-Themed Events and Gatherings

Unleashing the Fun: Italian Greyhound-Themed Events and Gatherings

Italian Greyhounds are not just beloved pets; they are an integral part of our families. Their elegance, charm, and unique personalities make them perfect candidates for themed events and gatherings that celebrate their special place in our lives. Below we will explore the world of Italian Greyhound-themed events and gatherings, showcasing a variety of exciting and engaging ideas that will bring together fellow Italian Greyhound enthusiasts and create unforgettable experiences.

Playdates and Meetups:

Italian Greyhound Socials: Organize Italian Greyhound-specific playdates and social gatherings at local dog parks or designated areas. These events provide a safe and secure environment for Italian Greyhounds to interact, play, and socialize with other dogs of their breed.

b. Breed-Specific Meetups: Join existing Italian Greyhound meetup groups or create one in your community. These gatherings allow Italian Greyhound owners to connect, share experiences, and build a supportive network centered around their beloved breed.

Costume Parties:

a. Halloween Pawties: Host a Halloween-themed costume party specifically for Italian Greyhounds and their owners. Encourage participants to dress up their dogs in creative costumes, and award prizes for the most innovative and adorable outfits.

Holiday Dress-Up: Celebrate festive occasions, such as Christmas or Valentine's Day, by organizing Italian Greyhound-themed costume parties. Embrace the holiday spirit by encouraging participants to dress their Italian Greyhounds in holiday-themed attire, creating a delightful and heartwarming atmosphere.

Lure Coursing Events:

Lure Coursing Competitions: Coordinate or participate in lure coursing events specifically tailored for Italian Greyhounds. These competitions allow Italian Greyhounds to showcase their natural agility and hunting instincts in a controlled and enjoyable environment.

Fun Runs: Organize non-competitive fun runs where Italian Greyhounds can chase a mechanical lure in a safe and enclosed space. This activity promotes exercise, mental stimulation, and camaraderie among Italian Greyhound owners and their dogs.

Fundraising Events:

Rescue and Adoption Drives: Collaborate with local rescue organizations or shelters to organize fundraising events that raise awareness and support for Italian Greyhound rescue and adoption. These events can include activities such as dog walks, silent auctions, or raffles.

Charity Walks and Fun Runs: Participate in charity walks or fun runs that support animal-related causes. Encourage participants to bring their Italian Greyhounds and create a team or group to represent the breed. This fosters a sense of community and demonstrates the commitment of Italian Greyhound owners to giving back.

Italian Greyhound Parades:

Breed-Specific Parades: Coordinate or participate in Italian Greyhound parades where owners and their dogs can showcase their Italian Greyhounds' beauty and grace. Parade routes can be organized in public areas or designated venues, allowing the community to admire these magnificent creatures.

Costume Contests and Floats: Incorporate costume contests and floats into the Italian Greyhound parades. Encourage participants to dress up their Italian Greyhounds in creative outfits or coordinate themed floats that reflect the breed's unique qualities.

Educational Seminars and Workshops:

1 Health and Wellness Workshops: Organize seminars or workshops focused on Italian Greyhound health, nutrition, grooming, and general well-being. Invite veterinary professionals, trainers, and specialists to provide valuable insights and share their expertise with Italian Greyhound owners.

Have Questions / Comments?

This book was designed to cover as much as possible but I know I have probably missed something, or some new amazing discovery that has just come out.

If you notice something missing or have a question that I failed to answer, please get in touch and let me know. If I can, I will email you an answer and also update the book so others can also benefit from it.

Thanks For Being Awesome :)

Submit Your Questions / Comments At:

---

1. https://xspurts.com/posts/questions

https://go.xspurts.com/questions

Get Another Book Free

We love writing and have produced a huge number of books.

For being one of our amazing readers, we would love to offer you another book we have created, 100% free.

To claim this limited time special offer, simply go to the site below and enter your name and email address.

You will then receive one of my great books, direct to your email account, 100% free!

https://go.xspurts.com/free-book-offer

---

1. https://xspurts.com/posts/free-book-offer

Also by Samantha D. Thompson

Dog Kidney Stones: The Complete Resource for Diagnosis and Treatment
The Ultimate Cat Care Guide: Expert Tips for Happy and Healthy Cats
Labrador Retriever 101: The Ultimate Guide for Labrador Lovers
Hip Dysplasia in Dogs: A Comprehensive Guide for Dog Owners
House Training 101: A Comprehensive Guide for Dog Owners
Canine Parvovirus: Everything You Need to Know
Dog Grooming Made Simple: A Comprehensive Guide for Pet Owners
Kennel Cough 101: A Comprehensive Guide for Pet Parents
Potty Training Your Puppy: A Complete Guide to Success
Secrets to Dog Training: The Ultimate Guide to Dog Obedience
Beagle 101: The Ultimate Guide for Beagle Lovers
Beagle Savvy: A Complete Guide to the Breed
Schnauzer 101: The Ultimate Guide for Schnauzer Lovers
Schnauzer Savvy A Complete Guide to the Breed
Afghan Hounds 101: The Ultimate Guide for Afghan Hound Lovers
Italian Greyhound 101: The Ultimate Guide for Italian Greyhound Lovers

Ingram Content Group UK Ltd.
Milton Keynes UK
UKHW020652060723
424661UK00015B/391